Beckett's Thing

Beckett's Thing

Painting and Theatre

David Lloyd

EDINBURGH
University Press

Edinburgh University Press is one of the leading university presses in the UK. We publish academic books and journals in our selected subject areas across the humanities and social sciences, combining cutting-edge scholarship with high editorial and production values to produce academic works of lasting importance. For more information visit our website: edinburghuniversitypress.com

© David Lloyd, 2016

Edinburgh University Press Ltd
The Tun – Holyrood Road
12(2f) Jackson's Entry
Edinburgh EH8 8PJ

Typeset in 11/13 Adobe Sabon by
Servis Filmsetting Ltd, Stockport, Cheshire,
and printed and bound in Great Britain by
CPI Group (UK) Ltd, Croydon CR0 4YY

A CIP record for this book is available from the British Library

ISBN 978 1 4744 1572 9 (hardback)
ISBN 978 1 4744 1573 6 (webready PDF)
ISBN 978 1 4744 1574 3 (epub)

The right of David Lloyd to be identified as the author of this work has been asserted in accordance with the Copyright, Designs and Patents Act 1988, and the Copyright and Related Rights Regulations 2003 (SI No. 2498).

Contents

Figures

Acknowledgements

As Samuel Beckett well knew, getting to know artwork is a slow if intensely pleasurable process. It demands in the first place persistent attention and, when possible, repeated occasions of viewing. There is no substitute for encountering the actual work in its material being. Unlike the books that those of us trained as literary critics are accustomed to work on, paintings cannot often be absorbed at home and their physical appearance – their texture and scale and dimensionality – is essential to their appreciation. So it requires much travel in order to see artworks and moreover the generosity of curators and collectors, private and institutional, who make these works available to view. In the course of writing this book, which has taken me more years than I care to confess, I have benefited in many ways from the kindness and hospitality of numerous individuals in the many cities in which I have had to track down works by artists that are widely dispersed and often not currently on display. I have also appreciated their patience with the stumbling efforts and slow vision of a novice in art criticism and the hours that many have given to allow me to view works held in storage or in collections of graphics and prints. They have made the difficult task of piecing together the work of insufficiently known artists inestimably easier. I am grateful to all the following individuals who have helped me in these ways over the years, and to those not known to me whose curation and care of the works enabled my access to them: Riann Coulter, Fionnuala Croke and Roisín Kennedy at the National Gallery of Ireland for their invaluable assistance in helping me access work by Jack B. Yeats; Helene Meyer, Brigitte Monti and Claude-Jeannine Ritschard at the Musée d'art et d'histoire, Geneva, for introducing me to the many works by Bram van Velde stored there; to Geurt Imanse and especially to Frank van Lamoen at the Stedelijk

Museum, Amsterdam, for patiently overseeing my viewing of work by both Bram van Velde and Avigdor Arikha; to Macha Daniel at the Cabinet d'art graphique at the Centre Pompidou, Paris, for access to graphic work by van Velde and Arikha; and to Sienna Brown at the Los Angeles County Museum of Art for enabling me to view graphic work and painting by Arikha. Mark Hamment and Kate Austin at the Marlborough Gallery, London, generously accommodated my numerous requests for information about Arikha's work and its location. M. Fernanda Meza of the Artists Rights Society and Liz Kurtulik Mercuri of Art Resource have been generous and patient resources in my many endeavours to locate artworks and permissions to reproduce them.

No less valuable to me has been the assistance over many years of several talented and long-suffering research assistants whose labours facilitated the location of artworks, turned up invaluable sources, and moved the project forward even when other work prevented me from focusing on it. My thanks to Annalisa Zox-Weaver, Erin O'Sullivan, Timothy Kreiner and Aaron Roberts – it has been a pleasure to work with you. Assistance of a rather different kind came to me from students in the several classes that I have taught over the years on Beckett, theatre and painting at the University of Southern California and at the University of Notre Dame: numerous sharp and insightful comments on both the paintings and the plays that we viewed have doubtless found their way into my own understanding of both Beckett's and the painters' work. Though the quick back and forth of class discussion precludes attributing every such insight, I am deeply conscious of how much I learned from our collective viewing of paintings and plays: it is one of the enduring pleasures of the classroom to be able to learn in collaboration. My thanks in particular go to the theatre students at USC whose production of *Come and Go* became so much more than a final project and taught me in crucial ways how to see that play.

The best research is always in conversation and this book has benefited in innumerable and never fully documentable ways from exchanges with so many friends and colleagues. Seamus Deane has been a perpetual inspiration as well as a brilliant editor; Colin Dayan has been an endless resource and support, especially during the almost daily conversations that took place in the first year I was able to devote fully to this project; and Breandán MacSuibhne sharpened both my prose and my wits with his own. Luke Gibbons is always the most acute of critics of visual work and an endless source of information and of humour. On Beckett, theatre and so much else, I am conscious how much I have learnt from Eyal Amiran, Ann Banfield, Patrick Bixby, Stan Gontarski, Daniel Gunn, Sean Kennedy, Mark Nixon, Alexandra Poulain, Mark Quigley and Rei Terada. And no one thinks the thing better than my friends and co-conspirators, Fred Moten and Denise da Silva.

Over the years, I have benefited immensely from the collective conversation that presentation of this work in lectures and colloquia has enabled. It would be impossible to list every occasion at which I have learnt from colleagues' responses and questions, but I want to signal in particular my gratitude to Victor Merriman and his colleagues at Liverpool Hope University's Department of Drama and Theatre Studies, whose hospitality over several years allowed me gradually to unfold this work to the most receptive and insightful of audiences. My thanks to Victor extend far beyond those occasions. Likewise, several opportunities to lecture at Notre Dame's Keough-Naughton Institute for Irish Studies graduate Irish Seminar not only livened my returns to Dublin but allowed me to sketch the first outlines of this work. My thanks especially to Kevin Whelan and to Brian Ó Conchubhair for these opportunities. For the last ten years, the Southern California Irish Studies Colloquium has sponsored the most convivial of occasions for the sharing of ideas and resources and I am particularly grateful to Enda Duffy and Laura O'Connor for keeping this initiative going despite the lean times.

Over the years, several grants and fellowships have enabled work on this book to proceed. I am grateful to the National Endowment for the Humanities for a year-long fellowship during which the main groundwork was laid, and to the University of Southern California for enabling me to accept that fellowship and for their support of research travel. The Keough-Naughton Institute for Irish Studies of the University of Notre Dame generously granted me a position as Faculty Fellow during which I was able to make considerable headway, and the University of California at Davis and at Riverside furnished teaching relief that has enabled me to complete this work.

It has been an exceptional pleasure to work with the editorial team at Edinburgh University Press on the production of this book and I wish to thank in particular Adela Rauchova, James Dale and, especially, Cathy Falconer, whose rare and meticulous copy-editing has saved me from many an error or inconsistency. Any remaining are entirely my own.

My constant companion throughout the writing of this book has been Sarita See, whose decolonised eye has taught my own to see again and again with fresh insight. To her this book is dedicated with my love and deepest respect.

Initial versions of some of the chapters have previously appeared in books and journals and I thank the editors of the following for enabling the publication of work in progress:

'Republics of Difference: Yeats, MacGreevy, Beckett', *Field Day Review* 1 (2005).

'The Gaze is a Thing: Beckett's Film and Bram van Velde', in *The Moderns* (exhibition catalogue), ed. Brian Cass and Christine Kennedy (Dublin: Irish Museum of Modern Art, 2011).

'Beckett's Thing: Bram van Velde and the Gaze', *Modernist Cultures*, 6.2 (2011).

'"Siege laid again": Arikha's Gaze, Beckett's Painted Stage', in S. E. Gontarski (ed.), *The Edinburgh Companion to Beckett and the Arts* (Edinburgh: Edinburgh University Press, 2014).

Other Becketts: Series Preface
General Editor: S. E. Gontarski, Florida State University

In 1997 Apple computers launched an advertising campaign (in print and on television) that entreated us to 'Think Different', and Samuel Beckett was one of Apple's icons. Avoiding Apple's solecism, we might modify the appeal to say that *Other Becketts* is a call to think differently as well, in this case about Beckett's work, to question, that is, even the questions we ask about it. *Other Becketts*, then, is a series of monographs focused on alternative, unexplored or under-explored approaches to the work of Samuel Beckett, not a call for novelty per se, but a call to examine afresh those of Beckett's interests that were more arcane than mainstream, interests that might be deemed quirky or strange, and those of his works less thoroughly explored critically and theoretically, the late prose and drama, say, or even the poetry or criticism. Volumes might cover (but are not restricted to) any of the following: unusual illnesses or neurological disorders (the 'duck foot, goose foot' of *First Love*, akathisia or the invented duck's disease or panpygoptosis of Miss Dew in *Murphy*, proprioception, or its disturbance, in *Not I*, perhaps, or other unusual neurological lapses among Beckett's creatures, from Watt to the Listener of *That Time*); mathematical peculiarities (irrational numbers, factorials, Fibonacci numbers or sequences, or non-Euclidian approaches to geometry); linguistic failures (from Nominalism to Mauthner, say); citations of or allusions to contrarian aesthetic philosophers working in a more or less irrationalist tradition (Nietzsche, Bergson or Deleuze, among others), or in general 'the simple games that time plays with space'. Alternative approaches would be of interest as well, with foci on objects, animals, cognitive or memory issues, and the like.

Introduction: The Painted Stage – Beckett's Visual Aesthetics

The work considered as pure creation, and whose function ceases with its genesis, is consigned to nothingness. A single art lover (a well informed one) would have saved it. Just one of these gentlemen, faces hollowed by unvalidated enthusiasms, feet flattened by innumerable stations, fingers worn by fifty franc catalogues, who look first from far away, then close up, and who, in particularly thorny cases, assess with their thumbs the depth of the impasto.[1]

Beckett's ironic but affectionate sketch of the art lover, this 'inoffensive nutcase who runs, as others do to the cinema, to the galleries, the museum, and even into churches' for the pleasure of viewing art, is as much a self-portrait as a satire.[2] It captures not only the reality of his own life-long love of painting, his genuine connoisseurship, and the independence of his critical views, but also the quality of attention that he was capable of giving to an artwork. It has often been noted that Beckett could stand for hours at a time before a canvas, absorbing its formal qualities, its material relations and rhythms as much as whatever image it conveyed.[3] Painting was in every sense Beckett's 'thing': he never seems to have lost his engagement either with individual paintings, or with the aesthetic questions that the contemporary fate of painting as an art form imposed. And his own work in the theatre gives new meaning to the well-worn phrase 'the painted stage'. Beckett's theatre, for stage and for film or television, this book insists, is not merely like painting or based on paintings, but is its own form of visual art. Visual art in painting and theatre furnished him with the space for an intense mode of thinking that is not confined to formal aesthetic appreciation, formidable as his capacity for that was. His absorption before paintings, his focused concentration on their singular existence as things in and of themselves, became

I

the means to explore a crisis in the modern subject that he early on named 'the new thing that has happened' and which would be the focus of his critical writing into the post-war period.[4] Engaging across his writing life a series of painters whose work confronts in profoundly different ways the problem of representation, or the question of the artist's gaze in relation to the object, he finds in them the terms and the means to work through the aporetic crisis of Western culture that he apprehends first as the breakdown of subject and object and then, in the wake of the Second World War, as 'a conception of humanity in ruins'.[5] Paintings that destroy or remake representation make space for the appearance of the 'thing' that resists representation at the very moment that humanity itself, and not merely its objects, has been reduced to the status of a thing. It is such a thing, the human broken and reduced to a thing among the things with which it circulates, that gradually comes to appear on Beckett's stage. It is this shattered but resistant and enduring human thing that is Beckett's peculiar preoccupation, the thing that comes after the subject and its objects and in which he sees through the interlocked crises, aesthetic, political and ethical, that his work persistently stages. From it I have borrowed the name of *Beckett's Thing*.

Increasingly, the formative influence of this 'passion for painting' on Beckett's oeuvre is becoming known to a wider public than critics and scholars, though the range and importance of his art criticism may still surprise even those who know his work well.[6] A passion for painting motivated Beckett's repeated visits to Dublin's National Gallery as a student, when he lived around the corner in the attic of his father's offices, and his regular trips to the galleries as a young man in London. It structured his extended stay in Germany in the 1930s, where he visited not only galleries, museums and churches in order to view medieval and baroque religious art, but also the cellars of institutions where art banned by the Nazi regime was stored. In Hamburg especially, he frequented the avant-garde circles of artists who, though in some cases banned, had not emigrated, and engaged in aesthetic discussions with them. All this he recorded in his lengthy and detailed letters to his friend Thomas MacGreevy, who had introduced him to the Irish painter Jack B. Yeats, and who would later become director of the National Gallery of Ireland. Later, settling in Paris in the late 1930s, he befriended a number of artists, who included not only the Dutch painters Geer and Bram van Velde, the latter of whom he championed with special attention and energy, but also Alberto Giacometti, André Masson, Pierre Tal-Coat, Henri Hayden, Stanley Hayter and Avigdor Arikha. Many of these he met through his close friend Georges Duthuit, the art critic and son-in-law of Henri Matisse, whose role in shaping and representing French art in the wake of the Second World War was critical. For a few years following his return to Paris after the war, Beckett worked closely with Duthuit on the English-language journal *Transition*, which sought to disseminate new French literature, art and criticism in the English-speaking world. It was in *Transition* and in the equally influential French journal *Cahiers d'Art* that Beckett's most substantial art criticism was published in the 1940s. Thereafter, Beckett virtually ceased to publish art criticism or, indeed, criticism of any kind, though he occasionally wrote brief if telling tributes to artists, as he did for Jack B. Yeats's Paris show in 1954 or for Arikha in the 1960s. But his engagement with the visual arts never ceased and continued to be reflected both in his own work and in his friendships and conversation, as the record of his long relationship with Arikha testifies.[7]

The impact on Beckett's writing of his intense engagement with the visual arts, and with painting in particular, has by and large been approached by critics in two ways: as a matter of direct allusions in his work to paintings he had seen, or as furnishing more general aesthetic analogies for his own procedures. On the one hand, Beckett frequently uses the citation of visual images within his works or invokes them as models or structures, especially in the dramatic work. Such evocations of images can range from direct reference, as to the 'tormented faces' of the 'Master of Tired Eyes' in the National Gallery in the early story 'Ding-Dong', to allusion, as with the figure of the Auditor in *Not I*, inspired by Caravaggio's *Beheading of Saint John the Baptist*.[8] In some cases, a specific painting is thought to have inspired the set or visual appearance of a play. The most famous instance of this is Beckett's own acknowledgement of the debt that *Waiting for Godot* owes, in the final passages of both acts, to the German Romantic painter Caspar David Friedrich's *Two Men Contemplating the Moon*, which he had seen in Dresden in 1937.[9] Beckett's visual memory was clearly formidable – he writes to Duthuit in 1948 with almost perfect recollection of a St. Sebastian by Antonello da Messina also seen in Dresden in 1937 – and it is easy to speculate on sources that might have influenced the visual elements of his works. Other candidates for *Waiting for Godot*'s scenario include two striking paintings by Jack B. Yeats that Beckett might well have known, *Two Travellers* and *The Graveyard Wall*.[10] Others have sought sources for the powerful, concentrated images of the later plays, as Graley Herren has done in relating the imagery and lighting of the television play *Nacht und Träume* to various representations of Christ in Gethsemane that Beckett may have seen.[11] We have, thanks especially to the painstaking work of James Knowlson, an almost exhaustive archive of the multitude of works that Beckett had seen, and the room for speculation on such immediate sources or prompts for his images and scenarios is vast.

But the identification of such sources is neither the only pathway into an understanding of Beckett's visual aesthetics nor always very instructive once the reference has been established. Other than anchoring *Godot* in a visual source that may be of use to a set designer, what does the allusion to Friedrich or to Yeats establish about Beckett's meaning or intentions? Though we can establish Beckett's fascination with numerous forms of art, as, for example, with German romanticism in poetry and music as well as in painting, such interests do not define him or his writing. It is clear that his work is a painstaking 'undoing' of its sources: citation and allusion function less as supports for the work than as materials to be dismantled and redistributed in new relations.[12] This uncertainty as to what use Beckett makes of his visual sources may be what has led critics to approach his relation to painting rather differently, drawing less on a kind of iconographical study of his work and more on the critical vocabulary that he developed through his writings on visual art, writings that often seem of a piece with his early critical writings on Joyce, Proust and other literary artists. Here, the interest is not so much in the connection between Beckett's work and specific images, or even in assessing what Beckett saw in particular paintings, as it is in tracking how Beckett forged his own *literary* aesthetic through his observations of the tendencies of contemporary painting. Dougald McMillan defined this approach succinctly: 'In writing about the predicament of the modern artists faced with fundamental questions of representation, Beckett has implicitly defined his own position.'[13] As early as the 'German Letter' of 1937, written to Axel Kaun in Berlin, Beckett had queried whether 'literature alone [was] to remain behind in the old lazy ways that [had] been so long abandoned by music and painting'. He speaks there already of language as 'a veil that must be torn apart in order to get at the things (or the Nothingness) behind it' and forecasts a 'literature of the unword'.[14]

Beckett's formulations in this letter form the bridge from the 1930 essay *Proust* to the later art-critical essays. In the former he claimed that 'The artistic tendency is not expansive, but a contraction. And art is the apotheosis of solitude. There is no communication because there are no vehicles of communication.' Accordingly, 'the artist is active, but negatively, shrinking from the nullity of extracircumferential phenomena, drawn in to the core of the eddy.'[15] In the 'Three Dialogues with Georges Duthuit', composed largely from correspondence and conversations and published in *Transition* in 1949, Beckett pushes towards a more radical formulation, that the artist must turn from the 'domain of the feasible', preferring 'The expression that there is nothing to express, nothing with which to express, nothing from which to express, no power to express, no desire to express, together with the obligation to express.' Consequently, as Bram van Velde is supposedly the first to acknowledge, 'to be an artist is to fail, as none other dare fail, that failure is his world and the shrink from it desertion, art and craft, good housekeeping, living'.[16] Though Beckett formulated these last statements, which we will explore further in Chapter 2, in the attempt to come to terms with the emerging directions of painting in post-war France, they have been taken along with his earlier critical statements to represent a self-reflexive effort to shape a literary aesthetic that would allow him to break with the overwhelming influence of Joyce and, to a lesser extent, of Proust. They contribute to a portrait of Beckett as a writer of exceptional, even exemplary integrity of purpose, whose career demonstrates a consistent and relentless trajectory: a ceaseless *via negativa* leading him towards 'the core of the eddy', carried out through a constant paring away of superfluity and excess, from the Joyceanic excesses of his early poetry to the spare and reduced forms of the late prose texts and plays. The art-critical writings, transferred wholesale from their initial objects, which were contemporary paintings, to Beckett's writings, furnish the critical grid within which that literary trajectory and its principles can be read.

There is no doubt that this mode of reading Beckett's writings on painting as a kind of preliminary map for the project of his own prose and drama has been enormously productive of insight, from Lawrence E. Harvey's pioneering work on the early critical writing down through Lois Oppenheim's invaluable *The Painted Word: Samuel Beckett's Dialogue with Art*.[17] Probably no study of the writer could dispense with that model, not least because the most substantial of Beckett's writings on painting, those of the 1940s on van Velde, notoriously coincide with the ruptures in his own work that ultimately defined him as a writer: the turn to writing in French and away from the English that was so contaminated with influence and competence; the vision of indigence and impotence that clarified the break he had to make with Joyce's 'omniscience and omnipotence' and that gave him the terrain that his work would explore; and the consequent frenzy of writing that gave us in a few years the short novellas, the *Trilogy*, *Godot* and the *Texts for Nothing*. For all Beckett's recurrent protestations of losing his way, of losing the capacity to write, of losing direction or the will to write, protestations all the more evident across the emerging volumes of letters, it is hard to avoid the sense of a single and remarkably consistent artistic career welling up from this crucial watershed of writerly break-through apparently enabled by a critical onslaught on the givens of modernism and on the longer traditions of Western art. From the commitment to failure attributed to van Velde to the desperate, spare 'Fail again. Fail better' of *Worstward Ho*, Beckett's seems one single, unswerving aesthetic and ethical quest.[18]

It is not the object of this book to contest this vision of Beckett's literary project or career, nor to question the value of seeking to understand his own work through his writings on others. Nor is it my main goal to contribute to the iconographic work of identifying the visual works that may have played some role in Beckett's realisation or imagination of his plays. But it does seem to be the case that such foci, productive of insight as they are, have come at the expense of looking attentively, as he notoriously did, at the works of the artists he admired and of seeking in them clues to Beckett's overall visual aesthetic. Relatively few critics have sought to 'read' specific paintings alongside Beckett's comments on them and to decipher why he admired these works to the extent that he would, against his own great and express reluctance, take the time to write on them.[19] That task, in some ways quite simple, shapes the principal aims of *Beckett's Thing*: to pursue as far as possible, drawing on Beckett's relatively spare comments about the painters whose work he admired and even promoted, what it was that he saw in them that detained his attention and defined his own approach to the visual presentation of his work. How far can we find in his appreciation of actual paintings clues not to any specific image that Beckett may have adopted, but to the visual principles that underlie and evolve through his work as a whole? The emphasis on actual paintings is crucial: theoretical reasoning on painting as an abstract category was not only painful for Beckett; it defied the principle that he articulated in writing on the van Velde brothers. 'There is no painting. There are only paintings.' And, further, 'impossible to reason on the unique.'[20] The task is, then, to try to see through specific paintings, primarily by painters he knew and admired, to what Beckett himself might have seen in them and to draw from them some sense of the visual imagination at work not only in his criticism but also in his dramatic work.

For perhaps obvious reasons, it is to the dramatic works, as written both for the stage and for television or film, that I turn to investigate those principles. Literary criticism tends to approach drama as text and narrative and to read it as such. It is rare that critics see plays as in themselves visual art, and even rarer that critics see the visual dimension of drama as work in itself rather than as mere backdrop or symbolic reinforcement of the text, dialogue or action. In *Beckett's Thing*, I bracket so far as possible any concern with the textual interpretation of the plays – which yield, in any case, less and less text to interpret in the later work – and focus primarily on their visual aspects. It is a striking fact about Beckett's dramatic work in any medium that one can arrest the action at almost any point and be rewarded with a tableau that is a virtual painting – a 'still' from any of the works appears as a calculated 'still life', to borrow one of his favourite word-plays. While this is true of earlier plays like *Godot* or *Endgame* – and Beckett's emphasis as a director 'shows his preoccupation with giving the play[s] a visual form'[21] – it is all the more the case with the brief later plays, whose painterliness seems especially profound. Accordingly, I read from Beckett's deep engagement with painting to his dramatic works understood in the first place as in themselves, and even above all, visual artworks.[22] This entails understanding Beckett's relation to art not merely in terms of particular paintings that inspired the appearance of a given play or the description of a character, nor even as a prompt for thinking analogically about the problems and solutions facing contemporary artists in different media, but primarily in terms of what it reveals about Beckett as a visual artist. What did he see in and learn from painters that eventually informed his own visual aesthetics? What are the implications of a body of drama that moves increasingly away from dialogue, from narrative, from the interaction of characters in realistic time or space, or from the unfolding of an event or series of events, and focuses instead on the visual, on gesture, rhythm or movement in the restricted space or 'box' of the stage, and on the set itself conceived as a painting in which the human characters are merely elements among others? And how does Beckett think through or with painting in order to arrive at so distinctive a visual aesthetic?

This is obviously a hazardous and often speculative undertaking, given how rarely Beckett spoke about his overall intentions, let alone his sources. And it goes without saying that the sources of his dramatic imagination were not solely found in painting. His acquaintance with theatre was at least as deep as his engagement with painting, from the Racine on whom he lectured in Trinity College to the J. M. Synge and W. B. Yeats in whose dialogical couples Beckett may have found suggestions for his own early scenarios and – in Yeats's case – inspiration for the dance-like movement and stylisation of the later ones. This book makes no attempt to track such influences on his dramatic style or even its visual elements. Its focus is narrower and hopefully more revealing as a result. In order to anchor my sense of how his visual imagination was formed, I have concentrated on painters on whom he wrote and with whom he had a long and sustained engagement, both as a friend and as a critical interlocutor. These are the painters with whose own aesthetic struggles and advances he lived most intimately and to whose practice and resulting canvases he would have been most steadily attuned. They are the painters whose oeuvre he experienced as it came into being and with whom, in different ways, he shared the evolution of his own work. Jack B. Yeats he met in 1930 through his friend Thomas MacGreevy after returning from his first extended stay in Paris. He seems subsequently to have made a point of visiting the older painter virtually every time he returned to Dublin, often taking long and apparently mostly silent walks with him, and usually viewing Yeats's recent work. Despite his financial difficulties at the time, he bought several works that remained with him for the rest of his life. His admiration for Yeats is detailed in the letters he wrote to MacGreevy, who was writing a study of the painter in the 1930s, and although Beckett saw Yeats little after his move to

Paris in 1938, his admiration never seems to have diminished. As Chapter 1 argues, Beckett's was an unconventional view at that time, not only in seeing Yeats in relation to the major 'independent' European artists rather than primarily as a 'national painter', but moreover in opening the impact of that national context on to a wider set of concerns. Those concerns include Yeats's gradual dismantling of the conventions of representation and the vital dynamic he establishes between the materials and the figural elements of his paintings, all of which have considerable political as well as aesthetic resonances in the context of the post-colonial Free State and of Yeats's radical republican affiliations.

In the late 1930s, as he was finally settling in Paris, Beckett got to know the van Velde brothers, Geer (Gerardus) and Bram (Abraham). Though initially Beckett was taken with the work of both brothers, he was eventually possessed almost exclusively by Bram's more uncompromising, painful turn to an increasingly non-representational mode of painting. More than any other artist, it was with Bram that Beckett identified, speaking of him as his 'familiar' and, it seems, working through a profound engagement with his paintings to the kinds of ruptures he had to make in his own writing. By the early 1950s, Beckett had come to regret his writings on Bram van Velde, not so much out of loss of respect as because he felt that his own quite idiosyncratic interpretation of the painter's project had overly shaped critical reception of his work, often to the painter's detriment. It is also clear that he believed that the direction of van Velde's work no longer coincided with his own aesthetic concerns. Nonetheless, some of Beckett's most important critical statements – and, indeed, the last extended critical works of any kind that he would write – emerged from this intense period of investment in van Velde's work and from his attempt to articulate the nature of its achievement. These efforts, ones he always considered provisional rather than definitive, brought him to confront not only van Velde's shattering of 'possessive' pictorial space and of the subject-object relation, but also his fragmentation of the gaze and of the human subject which that space had hitherto supported or held in place. This quality of van Velde's paintings of the 1940s, those with which Beckett's writings were most acutely concerned, has crucial implications for theatrical space and its elements, implications which, as I argue in Chapter 2, Beckett continued to work out in his own medium for a decade or more.

Beckett's relationship with the younger painter Avigdor Arikha was evidently of a very different nature, in terms of both its duration and its quality. Beckett and Arikha met in a Paris café in 1956, after Arikha had attended a performance of *Waiting for Godot*. Their friendship lasted until Beckett's death in 1989 and turned, according to Arikha's wife Anne Atik, around their mutual interest in art, music and literature, and occasional collaborations in the theatre or on artist's books. It embraced an almost familial intimacy that never characterised his relationships with the other painters.[23] It might be tempting to suggest that while Beckett learnt from Yeats and van Velde, Arikha in turn learnt from the older writer, whose reputation and distinctive modes of writing were largely established by the time they met. But there is little evidence of any direct aesthetic influence exercised by Beckett on Arikha, and Chapter 3 concerns rather the sense of a remarkable accord in their visual awareness and in what we might think of as their ethics as artists. It is the story of peculiar convergences rather than exact correspondences, but helps nonetheless to illuminate the visual, even specifically painterly qualities of Beckett's later theatre.

At the time of their meeting, Arikha was committed to abstract painting, and he remained so until 1965, when his experience of a Caravaggio show at the Louvre consolidated the dissatisfaction he had been feeling with abstraction and impelled him to return to 'drawing from observation', as he puts it. His work retains, nonetheless, the values learnt as an abstract painter and involves no simple return to figurative representation (terms he consistently rejected). His sense of pictorial space and of colorific relations throws into peculiar relief Beckett's own experiments with theatrical space and visuality in the later plays and highlights the debt that both owe to the example of Caravaggio. That debt involves not only the Italian painter's notorious use of chiaroscuro and his dramatic foreshortening of pictorial space, but also the refusal of *istoria* or narrative painting that scandalised his contemporaries. Both Arikha and Beckett seem to draw on a Caravaggiesque sense of visual space and to refuse narrative or epic means: their work implicates the viewer in the space of its occurrence, that space in which, as Beckett put it of van Velde, we find 'the thing that hides the thing', the object that 'always resists representation'.[24]

It will be evident that the artists who held Beckett's attention were not ones who occupied the mainstream of the European or

American art world. To be sure, each was a respected painter in his own right and well known in certain circles. None, however, belongs to any established school, even van Velde maintaining a somewhat oblique relation to what is somewhat loosely called the 'School of Paris'. Nor have they imprinted their style on later painting in the way, say, Cézanne, Matisse or Picasso forcefully shaped the future direction of art. They are, as Beckett himself was, despite his indubitable influence on subsequent writing in every genre, 'independents' and profoundly idiosyncratic in their manner of painting. So different are they as painters, indeed, that it may at first seem hard even to specify the common elements that might reveal Beckett's predilections. But what could be said to unite them with regard to the writer, or to the trajectory of his interests, is a particular relation to figure, to its appearance and disappearance. Beckett was consistently engaged by artists whose work haunts the line between figuration and abstraction, between the emergence of the image and its disappearance. Each of the painters I discuss in *Beckett's Thing* has a distinctive relation to issues of figuration and representation. Yeats may still be best known, if only on account of the circulation of prints and reproductions, for his early work that depicted the scenes of Irish life and landscape on which his reputation as a 'national painter' largely hangs. But the paintings that he began to produce after 1922, marked by the violence of the Irish war of decolonisation and the civil war that followed, seem to move towards the very edge of abstraction, the figures in them seeming to be swallowed by a ground that is composed of a thick, almost sculpted impasto. These paintings, with the peculiar obstacles they present to visual decipherment, were the ones that Beckett would have been most familiar with, seeing them as he generally did in the very moment of their production.

It may be that his familiarity with Yeats's work and with the trajectory of his oeuvre prepared Beckett to 'see' van Velde's, which pursued its own path from an early figurative work that synthesises the influence of German expressionism, on the one hand, and the still lifes of Cézanne and Matisse on the other. Increasingly, his work turns from representation, at first schematising the elements of figures or objects into masks or geometrical forms, and then reducing them to abstract motifs that seem to haunt his canvases with the memory of depicted things. One can, indeed, track through his work the precise logic by which an abstract mode of painting emerges from the masters of pre-war French art, a painting that pursues the spatial effects of Matisse and the colorific distribution of Cézanne into a terrain where the surface of the canvas becomes the turbulent site of ambiguous perspectives and shifting rhythms of colour and form, at once interior and epidermal.[25]

Arikha's work takes a different direction. In moving from a project of 'pure abstraction' back to what he prefers to call 'depiction' or 'drawing or painting from observation', Arikha seems to complete a dialectic immanent in Beckett's interests. For Arikha's work, informed as it is by his practice as an abstract painter and by his exceptional erudition as an art historian, both fully absorbs the lessons of abstract painting and deliberately seeks to displace the Cézannian colour grid that he sees as dominating both figurative and abstract painting in the twentieth century. If figure reappears or representation seems to return in his work, they do so within a very different pictorial space and with a very different aesthetic and ethical import.

Taken together, these three painters might form a constellation of 'minor' painting, in the sense of one that challenges the dominant givens of a canonical tradition, undermining it from within by means which imply another relation to mastery and to representation, a relation of refusal or abdication.[26] Where Yeats effectively refuses the role of Irish 'national painter' after 1922, in the wake of the failure of decolonisation, he does so by dissolving or troubling the relation of the represented and representative figure to the ground from which it stands out, thereby challenging the dominant aesthetic of nationalist paintings of representative types. Van Velde in turn produces a painting of 'incompletion', one in which lines 'go nowhere, have no apparent beginning or end and construct nothing' and where 'images are hinted at, yet come to nothing',[27] and thus deconstructs the legacy of Cézanne and Matisse that had become a virtual moral institution in post-war France's cultural reconstruction. If Beckett describes this 'painting of obstruction (*empêchement*)' in terms of a rigorous adherence to failure, he does so in the context of an equally robust and determined assault on the 'possessive' values that determine the Western art tradition and situate the subject and its gaze at the object. His interest in Arikha's work similarly tracked that painter's rethinking of the place of the gaze in pictorial space and his refusal of the grand moral narrative that continued discreetly

to determine post-war painting and its aesthetic claims. Art for
Arikha as for Beckett is neither representative nor figurative but
devoted solely to the depiction of the relation of the gaze to the
thing as it emerges into visibility.

It would thus be misleading to seek to assimilate Beckett's interest in an anti-representational painting to the tradition that dominated much of the formative period of his writing, American
abstract expressionism. Certainly, abstract expressionism also
emerged in response to the central developments of European
modernism, as, for example, in its 'loosening up [of] the relatively delimited illusion of shallow depth' in Picasso, Braque or
Léger, or more generally through the abandonment of 'expendable
conventions', as abstract expressionism's major critic and advocate Clement Greenberg described the genesis of 'American-Type'
painting.[28] Beckett's own critical thinking about painting indeed
seems to anticipate a major tenet of abstraction, its emancipation
from what Greenberg describes as the 'literariness' of representational painting, where 'the meaning . . . of what is represented
becomes truly inseparable from the representation itself' and
which presents 'the images of things that are inconceivable outside
of time and action'.[29] But where Beckett's critique of representation is aimed against the reproduction of the major tradition and,
as we shall see further throughout this book, at the relations of
domination that are inscribed in its possessive subject-object relations, abstract expressionism extends that tradition as its major
representative, with all that entails. It is, as Greenberg puts it, 'the
latest phase in the development of Western art as a whole' and
represents a further extension of 'the domain of the feasible', as
Beckett termed the ethical and aesthetic assumptions that he was
concerned to dismantle.

That continuity is perhaps most evident in the Kantian aesthetic
principle of disinterest that Greenberg sees fulfilled most purely
in abstraction. In continuing to mingle its purely formal attrac-
tions with those that derive from our interest in its subject matter,
representational art renders impossible the purely disinterested
and contemplative relation to the work that is properly aesthetic.
Abstract painting, on the other hand, 'has emerged as an epitome
of almost everything that disinterested contemplation requires'
and it is this that gives it its 'special, unique value'.[30] The abstract
work's effect is precisely to restore the subject to its integrity and
to suture subject and object:

It's all there at once, like a sudden revelation. This 'at-onceness' an abstract picture usually drives home to us with greater singleness and clarity than a representational painting does. . . . You are summoned and gathered into one point in the continuum of duration. . . . You become all attention, which means that you become, for the moment, selfless and in a sense entirely identified with the object of your attention.[31]

Nothing could be further from Beckett's steady insistence on the rupture of the lines of communication and the breakdown of the subject-object relation. As we will see in Chapters 2 and 3 of this book, it is neither the integrity of the subject by way of its gaze nor the rendering of the object to the subject that Beckett seeks in the artwork he admires, and certainly not the morally and culturally formative function of the aesthetic experience that Greenberg's critical writings espouse. And the quality of attention that Beckett's late work elicits is far from constituting the subject as a 'single point' in unity with its object but rather, as we will see, a sense of the dispersion and suspension of the subject in relation to things.

Beckett's resistance to the kinds of aesthetic principles that shaped the reception of American abstraction long preceded its full emergence as a major mode of art, and that almost visceral resistance also influenced his affinity for those artists with whom he worked most closely. The ground of his interest in a constellation of 'minor' artists is not the mere contingency of his decision to settle in Paris after it had ceased to be the art capital of the world or of his upbringing in a peripheral location like Ireland in the first half of the twentieth century. It is, this book argues, deeply bound up with principles of non-domination, which, if they were partly formed in relation to the Irish republicanism that he shared with Yeats, MacGreevy and others with whom he was intimate in the 1930s, find a further and more complex resonance in being referred to other locations and domains of work.[32] His interest in artists who remain at the margins of the international canon is of a piece with his insistence on continually undermining in his own work the redoubts of domination, of sovereign subjecthood or of aesthetic power, in that trajectory that leads him always to 'fail better'. His work is committed to the counter-sublime and to the refusal to perform what Deleuze and Guattari would call 'a major function'.[33]

Hence the models of abstract expressionism could not have offered him a visual correlative for his own work. Not only was it too evidently a continuation of the Western tradition into a new domain, but that domain was also one shaped by strikingly imperial claims. Sarita Echavez See has compellingly argued for the deep relationship between abstraction and imperialism, in its 'elision of colonial violence and dispossession', a relationship captured magnificently if unwittingly in Harold Rosenberg's celebration of 'American Action Painters':

> With the American, heir of the pioneer and the immigrant, the foundering of Art and Society was not perceived as a loss. On the contrary, the end of Art marked the beginning of an optimism regarding himself as an artist. The American vanguard painter took to the white canvas as Melville's Ishmael took to the sea.[34]

No better corroboration could be imagined for Beckett's discernment of the continuing force of Western possessive space in even the most 'advanced' art of his time, or of its role in restoring the place of the sovereign subject even in the face of the catastrophes that had overwhelmed mid-century Europe. Against the continued force of the sublime in the major art of the post-war period, Beckett aligns himself with an artist like Bram van Velde, whose works 'do not allow the eye to rest, do not allow the eye after a few moments of intellectual excitement to reconstitute the object of desire: man as the centre of descriptive power, as enunciating force'.[35] This is a work that resists what he calls, in one of his last extended critical tributes, on Henri Hayden,

> the recourses and subterfuges of a painting that is at a loss for referents, which no longer aim in the end to make more beautiful, as beautiful, otherwise beautiful, but quite frankly, to save a relation, a distance, a couple somewhat diminished whatever its components, the self [moi] in its capacity to act, to receive, and the remainder in its docility as the given.[36]

Nothing could have been further from Beckett's intentions, at any point in his writing career, than such an operation of salvage, particularly one that sought to retrieve at once the subject and the sublime.

If, after a relatively brief period of writing on art, Beckett almost entirely abandons both commentary and criticism, thinking 'the lenitive of comment' an impertinence, his desisting by no means spells the end of his vital engagement with visual art.[37] On the contrary, I argue, it is in his theatrical work that his dialogue with painting continues, as his virtual abandonment of criticism coincides with the success of *Godot* and with his increasing devotion to theatre as a medium. The development of his dramatic work in its visual dimension shows no steady and continuous development, though it can be related to the kinds of lessons he might have learnt from the painters with whose work he most intensely engaged at various moments. That learning is never direct, but involves a difficult work of intergeneric translation and a concomitant lag between what he sees in painting and what he is able to put into practice in another medium, whether stage, television or film. As Eyal Amiran has put it of his relation to van Velde, the latter's work 'may have served Beckett, up to a point, as a generative system, a structuring device which helped him to conceptualize and work through his own systematic enterprise'.[38] Although, as we have seen, on occasion Beckett used a specific painting as a visual prompt, generally speaking that is not his approach to thinking the relation of drama and painting as visual arts. After all, as he remarked to Duthuit regarding the designs for the set of *Godot*, 'Do you really think that one could hear anything, faced with a set by Bram, or see anything other than him?'[39] The work of translation is not to transform stage into painting, painterly as Beckett's scenarios can be, but to penetrate below the painting to a method of working, to a visual aesthetic and ethic that can be transformed under the constraints of another medium.

Such work implies, above all, that both painting and the visual dimensions of Beckett's drama are spaces of *thought*, means to extend rather than to suspend the critical work that he had engaged in language. This may not be surprising, given the extent to which the language of visibility, of the eye and the gaze have been fundamental to the philosophical underpinnings of the Western subject, even as they are to Beckett's own aesthetic and philosophical projects.[40] Ulrika Maude has succinctly summarised that 'history of vision' in which 'reason has been conceived and imagined in terms of sight', and she invokes Martin Heidegger's 'Age of the World Picture' to clarify the intimate relation between the placement of the subject before the picture and its stance before the world envisaged as its object:

'That the world becomes picture is one and the same event as man's becoming *subiectum* in the midst of that which is.' The separation of the self from the picture, in other words, is the precondition for grasping the enframed totality, just as the mind, in Cartesian thought, 'is said to be set apart from the material world it observes'.[41]

I explore further in Chapters 2 and 3 the relation between the eye and the subject of perspective that lays the ground for what Beckett describes as 'possessive space' and underwrites the subject-object relation. It is the gradual breakdown of that 'world picture' that can be descried across Beckett's theatre in a painstaking trajectory that is steadily informed by his engagement with painting. In part, the progress of his dramatic work involved the rupture with the dramatic image in which is preserved that dimension of the 'spectacle' that inherited, as Beckett's contemporary Guy Debord put it, 'all the *weaknesses* of the Western philosophical project which undertook to comprehend activity in terms of the categories of seeing'.[42]

That anti-spectacular trajectory can best be described as in the first place radically post-Kantian, despite an extensive tradition of criticism that has been preoccupied with Beckett's Cartesianism. His long-standing insistence on the breakdown of the subject-object relation, which forms the unifying thread of his writings from the essay on Proust to the notes for *Film*, is informed by his sense of the inaccessibility of what he calls 'the pure object', the thing in itself.[43] That inaccessibility of the object draws him, in ways that bear a remarkable affinity with Heidegger's thought of the time, into his rejection of representation, not only of any mimetic or naturalistic art, but also of representation as a larger aesthetic and political category. Indeed, Maude's invocation of Heidegger's essay suggests the complex of issues that, beyond the question of the visual articulation of the subject-object relation, leads both him and Beckett to interrogate the central categories of representation (*Vorstellung*) that link the aesthetic, the philosophical and the political within the process Heidegger calls 'representing production' (*vorstellenden Herstellen*).[44] Ironically, perhaps, it is through painting that Beckett thinks his way out of the space of representation that is defined by the 'world picture' of his moment.

What initially takes the place of representation for Beckett, perhaps under the influence of Proust's 'involuntary memory', is the image, a visual material that seems to rise, without the subject's willing it, as a correlative of subjectivity or 'self-consciousness'. Though he arrives at this formulation in his 1938 review of Denis Devlin's poetry, the most precise visual analogue for this non-representational image could be found in Jack B. Yeats's painting. As late as 1954, in his 'Homage to Jack B. Yeats', he speaks of those 'images of such breathless immediacy' that emanate from 'this great inner real where phantoms quick and dead, nature and void, all that ever and that never will be, join in a single evidence for a single testimony'.[45] Yeats's later paintings, by his own account, rejected representation of the world 'before' the subject, depicting instead images that arose from memory or imagination: 'people who walked into my imagination' to encounter artist and viewer who themselves 'stand within the picture' rather than at a remove.[46] Yeats's vivid sense of the painting as a theatrical space on to which images or persons step offers a valuable index of the visual qualities of Beckett's first stage plays, and it is no accident that his paintings have been suggested as sources for *Godot*. As I argue in Chapter 1, in keeping with Beckett's profound interest in the image at the time and with his conversations with Georges Duthuit on the topic, both *Godot* and *Endgame* are strongly unified by the theatrical images they present. Though that is most evident in their powerful sets – the tree and moon of *Godot*, the skull-like room of *Endgame* – it is also an emphatic visual quality of the tableaus that each play presents, tableaus that stylise or highlight the relations of domination and subjection that circulate among the couples that populate these plays, as they do the novels of the same period. Even against Beckett's insistence that these plays lacked any concealed meaning, their powerful theatrical images have impelled and sustained the innumerable interpretations of the plays that understand them in one way or another as symbolic.[47] Though, of course, such interpretations of these plays feed also on the texts, with their allusions and citations, parables and fragmented narratives, the apparent symbolic intent is conveyed by and inseparable from their visual aesthetic.

It is this strongly unified visual aesthetic, with its images of derelict but nonetheless distinct and even symbolic characters and props, that Beckett is obliged to break in his restless pursuit of a dramatic art adequate to his insight into what post-war France taught him to see as 'humanity in ruins'. It is a measure of the force of theatrical convention, perhaps, that effecting that rupture would take almost a decade after the writing of *Godot* and require a series of abandoned experiments, including the two *Roughs for Theatre* of the late 1950s that would surely have moved his dramatic writing in a direction closer, say, to Harold Pinter than to the profoundly radical works he produced in the 1960s. I argue in Chapter 2 that the extraordinary breakdown that he achieves in the elements of the theatre, starting with *Krapp's Last Tape* and determining the composition of every subsequent work, derives in part from his deep reading of Bram van Velde's painting and its own development. Van Velde undergoes his own slow and painful emancipation from the image in the course of the 1930s and 1940s, and the canvases with which Beckett was most familiar display an almost savage dismantling and redistribution of the elements of the image and of the subject's gaze across a visual field that hovers between abstraction and the vestiges of figuration. Though the mask-like forms that loom from the surfaces of van Velde's paintings will not find even a remote correlative till the very end of Beckett's career, in the phantom-like forms of the television version of *What Where*, Beckett's break with the dramatic image is signalled by his steady dismantling of the theatrical space and his distribution of the elements of both character and setting across the stage or the screen. This process involves more than what Daniel Albright has suggestively called Beckett's 'instinct . . . to fracture the theatre into distinct planes, in which action and speech never coincide'.[48] Just as van Velde discovers that the gaze is not a property or guarantee of the subject, so Beckett begins to disassemble the human figure and its properties into an assemblage of things – the body or its parts, voice, gaze, lighting or camera lens, tape recorder or visual image – that render the human subject a thing among its things.

One could say, indeed, that Beckett's theatre thinks the thing. It does so in a way that moves beyond Heidegger's contemporaneous essays on the thing, from 'The Origin of the Work of Art' of 1937 to 'The Thing' of 1950, refusing the philosopher's nostalgic identification of the thing with the pre-commodity, artisanal object in use and apprehending the consequences of late modernity for any conception of the human in its world. It is as if Beckett's dramas, like the great prose work that inaugurates his later work *How It Is*, relentlessly track the significance of an increasingly instrumentalised economic and political world. That world, as Theodor Adorno noted in his prescient essay on the play, was already symbolised in *Endgame*.[49] There already, and again in *Happy Days*, something of the subject's disintegrating relation to its objects is played out in the protagonist's fidgeting with broken and decayed objects – Hamm's handkerchief or his three-legged stuffed dog, Winnie's broken spectacles or deteriorating hairbrush. In the plays from *Krapp's Last Tape* to *Catastrophe* or *What Where*, those effects are not symbolised but staged and enacted.

And it is hardly incidental that these late plays become increasingly painterly, devoted to effects of light and colour, chiaroscuro and tableaus that foreground the action along a single strip of light, the movement of figures in and out of darkness, fading in and out or disappearing abruptly. Beckett had already recognised in van Velde the obdurate insistence of the painting as thing, 'the thing in suspension', 'the thing immobile in the void', rather than a representation of things.[50] His long association with Arikha, the last artist for whom he would write even the briefest tribute, the artist with whom he collaborated on artist's books, to whom he dedicated prose texts, and who designed the set for a New York production of *Endgame*, testifies to his continuing interrogation of the conditions of seeing as inseparable from the conditions of a new visual space composed by the human gaze suspended in its relations to things, in which the subject is implicated as itself a thing. Arikha is a painter for whom the gaze, the condition of seeing as itself an object of perception, is primary. His profound interrogation of 'what it is to be and to be in face of', to cite Beckett's brief but complex tribute, issues in work which, deliberately produced in the space of a single sitting, is itself dramatic, even performative, implicating the viewer in the space in which the thing appears suspended in view – as, indeed, his earlier abstract work staged the tumbling, shifting fall of shapes suspended in an ever-changing perspectival field.

To both Beckett and Arikha, in drama and in painting, the example of Caravaggio seems to have been of critical importance. The Italian master's influence was twofold, as I have already mentioned, involving both the painter's notorious predilection for effects of chiaroscuro achieved by single, elevated sources of light, and the resultant refusal of the pictorial depth that had become the means to imply narrative time by way of perspective. Arikha's dramatic experiments with pictorial space and colour relations find their correlative in Beckett's strikingly lit and foregrounded stage plays, where action seems to take place along a flattened frieze and figures emerge from and disappear into a pitch-black void, often deploying colour values to emphasise the rhythms of appearance. Paintings and plays alike emphasise ephemerality rather than narrative, moments of advent rather than events, and implicate audience and viewer as co-constituents of the work, caught up in the space of the thing that is happening in the instant itself.

Beckett's late plays thus deny the audience the position of spectator that is the theatrical equivalent of the punctual perspective which secured the subject its sovereign position in the possessive spatial relations of Western art. His dramatic work performs a relentless assault on the 'stage as moral institution' and the figure of Man that it reflected back.[51] Just as his dramatic work disperses and fragments the constituent elements of the theatre, dismantling the integrity of the human figure on the stage, it demands that the audience also undergo the frustration of any desire to unify its perception of the work, to reduce the dynamic of fragmentation and reification to coherence. The subject of Beckett's theatre is one suspended among the things that compose it. In the conclusion to *Beckett's Thing*, I seek to draw out Beckett's long-standing concern with the reification or thingliness of the late-modern subject, and with painting and theatre alike as media that stage this conception of the human reduced to the condition of a thing. Beckett's emphasis throughout his writings in every medium is famously negative, and has given rise to his reception as an artist of unusual pessimism, committed to meaninglessness and absurdity. At the same time, however, it is impossible to view Beckett as anything other than a profoundly ethical writer, attentive at every moment to the task of bringing 'light to the issueless predicament of existence, reducing the dark where there might have been, mathematically at least, a door', as he said of Yeats.[52] That steady illumination of the darkness that can appear so negative is, to be sure, a refusal to offer easy consolations in the face of apparent catastrophe, but it also entails the effort to think steadily through the implications of an era of increasing instrumentalisation and reification. Beckett's late plays, *Catastrophe* and *What Where*, stage with unusual directness his enduring concern with ethical and political questions. They present the human as a thing subject to administrative manipulation, incarceration and torture for which the stage itself becomes the medium. In the latter play in particular, the disembodied voice of the Law, Kant's voice of moral reason, reduced to the form of a prompt to torture, institutes the cycles of mutual interrogation and violence. And yet these human things, as in the final seconds of *Catastrophe*'s parodic Ecce Homo, continue to be objects that 'resist representation' in defiance of that Law whose dialectic both institutes the subject and subjects it to reification. With deliberate steadiness Beckett's work brings us to the threshold of a new theatrical space that is also that of the imagination of another ethical and political possibility for community. That community, imaged in the suspension of the audience in its relation to the stage, is thought *through* the conditions of reification and instrumentality, of dispossession and dereliction, rather than in compensation for them.[53] In the end, Beckett's thinking of the thing offers the possibility of imagining the outlines of the *res publica*, of a community founded not in the sovereignty of the subject over its objects but in the insistence of the human as a thing beyond representation, suspended in its relation to the things among which it dwells. We would for once be right to call such a conception a vision, not only in so far as its realisation remains a thing that is yet to come, but also in that it is ultimately apprehended in the visual and spatial rather than the textual elements of Beckett's theatre. What his profound engagement with the visual arts has to teach us, finally, is not only an aesthetic remaking of theatrical form, but an acute apprehension of the ethical and political implications of that form, 'perhaps even an inkling of the terms in which our condition is to be thought again'.[54]

Notes

1. Samuel Beckett, 'La Peinture des van Velde, ou Le Monde et le Pantalon', in *Disjecta*, p. 120. My translation.
2. Beckett, 'La Peinture des van Velde', p. 120. My translation.
3. See, for example, James Knowlson, *Damned to Fame: The Life of Samuel Beckett*, pp. 140 and 186.
4. Beckett, 'Recent Irish Poetry', in *Disjecta*, p. 70.
5. Beckett, 'The Capital of the Ruins', p. 28.
6. The phrase is drawn from the catalogue of the National Gallery of Ireland's ground-breaking centenary exhibition on Beckett and the visual arts: Fionnuala Croke (ed.), *Samuel Beckett: A Passion for Paintings*.
7. For this biographical information, see especially Knowlson, *Damned to Fame*. Valuable accounts of Beckett's absorption in visual art include Lawrence E. Harvey's pioneering *Samuel Beckett: Poet and Critic*; Dougald McMillan, 'Samuel Beckett and the Visual Arts:

The Embarrassment of Allegory'; and Anne Atik, *How It Was: A Memoir of Samuel Beckett*, especially for details of his relationship with Avigdor Arikha. For Beckett's relationship with Georges Duthuit, see Rémi Labrusse, 'Beckett et la peinture'. Increasingly it is possible to track Beckett's engagement with the visual arts through his own letters; see *The Letters of Samuel Beckett, Volume I: 1929–1940* and *Volume II: 1941–1956*.

8. See Croke, 'Introduction to the Exhibition, Part 1', in *Passion for Paintings*, p. 14; Atik, *How It Was*, pp. 4–6.
9. Knowlson, *Damned to Fame*, p. 236.
10. Knowlson, *Damned to Fame*, p. 342; Peggy Phelan, 'Lessons in Blindness from Samuel Beckett', pp. 1280–1; Beckett, *Molloy*, pp. 4–5.
11. Graley Herren, *Samuel Beckett's Plays on Film and Television*, pp. 163–6.
12. I borrow the term from S. E. Gontarski's still indispensable study of the genesis of the plays, *The Intent of Undoing in Samuel Beckett's Dramatic Texts*.
13. McMillan, 'Samuel Beckett and the Visual Arts', p. 31.
14. See 'German Letter of 1937 [to Axel Kaun]', in *Disjecta*, pp. 52–4, and its English translation by Martin Esslin, pp. 171–3.
15. Beckett, *Proust*, pp. 539–40.
16. Beckett, 'Three Dialogues', pp. 556 and 563.
17. Harvey, *Samuel Beckett*; Lois Oppenheim, *The Painted Word: Samuel Beckett's Dialogue with Art*. Jonathan Bignell comments on the shortcomings of efforts to address the pictorial qualities of Beckett's plays for TV in *Beckett on Screen: The Television Plays*, pp. 160–1.
18. Beckett, *Worstward Ho*, p. 471. It should be noted that Alain Badiou has presented a powerful challenge to this reading of the overall trajectory of Beckett's work, arguing instead that a marked break or rupture takes place between the writing of *Texts for Nothing* and *How It Is*. See his *On Beckett*, pp. 15–18 and 40–1.
19. A signal exception to this pattern is Eyal Amiran's regrettably brief section on Bram van Velde in *Wandering and Home: Beckett's Metaphysical Narrative*, pp. 41–55.
20. Beckett, 'La Peinture des van Velde', in *Disjecta*, pp. 123 and 127.
21. Dougald McMillan and Martha Fehsenfeld, *Beckett in the Theatre: The Author as Practical Playwright and Director*, Vol. 1, p. 91. See also Gontarski's remark on how Beckett's theatre after *Play* 'grew more overtly formalist and patterned as it became more visual', in *The Theatrical Notebooks of Samuel Beckett*, Vol. 4, p. xv.

22. In this formulation, I differ somewhat from Gerhard Hauck, for whom 'The fact that his plays approximate the representational conditions of visual art works is therefore a purely accidental by-product of the generally reductive process of composing plays.' For this and his larger argument, see Hauck's *Reductionism in Drama and the Theatre: The Case of Samuel Beckett*, pp. 175–6. Bignell, *Beckett on Screen*, p. 126, offers a range of painterly analogues for Beckett's visual effects on TV, including twentieth-century abstraction, Dutch interiors and Caravaggio. He also comments on the resemblance between the TV screen and the frame of the painting, pp. 138–9.

23. The record of their friendship is detailed in Atik's invaluable memoir, *How It Was*. Beckett dedicated a number of texts to Arikha, including the prose piece *Ceiling*, in Richard Channin et al., *Arikha*, p. 12, while Arikha designed the set for a New York production of *Endgame* in 1984 (Atik, *How It Was*, pp. 41–5) and produced prints to accompany an edition of Beckett's *Au Loin un Oiseau*. These prints, a set of which are in the British Museum, are reproduced in Duncan Thomson and Stephen Coppel, *Avigdor Arikha from Life: Drawings and Prints, 1965–2005*, pp. 59–63. On this work and Arikha's other artist's books with Beckett texts, *The North* and *L'issue*, see Oppenheim, *The Painted Word*, pp. 170–1 and 174–7.

24. Beckett, 'Peintres de l'empêchement', in *Disjecta*, p. 135. My translation.

25. The terms are those of Amiran, *Wandering and Home*, p. 55.

26. For a theoretical account of the 'minor' in this sense, see my *Nationalism and Minor Literature: James Clarence Mangan and the Emergence of Irish Cultural Nationalism*, chapter 1. Mark Nixon has commented insightfully on Beckett's general preference for the 'minor key' (*bémolisé*) in painting as against competence and sublimity: see his *Samuel Beckett's German Diaries, 1936–1937*, pp. 142–4.

27. Frances Morris, 'Bram van Velde (1895–1981)', p. 171.

28. Clement Greenberg, '"American-Type" Painting', in *Art and Culture: Critical Essays*, pp. 211 and 208.

29. Greenberg, 'The Case for Abstract Art', in *The Collected Essays and Criticism, Vol. 4*, p. 78.

30. Greenberg, 'The Case for Abstract Art', pp. 80, 82.

31. Greenberg, 'The Case for Abstract Art', p. 81.

32. See David Lloyd, 'Frames of *Referrance*: Samuel Beckett as an Irish

Question'.

33. Gilles Deleuze and Félix Guattari, *Kafka: pour une littérature mineure*.

34. Sarita See, *The Decolonized Eye: Filipino American Art and Performance*, p. 66; Harold Rosenberg, 'American Action Painters', cited in Joan Marter, 'Introduction: Internationalism and Abstract Expressionism', p. 2.

35. Serge Guilbaut, 'Disdain for the Stain: Abstract Expressionism and Tachisme', p. 49.

36. Beckett, 'Henri Hayden, homme-peintre', in *Disjecta*, p. 146.

37. Beckett, 'Homage to Jack B. Yeats', in *Disjecta*, p. 149.

38. Amiran, *Wandering and Home*, p. 46.

39. Beckett, *Letters, Vol. II*, p. 218.

40. Lois Oppenheim has argued forcefully for the ways in which for Beckett the visual relation of subject to object furnishes the model for that relation in general: 'For not only did the classic Beckettian themes—language (its expressivity or lack of), identity (its, at best, tenuous link to a fragmented self), and the ego-world relation—appear modeled on the sensory perspective of the eye and the verbal figuration of reality within the visual field constitutive, whatever the genre, of the Beckettian drama, but painting materialized (both in the creative and the critical work) as emblematic for Beckett of the creative process itself.' See Oppenheim, *The Painted Word*, p. 3.

41. Ulrika Maude, *Beckett, Technology and the Body*, p. 25. The embedded quotes are from Martin Heidegger, 'The Age of the World Picture', and Timothy Brennan, 'The World as Exhibition'.

42. Guy Debord, *Society of the Spectacle*, n.p., thesis 19.

43. Beckett, 'La Peinture des van Velde', in *Disjecta*, p. 126.

44. Heidegger, 'The Age of the World Picture', pp. 65–71. For an analysis of the interweaving of the political and aesthetic usages of 'representation', see my 'Representation's Coup'.

45. Beckett, 'Homage to Jack B. Yeats', in *Disjecta*, p. 149.

46. Jack B. Yeats, cited in Bruce Arnold, *Jack Yeats*, p. 333.

47. As Daniel Albright nicely puts it, 'in *Waiting for Godot*, Beckett isn't content simply to dispense with symbols; he must somehow find a way of showing that symbols could never properly constitute themselves anywhere. *Waiting for Godot* isn't an asymbolic play; it's an anti-symbolic play that insists on waving in the spectator's face the aborted fetuses of symbols, the cremains of symbols.' See Albright, *Beckett and Aesthetics*, p. 53.

48. Albright, *Beckett and Aesthetics*, p. 9.

49. In this respect, there may be more continuity between the preoccupations of the texts of the 1950s and *How It Is* than Badiou's insistence on a formal and conceptual rupture would allow (see note 18, above). I have analysed the ways in which *How It Is* extends Beckett's long-standing engagement with torture as an index of instrumentality in 'On Extorted Speech: Back to *How It Is*', in *Irish Culture and Colonial Modernity, 1800–2000*, pp. 198–220. For Adorno's remarks on *Endgame*, see 'Trying to Understand *Endgame*'.
50. Beckett, 'La Peinture des van Velde', in *Disjecta*, p. 126.
51. These terms are taken from Friedrich Schiller's 'On the Stage as Moral Institution'. For a discussion of this essay and its crucial place for any understanding of the history of representation, see David Lloyd and Paul Thomas, *Culture and the State*, pp. 53–7.
52. Beckett, 'MacGreevy on Yeats', in *Disjecta*, p. 97. Slightly paraphrased.
53. As Leo Bersani and Ulysse Dutoit have put it, speaking of Beckett's effort to respect the breakdown of the subject-object relation described in 'Recent Irish Poetry', 'To recognize the original truth of this unrelated state, as well as its inescapable consequences, may be the preconditions for any viable reconstruction of social relations.' See Bersani and Dutoit, *Arts of Impoverishment: Beckett, Rothko, Resnais*, p. 27.
54. Beckett, 'The Capital of the Ruins', p. 28.

Republics of Difference:
Yeats, MacGreevy, Beckett

I

Samuel Beckett's long personal and critical engagement with the Irish painter Jack B. Yeats provokes from the outset two puzzling observations: first, virtually every important study of Yeats invokes Beckett's testimony to the artist's singular greatness. There is nothing peculiar in that: Beckett's are eloquent and authoritative statements, for reasons that often have to do more with his stature than with the attention paid to his insights. Yet sketchy as Beckett's statements are, the accounts that invoke his authority make little effort to elaborate or to engage with the writer's quite idiosyncratic and solitary apprehension of Yeats's achievement and value. The invocation of the authority seems in no way to influence the approach to the paintings. Second, and no less puzzling, given the present general acceptance of the singularity and originality of Yeats's painterly technique in his later work, is how rarely critics undertake the formal analysis of it. His most indefatigable curator, Hilary Pyle, gives us in her exhaustive and indispensable catalogues detailed accounts of each of the works reproduced, but even these remain essentially descriptive rather than analytical and are marked by the impressionistic, tonal vocabulary that has been the hallmark of Yeats criticism to date: 'exuberant', 'ruminative', 'elated', 'sombre', even 'Wordsworthian'.[1] Such impressionistic accounts of the paintings seek to render their undoubted force, but they do so at great cost. On the one hand, they do not pause to attend to the remarkable artifice, the compositional exactitude, of Yeats's most powerful work, giving instead an impression of Yeats's virtually naïve, notoriously untaught spontaneity in his medium. In related ways, Bruce Arnold's peculiarly extended emphasis on the youthful artist's childlike fascination with miniature theatres and paper boats eclipses attention to the mature artist's reflections, political or aesthetic, in a way that ultimately sells short the seriousness of his engagements.[2] On the other hand, those impressionistic readings and the critics' fascination with the apparent spontaneity of the artist's procedures foreclose all too rapidly on the almost belligerent orneriness of the paintings and the unabashed difficulty with which they refuse to resolve to the viewer's gaze. Not for nothing did Yeats decline to permit reproductions of his works: prints, transparencies and digital images alike soften and flatten the sculpted dimensions of his brushwork, the stark transitions between virtually, sometimes even actually, bare canvas and astonishingly thick impasto, the unstable oscillation between the emergence of the figure and the foregrounding of the medium that dissolves even as it reveals. This difficulty that confronts the viewer has on occasion provoked hostility and mystification in face of the work and, precisely for that reason, should not be ignored or diminished. Indeed, if one wishes for an account of the difficulty of seeing a Yeats painting, an antagonistic and satirical cartoon in *Dublin Opinion* (Fig. 1.1) may serve better than much of what passes for art criticism.[3] Where the latter seeks to make the work explicable and palatable, the cartoon has at least the virtue of capturing the labour of attention that the paintings exact and concludes, however sardonically, with an acknowledgement of their possibly unsettling effects.

But if we wish to take Yeats's not-so-modest claim to be 'the first living painter in the world' with some seriousness, as I believe we should, we have surely to pay the paintings the more exacting attention they demand and begin at least to decipher the grounds of their originality and their continuing difficulty for the eye.[4] Beckett's valuation of him as being 'with the great of our time', which places him in the company of Kandinsky, Klee and Braque, amongst others, is scarcely to be dismissed: he was not given to flattery and his associations are hardly conventional.[5] The harder task is to decipher what Beckett's acute eye saw in Yeats's work (or, for that matter, to understand what Joyce meant in claiming that Yeats and he shared a 'method', or why an artist of the international stature of Oskar Kokoschka might have estimated Yeats so highly).[6] Beckett's remarks in his two published notices are not only too brief but also characteristically too enigmatic and reserved for us to do more than speculate on the grounds for Yeats's appar-

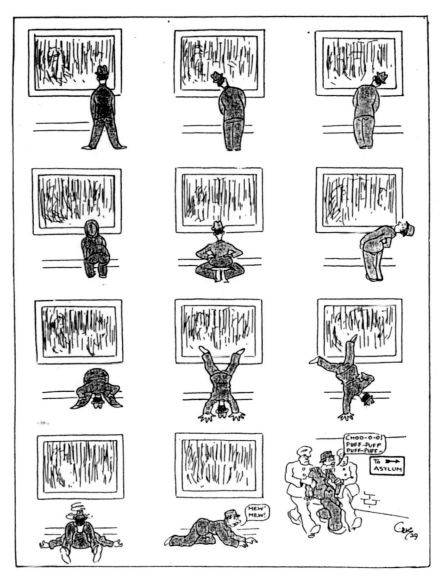

Fig. 1.1 *Dublin Opinion*, 'The Man Who Tried to Get the Hang of a Jack Yeats Picture' (1929).

ently powerful impact on him. Nonetheless, this chapter attempts to understand Beckett's homage to Yeats through an approach to what he may have seen as formally significant in the paintings. Beckett's capacity for *attention* to visual work is notorious, and it is clear that his regard for the paintings that he valued was based on the significance of their forms rather than on any symbolic or allegorical meaning they might secrete. Indeed, as we shall see further, the whole tendency of Beckett's writings on art (and not solely on Yeats) was antagonistic to either symbolism or allegory and even to representation itself. That antagonism places him, rightly or wrongly, in direct opposition to the predominant reception of Yeats, whether he be seen as the painter who gives expression to the spirit of the nation or as one whose works are achieved, if enigmatic, symbols of emotional states or of individual memories. The question here is not so much whether Beckett was correct in his readings as it is to see what in Yeats's paintings might lend itself to such a radically antithetical vision.

The dominant view of Yeats in Beckett's own moment, which gave occasion for his first extended remarks on the painting, was that of their mutual friend Thomas MacGreevy. According to Beckett, the leading conviction in MacGreevy's short essay is that Jack B. Yeats is, in every sense, the most representative painter of the Irish nation. Beckett quotes MacGreevy as follows:

What was unique in Ireland was that the life of the people considered itself, and was in fact, spiritually and culturally as well as politically, the whole life of the nation. Those who acted for the nation officially were outside the nation. They had a stronger sense of identity with the English governing class than with the people of Ireland, and their art was no more than a province of English art. The first genuine artist, therefore, who so identified himself with the people of Ireland as to be able to give true and good and beautiful expression to the life they lived, and to that sense of themselves as the Irish nation, inevitably became not merely a *genre* painter like the painters of the *petit peuple* in other countries, and not merely a nation's painter in the sense that Pol de Limburg, Louis le Nain, Bassano, Ostade or Jan Steen were national painters, but *the* national painter in the sense that Rembrandt and Velasquez and Watteau were national painters, the painter who in his work was the consummate expression of the spirit of his own nation at one of the supreme points in its evolution.[7]

MacGreevy's reading of Yeats's painting as 'the consummate expression of the spirit of his own nation' may itself be the consummate expression of a cultural nationalist aesthetic. Intrinsic to this aesthetic, which in Ireland dates back at least to the Young Ireland movement of the 1840s, is the conception of both the artwork and the artist as representative. As MacGreevy puts it:

> Actually the peoples [sic] are represented only by disinterested men, and more particularly by artists. In resurgent Ireland the pioneer and first representative man in the art of painting was Jack B. Yeats. (JBY, 32)[8]

The play on the relation between the political and the mimetic usage of the term 'representation' is deliberate and explicit. The artist himself becomes representative of the national spirit by representing the life of the nation in painting. Not, as MacGreevy makes clear, that representing the national spirit requires 'strict adherence to the observed fact'; on the contrary, for a nationalist aesthetic, the transformative capacity of imagination redeems a damaged nation. One might say, drawing again on familiar Romantic precepts, that the act of representation is redemptively transformative in itself, in so far as it raises the scattered particulars to the permanent and universal, or to what MacGreevy terms 'the unchanging elements of reality' (JBY, 28). In such terms, representation is not mere depiction of the particular but an always transformative elevation of the particular to the universal that is a return of the nation to its essential self. The poetry of this painting is 'the splendour of essential truth' (JBY, 27). Even without MacGreevy's emphatic evocation of the symbolic dimensions of paintings like *In Memory of Boucicault and Bianconi*, his insistent deployment of a vocabulary of translucence – 'glowing', 'mystic brilliance', 'light and fire', 'inward intensity', 'radiance' – would be sufficient to betray MacGreevy's investment in a symbolist reading of Yeats, a reading which has certainly been influential in subsequent assessments of Yeats's work.[9]

In the terms of this nationalist/symbolist aesthetic, the representation of the particular is the outward manifestation of an inward spirit – the '*expression* of the spirit of [the] nation', as MacGreevy puts it. An expressive aesthetic of this order thus assumes as given a discrete spirit or essence. This spirit is translucent in the outward form. The fragmented particular becomes consubstantial with the whole of which it is part. Representation here has the double sense of standing in for and of manifesting something. Thus the very process of representation restores the fragmented elements of the nation to wholeness by making each an aspect of the expression of the national spirit. In MacGreevy's account, Yeats's work answers to the need of the Irish in the early twentieth century 'to feel their own life was being expressed in art' (*JBY*, 19). The very term 'life' here marks the threshold at which the expressive act is situated, on the boundary that marks the difference between and the fragile continuity of the inner life of a people (its spirit or vital force) and the outward manifestations of a more or less unreflective 'daily life': the labours, pleasures and habits of a people. Painting, as it were, opens a door between the damaged life of a heretofore hidden Ireland and the secret realm of its spirit.

The nationalist view of art, in which a political and an aesthetic *parti pris* are combined, that which governs MacGreevy's essay on Yeats, could only be anathema to Beckett. His review of the work articulates what appears to have been a long-standing and well-understood difference in the two writers' approaches to Yeats and to art in general. Beckett pointedly distinguishes in the subtitles of his review between the aspect of Yeats that MacGreevy emphasises, *The National Painter*, and the one he promotes, *The Artist*, insisting that the 'national aspects of Mr. Yeats's genius have . . . been overstated'. He proceeds to imply, briefly, curtly even, both the interested or aesthetically 'impure' grounds for that overstatement and reasons to suspect the validity of ascribing to Yeats an 'imaginative sympathy' with the Irish people ('How sympathetic?' the review almost maliciously enquires) (*D*, 96). In what must be one of Beckett's most resonant locutions, he dismisses any notion that Yeats's paintings might represent a doorway between inner truth and outer reality, preferring instead a powerful image of closure: Yeats 'is with the great of our time . . . because he brings light, as only the great dare to bring light, to the issueless predicament of existence, reduces the dark where there might have been, mathematically at least, a door' (*D*, 97). Beckett's image here is at once deft, succinct and devastating. The very valence of light, as that which shines through the particular to imbue it with possibly universal meaning, is reversed here, as the light becomes a dismally demystifying force, reducing darkness only to expose the absence of communication, of doors in or out. Not only does the image uncannily predict Beckett's later short texts and plays,

like *Lessness* (1970) and *The Lost Ones* (1970), *Not I* (1972) or
Eh Joe (1966), it also catches the ambiguous quality of many of
Yeats's paintings, where the angled beam of light seems to be no
conventional indicator of optimism or hope, but a baleful and
melancholy illumination that serves only to enhance the gloom.

Clearly, for Beckett, what is illuminated in the imaginative glow
of Yeats's painting is not the particular restored to wholeness, but a
series of disjunctive images deprived of either connection or deter-
minate significance and expressive only of the missed encounter:

> The being in the street, when it happens in the room, the being in the
> room when it happens in the street, the turning to gaze from land to
> sea, from sea to land, the backs to one another and the eyes aban-
> doning, the man alone trudging in the sand, the man alone thinking
> (thinking!) in his box – these are characteristic notations . . . (*D*, 97)

Beckett's terse and uncompromising statement of his utterly different apprehension of the painter can scarcely have surprised
MacGreevy. Beckett had already made his understanding of Yeats
clear in letters (to some of which MacGreevy alludes) that emphasise, in similar tones, his perception of the paintings as images
of alienation, suspension, disjunction – anything but representations of the continuity of artist and people, inner and outer, spirit
and body. Beckett's view of Yeats resonates rather with the post-
Cartesian predicament of scission and disaggregation, between
mind and matter, subject and object, that notoriously informs all
of the writer's early work. As he wrote to MacGreevy, even as the
latter was composing the first draft of the essay on Yeats:

> I find something terrifying for example in the way Yeats puts down a
> man's head & a woman's head side by side, or face to face, the awful
> acceptance of 2 entities that will never mingle. And do you remember
> the picture of a man sitting under a fuchsia hedge, reading with his
> back turned to the sea and the thunder clouds? One does not realize
> how still his pictures are till one looks at others, almost petrified, a
> sudden suspension of the performance, of the convention of sympathy
> and antipathy, meeting and parting, joy and sorrow.[10]

It is probably impossible to tell to which of Yeats's paintings
Beckett is referring in recalling 'puts down a man's head & a
woman's head side by side, or face to face', though the second

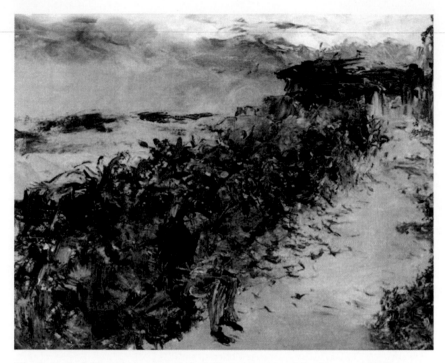

Fig. 1.2 Jack B. Yeats, *A Storm* (oil on canvas, 46 × 61 cm, 1936),
© Estate of Jack B. Yeats. All rights reserved, DACS/ARS 2016.

painting is identifiable as *A Storm* (1936; Fig. 1.2). But it is clear
that what holds his attention is precisely not what MacGreevy
celebrates in the painter – 'movement and colour', fluidity and,
of course, translucence of expression (*JBY*, 27). It is, rather, this
quality of petrification and suspension that seems to him quite
antithetical to the 'sympathy' that MacGreevy names as a dominant quality in Yeats. In the same letter, Beckett insists on the
separateness, not only of human beings from one another, but also
of the human and the natural in Yeats's work: 'What I feel he gets
so well, dispassionately, not tragically like Watteau, is the hetero-
geneity of nature and the human denizens, the unalterable alien-
ness of the 2 phenomena.'[11] Unlike the painting of Constable or
Turner, whose 'nature is really infested with "spirit"', Yeats's 'final
quale' is 'the ultimate *inorganism* of everything'. This inorganism
is for Beckett not merely a quality of the represented of the paintings, but a matter of what the *forms* of the paintings articulate: 'A
painting of pure inorganic juxtapositions, where nothing can be
taken or given and there is no possibility of change or exchange.'[12]

Nothing could be further, it seems, from MacGreevy's assertion that Yeats's 'concern with the natural scene itself was a human concern. He occasionally depicted it unpeopled, a solitude, but such a solitude as could clearly provide an enlargement of one's human experience' (*JBY*, 12).

Such intense differences in perception and in the evaluation of the paintings signal, perhaps, the capaciousness of the paintings themselves, their openness to divergent readings that Yeats himself is known to have desired. At the same time, they derive from a marked difference in the aesthetic *and* the political assumptions of each writer. For MacGreevy, as we have seen, Yeats is the first and quintessential national painter; for Beckett, Yeats explores rather what he had described in a 1934 review, 'Recent Irish Poetry', as 'the new thing that has happened, or the old thing that has happened again, namely the breakdown of the object' or 'the breakdown of the subject' – in either case, the rupture of communication (*D*, 70). Awareness of this situation makes it the artist's task to achieve a statement 'of the space that intervenes between him and the world of objects'. And, already in 1934, it is 'a picture by Mr. Jack Yeats' that he invokes, alongside T. S. Eliot's *The Wasteland*, as exemplary of this awareness. MacGreevy appears to assimilate Yeats to a nationalist agenda, emphasising the representative status of both the artist and his figurations, foregrounding those elements of his work that can be read as expressive of the national spirit, and appropriating Yeats to an aesthetic that affirms the continuity of the spirit in the face of the disintegrative force of an *unrepresentative* colonial power. Beckett emphasises rupture and discontinuity and the radically unreconciled relation of subject and object, and appropriates the painter no less forcefully to his own apprehension of the 'issueless predicament of existence'. Yeats's paintings become the contested zone of two radically opposed conjunctures of aesthetic and political principles.

But doubtless, in following the terms that Beckett establishes in his review of MacGreevy on Yeats, one is drawn to exaggerate the differences, stark as sometimes they are. MacGreevy's essay is in some ways a much less coherent production than at first appears, and is marked by contradictions and countercurrents that trouble its ostensibly nationalist agenda. While Beckett's contempt for the *Saorstát* (the post-treaty Irish Free State) has often been emphasised, less has been made of the long-standing republicanism that MacGreevy and Yeats shared and which forms a barely occluded

subtext of the essay. In the wake of the Civil War, which pitted
republican radicals against the forces of the new Free State – to
which MacGreevy refers disparagingly as 'the little almost republic of Ireland' – the identification of nationalism and republicanism
is no simple matter.

Indeed, MacGreevy's essay on Yeats not only makes no secret of
his own political affiliations, but also insists on articulating both
a republican interpretation of recent Irish history and his sense of
the relation of Yeats's work to republicanism. This subtext ranges
from references to 'the tanks and lorries of imperial terrorists' to
an openly republican interpretation of partition:

> The end of the prolonged struggle was that Ireland had not the one
> parliament that it wanted but the two it didn't want imposed on it.
> *Divide and rule.* The country was partitioned. The imperial connec-
> tion remained. And with the adroitness of experienced politicians the
> imperialists laid the final odium of moral defeat on the Irish them-
> selves. Ireland was launched on a civil war. (*JBY*, 25)

In this context, MacGreevy's discussion or even invocation of
several paintings of Yeats's gains implicit political significance:
Bachelor's Walk, In Memory (1915; Fig. 1.3), with its reference
to the murder of Irish nationalists by the British army; *Singing the
Dark Rosaleen, Croke Park* (1921), which depicts the singing of
that patriotic ballad at the Gaelic sports arena that had become
infamous for the Black and Tan massacre of Bloody Sunday the
year before the painting's completion;[13] *The Funeral of Harry
Boland* (1922), commemorating the death of the prominent
republican leader; *Communicating with Prisoners* (c. 1924),
which represents a group of women shouting up to republican
women prisoners in Kilmainham Gaol during the Civil War;
and, in his postscript added in 1945, the reference to a peculiarly
sombre painting *Going to Wolfe Tone's Grave* (1929), of which
MacGreevy parenthetically and somewhat redundantly remarks
'the national note is struck as clearly as ever in the past' (*JBY*, 37).
As if it were necessary, that last remark serves to underline the significance of this canon of Yeats's paintings and the kind of historical and political claim that is entailed in the assertion that Yeats is
the pre-eminent Irish painter. In the first place, by establishing that
the painter's work affiliated him with republicanism and that his
claims as a historical painter rest on paintings that commemorate

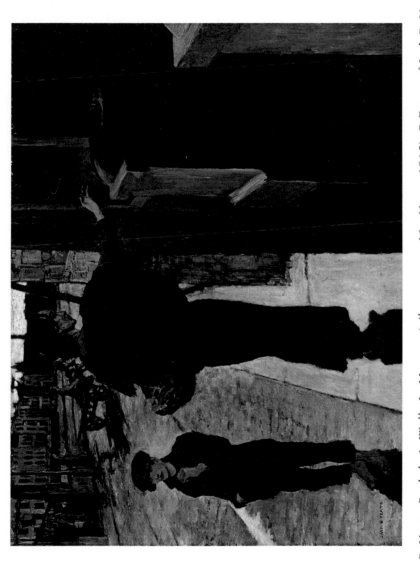

Fig. 1.3 Jack B. Yeats, *Bachelor's Walk, In Memory* (oil on canvas, 46 × 51 cm, 1915), © Estate of Jack B. Yeats. All rights reserved, DACS/ARS 2016.

the high points and the defeats of republican struggle, MacGreevy links Yeats's own trajectory as an artist to disaffiliation from the present order and to a more or less proleptic relation to the nation he represents. Betrayed by the collusion with its imperial saboteurs of the nation that claims to be 'once again', the republican artist represents the nation that is 'yet to be', the still damaged but recalcitrant people. If, in the immediate aftermath of the Civil War, 'fact and poetry had parted company', it becomes inevitable that 'Jack Yeats's work became a passionate recall to poetry' (*JBY*, 27). It is to this moment also that MacGreevy dates the major 'modification of technique' that begins to constitute Yeats's later, more aesthetically uncompromising style. Both stylistically and politically, MacGreevy suggests, Yeats's work is a refusal of the status quo, of the state that is in being.

This trajectory of Yeats's work, which MacGreevy understands as belonging with the 'subjective tendency' of post-war Ireland, correlates to an 'objective tendency' both in the painter's work and in Ireland itself. In these tendencies, we might say, republicanism withdraws into a kind of permanent if 'obscure' and dispersed opposition.[14] The objective tendency, which is 'to insist on the need for a definitive solution of Ireland's political and, more particularly, social problems', maintains the legacy not only of the spiritual nationalist Patrick Pearse, but also of the national Marxist labour leader James Connolly.[15] Its oppositionality, in the moment, is 'that it fulfills the perennial need to check up on authority's liability to abuse its privileges' (*JBY*, 26). What may appear here as a strangely muted version of republican ideals in fact embodies an understated but no less significant principle of non-domination that, as Philip Pettit has argued, is critical to the specific understanding of freedom that is articulated throughout republican political thought.[16]

If the 'subjective tendency' of the movement manifests itself in the formal changes in Yeats's work, MacGreevy locates the 'objective tendency' in the content of his work. However, the changes are less marked than the continuity. Yeats's long-standing devotion to depicting the common people of Ireland links him to the radical tradition of republicanism. MacGreevy's implication, scarcely muted here, is that Yeats's work has always allied him to the left-wing republicanism of 'the sociologist [*sic*], James Connolly':

It is not likely that Jack Yeats has remained untouched by this objective tendency. But as he has always painted the people, 'the workers,' in town and country, it would be difficult to trace any such influence as a new thing in his art. It is not yesterday or today that Jack Yeats discovered labouring humanity. At the Celtic Race Congress in Paris in 1923, he read a paper in which he gave it as his opinion that the most stirring sights in the world are a man ploughing and a ship on the sea. He still paints the people, and with an even more passionate directness in recent years than in his earlier days. Sometimes there is more outward calm but more inward intensity, fire and imagination than there used to be. I think here particularly of the timeless figure of *The Breaker-Out* [1925; Fig. 1.4]. Impassive now, but still desperate, he might be the child of *The Big Turf Fire* [1898; Fig. 1.5] painted twenty-five years later. (*JBY*, 26–7)

MacGreevy's final allusion connects the 1925 oil of a departing sailor, *The Breaker-Out*, with an early sketch of unmistakable political import that he analyses earlier in the essay:

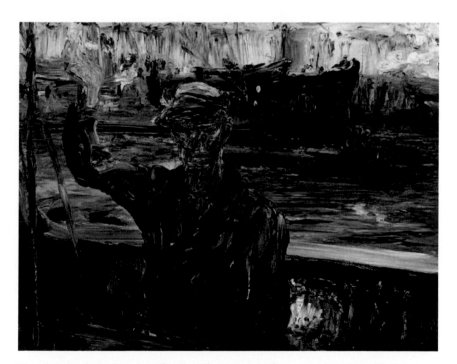

Fig. 1.4 Jack B. Yeats, *The Breaker-Out* (oil on canvas, 51 × 68.5 cm, 1925), © Estate of Jack B. Yeats. All rights reserved, DACS/ARS 2016.

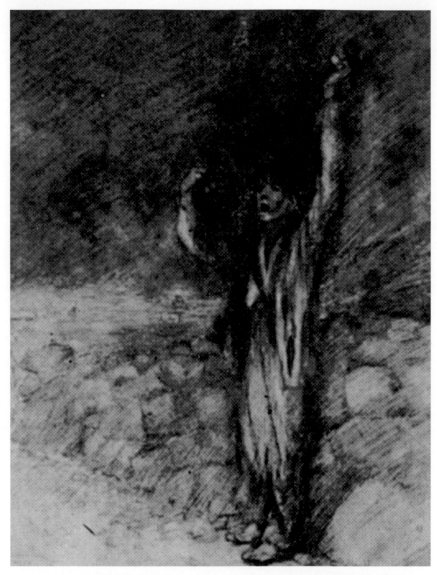

Fig. 1.5 Jack B. Yeats, *Singing The Big Turf Fire* (pen and ink on card, 15.8 × 6.3 cm, 1898), © Estate of Jack B. Yeats. All rights reserved, DACS/ARS 2016.

Jack Yeats found no occasion to go outside of the everyday scene for his material and there is no excess of emphasis in his statement. We may read satire and revolution into that early sketch in which a ragged boy tries to gain a few coppers standing on the roadside on a stormy night singing, of all songs, *The Big Turf Fire*. His arms are raised above his head in a wild gesture of desperation as he marks the rhythm with a pair of bones in his hand. But the artist was more than a satirist or revolutionist in the everyday sense. The incident was one of a variety of incidents he noted, and he perceived the import of it and found the appropriate statement of it as he perceived the import and found the appropriate statement of others that were utterly dissimilar. Of course every genuine artist is a revolutionist by the mere fact of being a genuine artist. Genuineness, truth, however peaceable, is always revolutionary – it is usually the counter-revolutionaries who make revolution bloody. (*JBY*, 23)

The 'truth' that is so revolutionary, and that the Irish counter-revolution of the Civil War period had bloodily suppressed, entails a different Ireland from that established and made respectable by the official and conservative Catholic nationalism of the Free State. The Ireland mobilised by the left-wing republicanism of Liam Mellows, Ernie O'Malley, Peadar O'Donnell or Constance Markievicz was not that of the big farmers and graziers, the 'nation building' class of the new order, nor that of the small and larger business interests that, as Connolly had always predicted, would ultimately continue to serve the interests of British capital – what MacGreevy termed 'imperial masters' – even in a formally independent nation. It was, rather, the Ireland of the dispossessed, of the landless labourers and the workers who had fought for unionisation and, in some cases, for soviet-style co-operatives. It was an Ireland of the marginal people, the 'tinkers' and tramps, the rogues and derelicts, the ballad singers and roving musicians that populate Yeats's pre-war images of Ireland and who, in actual practice, so often proved recalcitrant to assimilation into the official nationalist movement with its need to refine and purify the spirit of the nation.[17] In this respect, Yeats's art could be seen to continue the traditions of recalcitrance to the law that MacGreevy sees as characteristic of an Irish anti-colonial mentality, so that his later painting projects decolonisation as a process continuing beyond the moment of formal independence.

It is, indeed, no accident that when MacGreevy seeks to

characterise the mentality of the dispossessed Irish on the eve of the War of Independence, it is not to a conventional historian that he turns but to the recently published memoir of Ernie O'Malley, the republican guerilla imprisoned by the Free State during the Civil War, who became a close friend of the painter and one of the earliest commentators on his work.[18] Such pointers throughout the essay ask us to re-examine the pre-1922 body of Yeats's work in Ireland, on which – rather than on the later and most formally innovative paintings – his reputation as Ireland's foremost *national* painter is still based. Indeed, in so far as its broad public acceptance is concerned, that reputation probably rests on a mere handful of works, and principally those most frequently reproduced under his sisters' Cuala Press imprint and in subsequent mass-produced reproductions. Little wonder that in the 1930s he refused to permit reprints of those editions and, indeed, virtually repudiated them. Even his determined, if fruitless, attempt to ban reproductions of his work beyond his own death signals his vivid appreciation of the function of selection in defining – and domesticating – the reception of his oeuvre as much as it does his desire to preserve the artistic integrity of his paintings *as* paintings.

II

The most cursory survey of Yeats's earlier drawings, paintings and illustrations of Irish material indicates how the selection and dissemination of his work has operated to contain and limit its range. The tendency of the most widely circulated reproductions is to emphasise the element of gentle whimsy in his depictions of Irish rural life, or the elements of fanciful, even boyish romanticism in the Cuala Press prints and broadsides.[19] A full sense of his engagement with a certain demotic or even daemonic energy in the margins of Irish life (the sort of energy MacGreevy indicates in his description of *Singing The Big Turf Fire*, an energy of contradiction and deprivation) seems to slip away through the refining filters of selection. This loss is not merely a matter of the *content* of the representations, though it is true that a principle of selection that emphasised his rogues and derelicts would give a quite different impression of his understanding of the 'national spirit'. It is also a matter of what gets lost if one overlooks the compositional qualities that underwrite the scenes that energise him, qualities that emphasise an unruliness and insubordination that MacGreevy may be right to find more deeply internalised in the post-1922 paintings. As with his friend and travelling companion J. M. Synge, whose works on Aran and West Kerry and whose articles on the Congested Districts of Connemara he illustrated, it would prove too easy for even the most acute of critics to dismiss Yeats's work in this area as mere ethnographic romanticisation.[20] The ethical comfort with which by now we dismiss the supposedly ethnographic gaze of early twentieth-century nationalists, as if they were simply primitivising in the manner of Robert O'Flaherty, or as if the undoubted element of projection in their critiques of modernity fell on nothing more than a blank screen, risks missing their perception of more complex and subversive dynamics in the West's negotiations with modernity. But even as gently comic a drawing as *The Poteen Makers* (1912; Fig. 1.6), with its deft caricatures of the magistrates and of the onlookers – at once sympathetic and malicious – secretes an observation on Irish social life that easily passes unnoticed. For its focus on the magistrates' bench distracts from the peculiar fact that the accused themselves, whom the picture claims by its title to depict, are strangely absent from the scene. Their backs are turned to us; it is as if they abscond from our gaze as, perhaps, they seek to elude the force of the law that condemns them. Or in *The Wake House* (c. 1908; Fig. 1.7), the scene of the crowded room frames the intent figure of a speaker occupying the vital site of the hearth, the mourning of the dead deflected, or, it may be, more fully realised, in what seem to be the passions of political speech.[21] The faces of the crowd are again turned from artist and viewer, disregarding the act of representation as if the focus of the action is tangential or oblique to the gaze that seeks to render and make sense of the occasion.[22] Or, to end with but one more of dozens of such images, in *The Felons of our Land* (1910; Fig. 1.8), as in the later *Singing the Dark Rosaleen*, the action of the ballad singing is depicted at the margins of the sporting event, the ragged and derelict-looking assembly taking place at the edges of the main social gathering in which a nationalist like Daniel Corkery, or even MacGreevy himself on occasion, would have traced the image of the nation performing itself.[23] The title of the drawing in turn nicely poses the ambiguity as to whether 'felons' refers to the ballad itself or to those who sing and listen to it.

My point is, of course, that there is something in such works, modest in their 'appropriate statement' as they are, that already

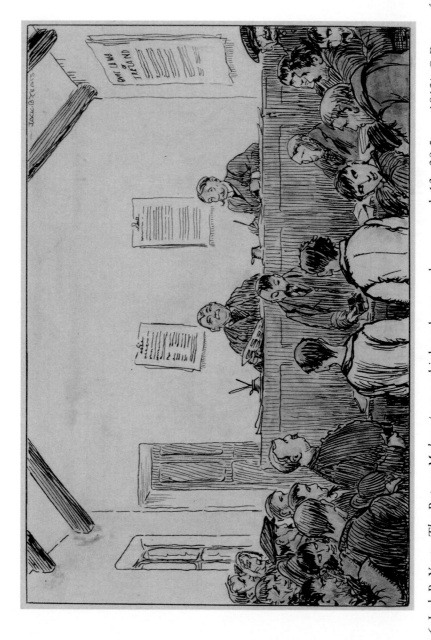

Fig. 1.6 Jack B. Yeats, *The Poteen Makers* (pen and ink and watercolour on card, 13 × 20.5 cm, 1912), © Estate of Jack B. Yeats. All rights reserved, DACS/ARS 2016.

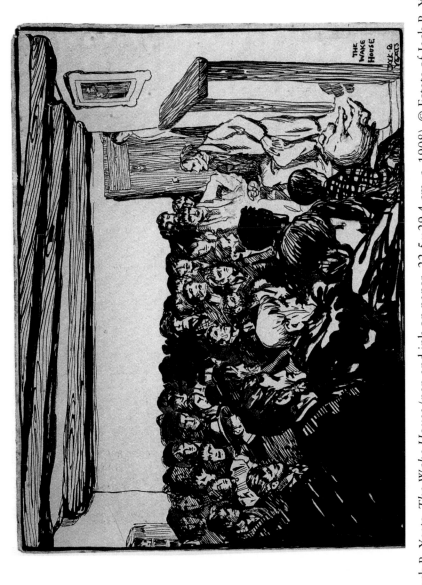

Fig. 1.7 Jack B. Yeats, *The Wake House* (pen and ink on paper, 22.5 × 29.4 cm, c. 1908), © Estate of Jack B. Yeats. All rights reserved, DACS/ARS 2016.

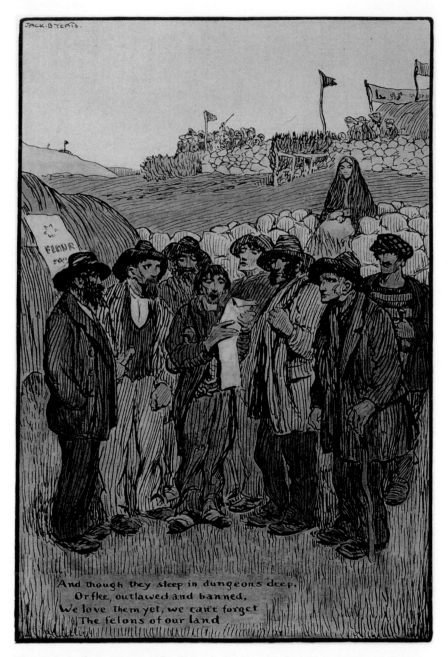

Fig. 1.8 Jack B. Yeats, *The Felons of our Land* (ink and watercolour on card, 30.5 × 19.5 cm, 1910), © Estate of Jack B. Yeats. All rights reserved, DACS/ARS 2016.

exceeds the merely ethnographic, as it does the simply nationalist, precisely by foregrounding what MacGreevy seems also to
have observed, that 'in Ireland, the whole people were below the
law' (*JBY*, 15). There is something in these events that defies the
force of the law, the social order of the state and the gazes of its
representatives, whether the police, the magistrate or the ethnographic stranger – including ourselves as viewers. As these are
representations of those who 'cannot represent themselves' and
therefore 'must be represented', they are also no less representations of that which eludes representation, which disappears from
representation even in the glare of what it renders visible.[24] It is
no paradox, then, as MacGreevy seems to suggest, that the condition under which Jack Yeats becomes the representative national
painter is precisely one of a failure of representation in which the
petit peuple is set over against 'an unrepresentative possessing
class' and in which 'those who acted for the nation officially were
outside the nation' (*JBY*, 9, 17). The counter-revolutionary Free
State does not, from a republican perspective, overcome that rift
in representation, but in a sense exacerbates it, dividing the people
from itself rather than unifying it, as a decolonising nationalism
seemed to, against the imperial power. The rift cannot be healed
by the official nationalist means of offering a symbolic common
ground, an idealised west, for example, in which difference might
appear to be sublated. For this reason, MacGreevy could never
consider Paul Henry as a potentially representative Irish artist in
the same way as he did Yeats. For in Henry, more often than not,
the effect of Irishness (the spirit of Ireland, in nationalist terms) is
rendered through the evacuation of the landscape of the population that works it, fights over it, fights for it, that makes it a site
of struggle rather than of reconciliation or repose. Or, where the
peasants are represented, they are represented as an element, if
a naturally embattled element, of the landscape itself, as in *The
Potato Diggers* (1912; Fig. 1.9).

Refusal of the subordination of the human figure to the landscape or, by the same token, of the heroic domination of the
landscape by the human is intrinsic to Yeats's work, according to
both MacGreevy and Beckett. Indeed, it is precisely here that the
critics converge, in their recognition of Yeats's recalcitrance to any
mode of premature reconciliation. Where Beckett apprehends this
in terms of the 'petrification' of figure and landscape, MacGreevy
approaches it through what he understands as Yeats's singular

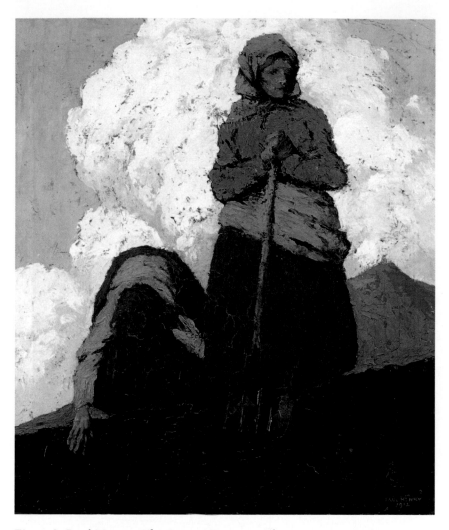

Fig. 1.9 Paul Henry, *The Potato Diggers* (oil on canvas, 1912),
© Estate of Paul Henry/Artists Rights Society (ARS), New York/
IVARO, Dublin, 2016.

innovation in the history of painting, the striking of 'a new balance between the landscape and the figure':

> With Jack Yeats, the landscape is as real as the figures. It has its own character as they have theirs. It is impersonal. They are the reverse. But the sense of the impersonal is an enrichment of the humanity of the figures. And conversely, the opposition heightens the sense of the impersonal character of the landscape. . . . I do not think I am claiming too much for Jack Yeats when I say that nobody before him had jux-taposed landscape and figure without subduing the character of either to that of the other. . . . Association and apartness at one and the same time have never been more clearly stated in terms of art. (*JBY*, 13–14)

This is an extraordinary insight by MacGreevy into what provides the underlying dynamic of so many of Yeats's later works. Its just-ness is exemplified by any number of paintings, from *O'Connell Bridge* (1925), where the landscape is urban, to *Men of Destiny* (1946) or *Many Ferries* (1948). I would only want to extend his observation from the relation of landscape to figure to other rela-tions, formal and figurative, in the paintings – from the relation-ships among figures themselves to the relation of figuration to the material aspects of the medium itself. What MacGreevy variously comprehends as balance, or as 'association and apartness', seems to me to lie at the heart of the dynamic tensions that trouble the viewer's gaze before the most achieved of these canvases. It is as if the recalcitrance to representation that was depicted over and over again as a quality of the figures in the early works is drawn into the very process of figuration, as if, to bend MacGreevy's terms only slightly, an objective tendency in relation *to* representation becomes a subjective tendency *of* representation.

It is well known that the most immediately striking aspect of the transformation of Yeats's style through the 1920s and 1930s is his gradual abandonment of line. The early oils are marked by the pre-dominance of sharp outlines bounding the figures and the visual foci of the image, what Bruce Arnold aptly refers to as '*drawing* in oil paint'.[25] This is true not only for the illustrations to *Irishmen All*, whose technical qualities Arnold nicely analyses, associating them with the line drawing of *A Broadside* or with Yeats's experi-ence of poster-work. It is no less true of free-standing oil paintings like *Bachelor's Walk* or *The Double Jockey Act* (1916; Fig. 1.10). In the former, the figures of the flower girl and the boy at her side

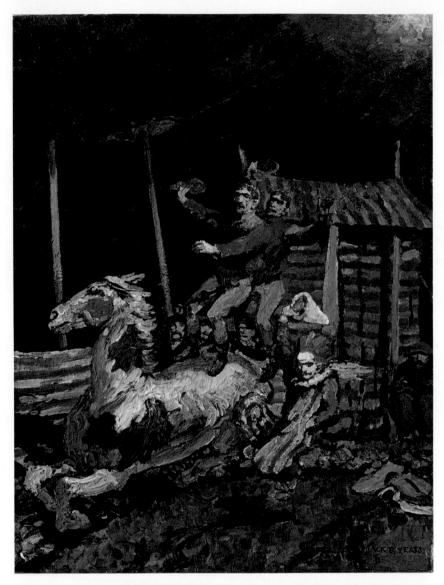

Fig. 1.10 Jack B. Yeats, *The Double Jockey Act* (oil on canvas, 61×46 cm, 1916), © Estate of Jack B. Yeats. All rights reserved, DACS/ARS 2016.

stand out starkly from the street, the pavement and the walls behind them, as if backlit, or even as if collaged on to the already-painted scene (Yeats's miniature theatres come to mind at once). Facial features and the divisions of skin from fabric, as well as from the background, are clearly delineated. Here, figure stands out from its ground emphatically. In *The Double Jockey Act*, painted only a year later, already *within* the figures a freer brushwork seems to be emerging – the different tones of the skewbald horse and the features and clothing of the jockeys and the clown have lost sharpness of definition and boundary in a way that contributes to the demotic sense of energy that radiates from the painting. The effect of the very visible brushstrokes here, and of the pointillistic texture of the arena floor, begins to oppose Yeats's tendency to work within a bounding line.[26] Nonetheless, the overall composition is strongly delineated, the red-striped canvas of the tent and the upright poles clearly distinguishing and outlining the various fields and depths of vision. There is a palpable tension in the work between the impulse of the draughtsman and that of the painter.

Just as the sharp illustrator's outlines make the often-reproduced drawings of *Life in the West* and other Irish scenes susceptible, if wrongly, of an ethnographic or a sentimentalising appropriation, so the clear outlines and the relief into which they throw the figures against the background predispose a painting like *Bachelor's Walk* to being 'used as a nationalist ikon, and a symbol'.[27] The very 'standing out' of the human figures projects them into a representational status that is both their 'standing for' the nation as its types *and* a mode of pictorial clarity or accessibility. Nothing obscures the significance of the act and its pathos. Indeed, by a kind of visual pun one might say that the clarity of outline correlates with the clarity of expressive visual communication, the translucence of the meaning in the image, of the general in this particular, that composes the symbol. In such a painting, in fact, Jack Yeats comes closest to the formal qualities of an epic historical and unambiguously national painter like Sean Keating, whose canvases are marked by strong typological figuration, deliberate symbolic, even allegorical significance, and, above all, a stark outlining of figure against background.

This is not intended as a reductive comparison, but rather to mark the technical and formal transfiguration of Yeats's work in both its radical nature and its political significance. Neither of them lies simply in a shift in content or subject matter, from 'a perception of countrymen in relaxation' to 'the loneliness of the individual soul', as Ernie O'Malley put it, or from specificity to images 'less firmly fixed in time and space', as John Rothenstein claimed.[28] There is, obviously, nothing intrinsically less poetic or less lonely and individual, or even more specific, in *The Circus Dwarf* (1912) or *Derelict* (1910) than in *No Flowers* (1945) or *A Morning in the City* (1937). We are obliged to turn to the significance of the actual mode of representation rather than to the objects represented to grasp the import of the paintings, of the way in which they seize and work on the viewer's gaze.

Any number of Yeats's later paintings would serve to exemplify the activity of the gaze that his canvases demand and provoke. We will focus here on two, *Two Travellers* and *The Old Walls*, that manifest somewhat different aspects of the painter's technique and its effects. *Two Travellers* (1942; Fig. 1.11) is one of Yeats's better-known paintings, partly because the Tate Gallery purchased it, partly because it has been associated with the set of Beckett's *Waiting for Godot*.[29] Thematically, the painting resumes many of Yeats's visual preoccupations. Two men, in well-worn clothing, encounter one another on a rough track in a coastal landscape. Heavy clouds suggest an imminent rainstorm, though the skyscape is lighter over a choppy sea in what is presumably the west, where a faint rose light illuminates the clouds and falls on one traveller's face. The encounter remains an enigma: are they strangers or acquaintances? Of what do they speak? How far are they travelling? What brings them to this otherwise desolate and apparently uninhabited terrain? Where is each heading? In this respect, the painting is of course susceptible cither of Beckett's understanding of Yeats's images as disjunctive and suspended, or of MacGreevy's reading of this painting as 'an apparently casual encounter in a world of mystery', revealing a new 'exalted tragic consciousness' (*JBY*, 37). It is also potentially open to Brian O'Doherty's hastily dismissive criticism of Yeats's romanticisation of the figure of the traveller, in the course of which he effectively reduces the later work to identity with the early illustrations and broadsides, all equivalent in their representation and mythologisation of the national character as that of the outsider.[30] And yet to turn from the thematic paraphrase of the painting (the aspect of the painting that reproduction tends to foreground by flattening out the texture of the medium) to its formal and technical qualities is to engage

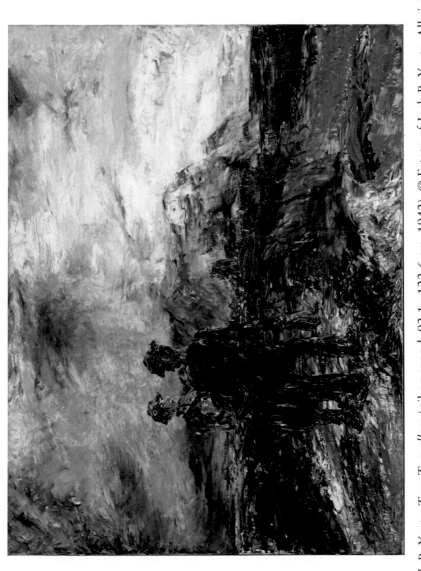

Fig. 1.11 Jack B. Yeats, *Two Travellers* (oil on wood, 92.1 × 122.6 cm, 1942), © Estate of Jack B. Yeats. All rights reserved, DACS/ARS 2016. Photo credit: Tate London/Art Resource, New York.

with a much less stable phenomenon that obliges what Beckett calls the 'labour' that is engaged 'between such a knower and such an unknown' (D, 95). The obligation to labour constitutes the difficulty that obtrudes in almost every instance of the later painting between a thematic statement that can be reduced for conventional consumption, or, as O'Doherty complains, national self-flattery, and the work itself, in every sense of that word. That labour evoked by the work departs markedly from the lucidity of representation that makes earlier paintings like *Bachelor's Walk* so much more readily available for iconic use.

Confronting *Two Travellers*, one is almost certainly struck at once by the paint surface itself and by the difficulty of resolving the image out of the paintwork. The same effect can be observed in many of Yeats's late paintings, notably, for example, *Grief* (1951; Fig. 1.12) and *Above the Fair* (1946; Fig. 1.13): it is often extremely difficult to achieve a total image of the painting no matter where one stands before the canvas, and wherever one stands, one has the impression of seeing the work at a different depth of focus, so to speak. It is as if the represented of the painting continually dissolves back into the medium of the representation, resisting totalisation and renewing the work of the gaze at every turn.[31] In *Two Travellers*, not atypically, the layering of the oils is at very different thicknesses, ranging from the thinnest of layers to a dense impasto. The grey cloudscape that stretches from the expanse of sky in the upper left corner across the line of the hill or mountain that becomes an abrupt cliff to the right is a thin film through which the bare canvas can at points be glimpsed. To the far mid-right, the dark blue of the sea is thickly layered but scored at points by brush handle or palette knife to reveal bare canvas, producing the effect of lines of surf foam at the cliff's base. Just right of centre, along the side of the road or path that bisects the painting, an extraordinary stretch of primary colours – predominantly yellow, red and green – is dashed unmixed and thickly on to the canvas and apparently, to judge from the absence of brush-marks, applied directly from the tube or perhaps the finger to the canvas. Similar patches of bright primary colour appear to the left of the two figures, but in neither case do these vivid and heady patches of colour resolve into the conventional outlines of the vegetation they must be taken to represent. The thickest impasto composes the two figures. In evident contrast to the earlier oils, however, no firm bounding lines enclose them. On

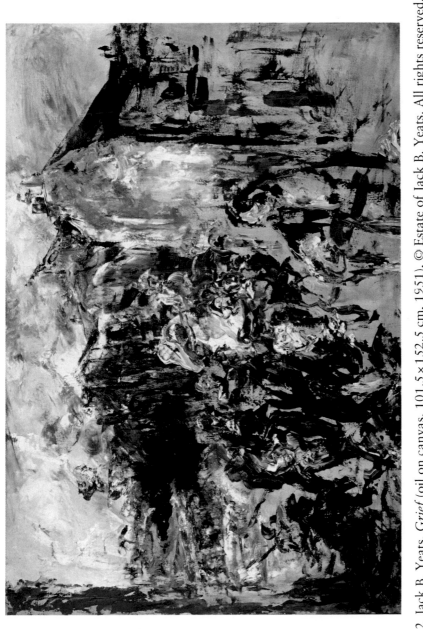

Fig. 1.12 Jack B. Yeats, *Grief* (oil on canvas, 101.5 × 152.5 cm, 1951), © Estate of Jack B. Yeats. All rights reserved, DACS/ARS 2016.

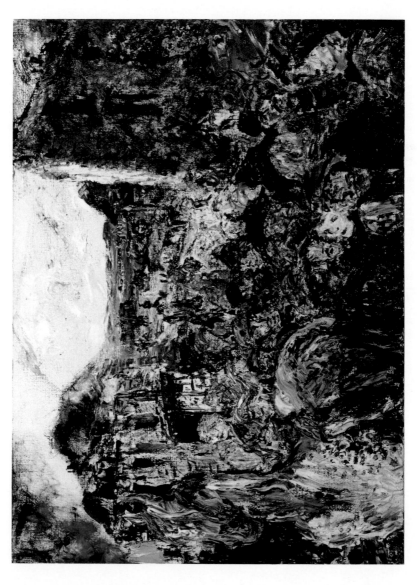

Fig. 1.13 Jack B. Yeats, *Above the Fair* (oil on canvas, 91 ×122 cm, 1946), © Estate of Jack B. Yeats. All rights reserved, DACS/ARS 2016.

the contrary, they are composed largely out of the same oil tones as the landscape immediately surrounding them; at points, such as the right leg of the left-hand traveller, they are literally carved out of the depth of the paint by, presumably, the tip of the brush handle. The figures seem at one moment to be sculpted almost three-dimensionally out of the surface of the oil paint, at another to merge back into it, the figure becoming consubstantial with the medium. In such a technique, 'drawing in oils' takes on an entirely new meaning.

The mobility of the gaze that is obliged by this highly plastic application of the oils is reinforced by the overall composition of the painting. With an effect that is again largely lost in the flattening of reproduction, the canvas appears to be constructed of overlapping and competing zones of focus. While at one moment the two figures in the foreground appear to dominate, the eye is almost immediately led either to the upper left quadrant of the lowering sky by the figure's vertical posture, or, by the intense primary colours, to the roadway, and then, by a sharp rightward turn of the line described by those pigments at the base of the cliff and its continuation in a fine line of red, to the sea and skyscape of the upper right quadrant. These various zones of focus are not discrete, however, but overlap and penetrate each other while being linked by the roadway whose line of sight projects diagonally from the lower left through the standing figures towards the upper right. The effect of these distinct but overlapping compositional zones is to prevent the eye from coming to repose. In this sense, the painting forcefully confirms MacGreevy's insight, based on earlier work of Yeats's, as to the 'balance' between figure and landscape, but does so in a way remarkably more dynamic in every respect. It is not only that within the representation the eye moves without dominative hierarchy between what would otherwise be 'figure' and 'ground', but that the gaze moves, is obliged to move, simultaneously between the representation, the image in the painting, and the medium of the representation, the material of the painting. The dimension of artifice, the material that composes the image, is not subordinated to the image: rather, its surfaces, depths and plastic textures are foregrounded in a way that dissolves the figure even as they supply the medium through which it emerges. The oscillation of the eye between material and representation produces the paradoxical effect of suspension to which Beckett refers, like a sustained tremolo in musical composition.

In this relative autonomy of medium and representation, Yeats's rejection of reproductions is aimed at the preservation of the work *as work*, as the difficult locus of an unachievable labour of looking. The rejection does not have as its aim a reactionary preservation of aura, in which the symbolist translucence of the image through the transparent medium might be maintained. Instead it is based on the wish to retain the sometimes vertiginous oscillation between the image and its material medium. The relation here between the visual 'content' and the formal or technical means resembles Theodor Adorno's description of the relation between content and technique in the new music that was emerging more or less contemporaneously with Yeats's career as an artist:

> Content and technique are both identical and non-identical because a work of art acquires its life in the tension between inner and outer; because it is a work of art only if its manifest appearance points to something beyond itself. . . . The unmediated identity of content and appearance would annul the idea of art. For all that, the two are also identical. For in composition, that which has been made real is all that counts. Only philistines can entertain the notion of a ready-made and self-contained artistic content that is then projected into the external world with the aid of a technique conceived of in similarly thing-like terms. Inner experience and outer form are created by a reciprocal process of interaction.[32]

This dialectic of content and technique is less formally implied in Yeats's own remarks to a Japanese interviewer, Shotaro Oshima, concerning the stylistic changes in his work: 'Things in the external world may seem always the same to some people, but an artist finds them different when a change is brought about in him. He must not try to go against this inner change.'[33]

What this conception of the mutual autonomy of content and technique suggests is no less that every occasion, every image to be produced, requires a different technical solution; that composition, in painting as in music, requires different modes of deployment of its medium, specific to that occasion. To turn from *Two Travellers* to *The Old Walls* (1945; Fig. 1.14) is to see Yeats deploy a similar repertoire of techniques modified for a quite different conjunction and to equally different effects. Here, a solitary figure stands enclosed by a space of ruins, the whole being suffused by a yellow light that is totally appropriate to those melancholy

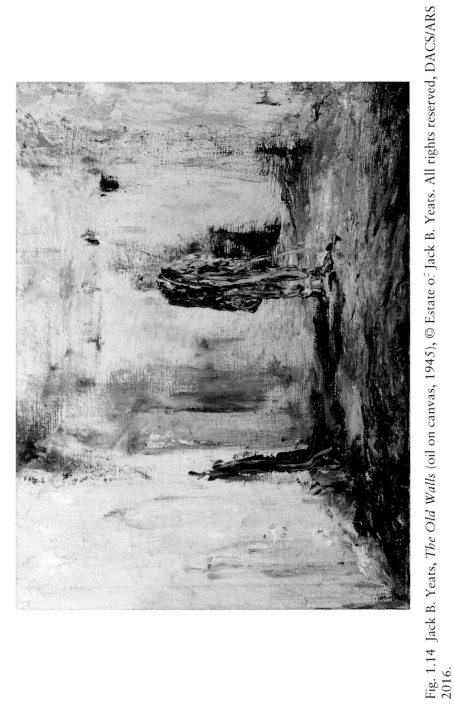

Fig. 1.14 Jack B. Yeats, *The Old Walls* (oil on canvas, 1945), © Estate of Jack B. Yeats. All rights reserved, DACS/ARS 2016.

light effects that I referred to earlier. If the dark patch to the left of the standing figure is, as it appears to be, his shadow rather than a bush or clump of weeds, then the light that enters the ruined structure is the low light of a rising or setting sun. This painting, which Beckett could have seen on his immediate post-war visit to Ireland, shares some of the colour tones of *A Storm*, on which he commented in his letter to MacGreevy, and of *A Morning* (1935–36) that he had purchased from Yeats in the mid-1930s. Here, the variation in the application of the oils is no less marked than in *Two Travellers*, but to quite different tonal effect. The figure upper centre and his shadow to the left are zones of thick, dark impasto, while the walls that constitute the upper segment and the sides of the painting are composed of an astonishingly thin layer of paint, in many places consisting of virtually bare canvas. There is a certain bravura in this willingness to compose so much of the painting from the exposed canvas that underlies the image, pushing what MacGreevy refers to as the 'swift and summary . . . brushwork' that shapes his figures to a further limit (*JBY*, 15). Here, however, the treatment is not of the figure, but of the walls between which the figure stands, a structure that becomes attenuated to apparent translucence: it is virtually the formal antithesis of the two paintings that MacGreevy singles out on account of the disappearance of the figures into, respectively, background and motion, *Going to Wolfe Tone's Grave* and *The Salt Marshes* (n.d.). In *The Old Walls* it is the human figure that bears the substance of the painting, while the ruins around him seem to fade and dissolve from representation. It is an effect that recurs with remarkable frequency in the later paintings, where even what appear to be still-intact structures lose substance and solidity in relation to the light and to the human figures that move across them (see, for example, *The Breakfast Room* (1944), *A Silence* (1944), *The Music* (1946), *In the City's Heart* (1950) and *Grief* (1951)). The paradoxical effect of this is, on the one hand, to make the human figure seem more solid and substantial than its material environment: we might then see the contemplative figure of *The Old Walls* standing out against the structures he has outlasted; on the other, it is to make the human presence seem, by virtue of its very solidity, a ghostly remnant of things that have passed away, seeking to summon them once more to presence.[34] The very application of the paint thus enacts the oscillation of memory and loss, representation and the evanescent present, staging technically the insubstantiality of substance and the accumulated patina of perception and reflection that makes memory a filter or screen rather than a translucent medium. The formal as well as iconic tension that insists here between the figure and its ground transforms the 'balance' between landscape and figure that MacGreevy noted into a reflection on the medium of representation itself. The canvas as painted becomes in its technical bravura an index of the extent to which the opacity of the subject, with its dense layerings of memory, obtrudes between the representation and the object that eludes it, fading ultimately into ruination.

This rigorous foregrounding of the technical problems of representation constitutes the enduring difficulty of viewing Yeats's paintings as visual totalities: standing before his canvases, one is constantly forced to move back and forth between technique and image, figure and medium, undecided as to which dominates. This recalcitrance to visual consumption of the image belies equally those who seek to celebrate Yeats for his romantic nationalism and those who, like Brian O'Doherty, deprecate him for the same. Both appropriations of his work are as reductive of the aesthetic concept of romanticism as they are of the paintings themselves, levelling one to mere fanciful idealisation and the other to a mere iconic thematics. Yeats's painting defies every effort to reduce it to figurative translucence, whether in the form of the translucence of the symbol that informs a nationalist aesthetic or in that of a classical painting in which, as Louis Marin has argued, 'the material "canvas" and "real" surface must be posited and neutralised in what is essentially a technical, theoretical and ideological assumption of transparency'.[35] On the contrary, Yeats's painting foregrounds its material conditions of representation with an effect that is the antithesis of mimetic reflection of the world.

III

It is to this formal recalcitrance of Yeats's painting, rather than to a contingent affinity with his representations of tramps, clowns or derelicts, that we can most fruitfully trace Beckett's high estimation of the painter. The period during which Beckett befriended and engaged most closely with Yeats was also that in which he was beginning to articulate his own approach to art and was singularly exercised by the problem of representation and with the problematic relation, already cited, of subject to object. Where for

Yeats the difficult relation of representation to represented was articulated in a painting that foregrounded the tension between figure and medium, for Beckett, most notably in his critical essays of this period but also throughout the restless experimentation of his writing, an analogous tension first emerges in the relation between language and its objects. For Beckett, that relation never ceased to be phrased as a question of *two* distinct domains – whether of language and self-consciousness or of language and percepts – and was (as for Adorno and Yeats) more precisely a question of a tension in which medium and representation in turn, and always undecidably, dominate perception of the work. As he put it, form and content are not consubstantial, as in a symbolic or expressive mode, but form 'exists as a material separate from the material it accommodates'.[36] This conviction gradually became, as we shall see in the next section, both crucial to the achievement of the first plays, *Waiting for Godot* and *Endgame*, and intrinsic to his sense of their limits.

It was across the 1930s and 1940s that Beckett began to articulate the problem of the writer through what was apparently a difficult but increasingly necessary distinction between form and content – difficult because it demanded a rupture with the Joyce for whom 'form *is* content, content *is form*'.[37] As he writes in 1937 to his German friend Axel Kaun:

> And more and more my own language appears to me like a veil that must be torn apart to get at the things (or the Nothingness) behind it. . . . As we cannot eliminate language all at once, we should at least leave nothing undone that might contribute to its falling into disrepute. To bore one hole after another in it, until what lurks behind it – be it something or nothing – begins to seep through; I cannot imagine a higher goal for a writer today. Or is literature alone to remain behind in the old lazy ways that have been so long ago abandoned by music and painting? (D, 171–2)

Language for Beckett at this point remains conceived of metaphorically as a *veil* between the object external to it and the representation that it constitutes, although the counter-analogy with music and painting suggests that he may already be grasping for a notion of an art in which there is no distinction between form and matter.

As he proceeds, he articulates a project that, though the analogy here is to music, remarkably resembles Yeats's use of his artistic materials:

Is there any reason why that terrible materiality of the word surface should not be capable of being dissolved, like for example the sound surface, torn by enormous pauses, of Beethoven's seventh Symphony, so that through whole pages we can perceive nothing but a path of sounds suspended in giddy heights, linking unfathomable abysses of silence? (*D*, 172)

And it is, as we know, to painting that Beckett most consistently turns to find analogies for his own predicament as a writer. What is striking, however, is that despite the antagonism to representation and to expression that informs his criticism of MacGreevy and his art criticism in general, Beckett does not turn for a solution to abstraction, as one might expect, but rather to artists who seem to be linked only in their exploration of the limits of figuration: Yeats, Bram van Velde and, later in his life, Avigdor Arikha. He remarks in his review of Denis Devlin's *Intercessions* that 'it is naturally in the image that this profound and abstruse self-consciousness first emerges with least loss of integrity. . . . First emerges' (*D*, 94). That insistent repetition (separated from the first instance by several sentences, thus requiring a palpable effort of recall) is also a qualification. Beckett's fascination with the qualities and paradoxes of the image remains a constant of his work, so much so that the images he isolates from Yeats's paintings remarkably anticipate those of the short texts and plays of the 1960s. But the condition of the image's emergence, as the representative of self-consciousness, is no less the condition of its fading, a point on which those texts, with their cyclical fadings in and out of visibility, insist. This is already for Beckett, in his writings on painting, the crux of the gaze that painting obliges in its staging of the undecidable relation between image and medium:

Whence comes this impression of a thing in the void? Of artifice [*de la façon*]? It's as if one were to say that the impression of blue comes from the sky. (*D*, 125; my translation)

This perplexity as to the object of representation, in representation, and to its referents is bound up with the act of looking itself in which the viewer's disequilibrium becomes a kind of self-referential slapstick. Beckett's 'amateurs' in the museum or gallery 'look first from far away, then close up, and . . . in particularly thorny cases, assess with their thumbs the depth of the impasto'

(D, 120; my translation). Though this passage concerns painting in general and the van Velde brothers in particular, perhaps no better or more succinct account of the process and difficulty of looking at a Yeats painting could be achieved.

But none of this resolves the question of the relation of the medium to the represented. Which is it that is recalcitrant: the figure that insists on its emergence or the medium into which again it dissolves before the oscillating gaze? For Beckett, this 'issue-less predicament', the aporia into which so reflexive an artwork throws the viewer, is thoroughly melancholic. It is a condition that leads him to speak, writing still of the van Veldes, Geer and Bram, of *le deuil de l'objet*, mourning for the object (or the mourning *of* the object – the ambiguity of the French genitive is carefully poised). This mourning is not one that can be alleviated, least of all by abandoning the attempt to represent:

> It seems absurd to speak, as Kandinsky did, of a painting liberated from the object. That from which painting is liberated is the illusion that there exists more than one object of representation, perhaps even of the illusion that this unique object would let itself be represented . . . For what remains of representation if the essence of the object is to abscond from representation? (D, 136; my translation)

The persistence of an obligation to represent, because painting cannot be freed from the very object that eludes it, leads to a painting whose condition is a ceaseless unveiling that reveals only further veils, as if the medium cannot dispense with the medium that hinders its ends, any more than language, as The Unnamable will discover, can put an end to the obstruction of language: 'An endless unveiling, veil behind veil, plane on plane of imperfect transparencies, an unveiling towards the ununveilable, the nothing, the thing yet again' (D, 137; my translation). This thing that insists and yet is no-thing, this thing that eludes representation, remains the melancholic 'core of the eddy', encrypted beyond the reach of a subject that nonetheless cannot abandon the urge to capture it (D, 152).[38] Though it may seem absurd to align Jack B. Yeats with the van Veldes, whose work, as we shall see, in quite different ways pushes the boundaries between figuration and abstraction to the very limit, it is the association that Beckett makes from the outset. All are painters whose work, like 'the best of modern painting', is a critique, a refusal 'of the old subject-object relation'.

In each case, and not least in Yeats's, it is the dynamic oscillation between material and image that sets that critique in play. The dynamic of Yeats's paintings, then, is the enactment of a failure of representation, a failure either to retrieve or to abandon the object. The formal means employed in this virtually obsessive work of representation are at once the analogue and the performance of that predicament. It is a predicament to which Beckett himself continually recurs in his writings and that links his own pro-foundly obsessive, or single-minded, practice with Yeats's own. His critical works, from *Proust* (1931) to the 'Three Dialogues with Georges Duthuit' (1949), repeatedly address it, and the early writings in English through to *Watt* (1953) continually thematise it, but it is not, as I will argue, until the late plays, beginning in the early 1960s, that he achieved the capacity to enact or to stage with assurance the disaggregation of medium and representation that Yeats's paintings assume in their own domain.

It is well known that Yeats produced his own late paintings through acts of memory, the records of which are the voluminous sketchbooks that he mined for later treatment.[39] This is, of course, a remarkable transition for an artist whose early work was, often perforce, based on the rapid notation of daily events. Painting from memory, even without the intermediary of the retrieved sketch, is inevitably the representation of an object already internalised, the representation of a (mental) representation, rather than that of an object presented to view. It is painting as anamnesis rather than mimesis. Memory here is neither the retrieval of time past nor the repossession of a lost object, but the performance of that occultat-ing light in which the figure merges and dissolves. Thus many of Yeats's later paintings foreground a figure watching, gazing, as if the painter's or the viewer's gaze passes perforce through anoth-er's. Beckett's term 'suspension' again seems utterly apt, rendering acutely not only the sense of the figure's apprehensive fixation before the scene, but also the suspension in turn of the viewer's gaze as the medium dissolves the specular image of the gazing figure, even as it emerges. In these paintings, memory is presented not as the past regained, but as an enigma for the present. And that enigma is only reinforced by the teasing, highly literary titles affixed to the paintings, titles that seem to allude to an explana-tory framework outside the canvases, to a tale in which they might become clear, but which yet eludes the viewer. They transform what might have been symbols into allegories, but into allegories that cannot be reduced to conceptual clarity, to interpretative mapping. This is a figuration without a possible turn to the literal.

We face, then, an oeuvre that answers in advance to Beckett's desire for an art that abandons the 'possessional' drive that has continually renewed Western representational art (*D*, 135). The internal dynamics by which figure and ground, material and image, technique and content are held in suspended, oscillating equilibrium correlates to a refusal of domination that is the aesthetic counterpart of a radical republicanism, a republicanism, that is, that remains profoundly at odds with the representational structures that undergird the cultural projects of nationalism and the modern state. I do not, evidently, mean to suggest that either Yeats or, least of all, Beckett programmatically set out to subserve the political projects of Irish republicanism, though Yeats's commitment to depicting the marginal sectors of Irish social life, urban and rural, has often enough been understood in those terms. It is, rather, that the post-colonial disaffection of both artists from the nation-state that emerged not only stands as an acknowledgement of the failure of a certain political promise but also spells the disintegration of a coeval aesthetic project of representation. Pettit has suggested that the displacement of a long-standing tradition of republican thought by the emergence of political liberalism and representative forms of democracy in the early nineteenth century follows from the radicalisation of republicanism in the late eighteenth century into a will to extend the principle of non-domination universally, rather than restricting it to white men of property.[40] This displacement in political thought coincides with the emergence, no less in reaction to radical republicanism, of an aesthetic and cultural philosophy that detours the antagonistic and potentially revolutionary claims of democratic social movements into and through representation. In this tradition, which runs most evidently from Kant and Schiller in Germany through to Mill and Arnold in Britain, distinct domains of representation are conjoined and articulated together to produce a field of identities in which the disinterested ethical citizen willingly learns to be represented. Aesthetic representation prefigures political representation, regulating the identification of the subject with the common ground of the state.[41] One might say that the whole tendency of the aesthetic that is devoted to the moment of representation, in which the formal supervenes on the material, derives from and corresponds to the continuing anxiety provoked by the radical claims of a republicanism of differences. The need for an aesthetic education to produce in the spectator that disposition by which he (*he*) becomes representative of the species is no other than the moment in which Kant responds to the French Revolution by proclaiming a republic that would be restricted to the learned, to the philosophers. In each case, the subordination of the singular, potentially eruptive manifestation of difference to a narrative of representation establishes a trajectory whereby the spectre of intractable elements can be contained and assimilated to identity. Realism, in which the multiplicity of social forms is disciplined into narrative resolutions that integrate the individual into the 'second nature' of the social, and symbolism, in which the particular stands in, translucently, for the universal, are the twin stylistic modes of this trajectory.

Cultural nationalism by and large reproduces that model in forms complicated by the need that MacGreevy acknowledges to find in culture alternative institutions to those that the coloniser occupies politically. This at first insurgent cultural nationalism seeks to enter into representation a people that has never before been represented, and to regulate the forms of representation in such a way that the unity and identity of a heterogeneous and fragmented population can be produced and affirmed. The failure of the national project thus throws into relief both the logical contradictions of the drive to representation, revealing the necessarily selective requirements of its inclusive claims, and the dominative ends that subtend it. The nationalism that proclaims the unity of the people in difference from the imperial state cannot accommodate the proliferation of difference that constitutes the inner space of the popular. And in so far as the contradictions of nationalist culture repeat those of the metropolis, only in forms writ larger by the exacerbated conditions of the colony, the foundering of this model of representation in the periphery resonates at the centre also. It is no accident that the modernist critique of representation was so often generated from peripheral cultural locations, since it was at the margins and in sites of more or less violent struggle that the aesthetic politics of the nation-state began to unravel.

The critical aesthetic impulse that draws together Yeats the painter and Beckett the writer dwells, with a certain compulsion born of necessity, on the ruin of representation that follows in the wake of the national project. It is not that either artist promotes an immediately cognisable political aesthetic. On the contrary, it is rather the inevitable imbrication of the political with the aesthetic within nationalism that makes of their intense preoccupation with the conditions of representation a deeply implicit political affair. The disengagement of the aesthetic from apparent political ends serves in their case no longer as the means to furnish the separate space for aesthetic formation in a well-articulated state. We might view it rather, to borrow a term from Pettit, as the aesthetic correlative of a 'deontological republicanism', one that regards the ethical foundations of 'freedom-as-non-domination' rather than the institutions that promote or safeguard its realisation.[42] In other words, where an aesthetic of representation that had become tied to a mode of political thinking becomes, along with the political state, a means to domination, only in the ruins of that aesthetic can an alternative be excavated. The excavation that follows is at once positive and negative – positive in its making space once more for the recalcitrant, for figures of those that had been denied representation: the tramps, rogues and derelicts that populate both artists' works; negative in the relentless interrogation of the *means* of representation that engage both formally and technically. However, it is precisely the tension between the act of figuration and its formal questioning that prevents the dimension of the political in either artist's work from ever congealing into a concrete utopian project. The space of their work is, rather, the place made over and over again for the unfit in representation, for those that dwell only among the ruins. In the ruins of representation alone, where the nation meets its end, the anticipatory trace of a republic emerges as that thing that yet eludes representation.

IV

No more obvious or notorious example of the representation of the tramp and the derelict could exist than the play on which Beckett began working shortly after he wrote his review of MacGreevy on Yeats. Frequent attempts have been made by critics to identify the visual sources of Beckett's plays, and for none more than *Waiting for Godot*, the first to be produced and the only finished play to be written and performed during Yeats's lifetime. Although the painting most often associated with *Godot* is Caspar David Friedrich's *Two Men Contemplating the Moon*, an association that Beckett on occasion confirmed, the visual effect of the play has also been identified with more than one painting of Yeats's, including, as

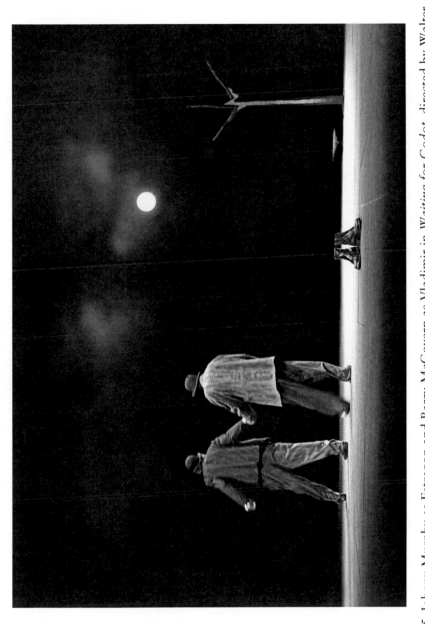

Fig. 1.15 Johnny Murphy as Estragon and Barry McGovern as Vladimir in *Waiting for Godot*, directed by Walter Asmus, Gate Theatre (Dublin) production at the Barbican, London, 1999. Photo © John Haynes/Lebrecht Music & Arts.

we have seen, *Two Travellers* and, more recently, *The Graveyard Wall*.[43] Such identifications, inconclusive as they must be where Beckett never confirmed them, have a prima facie plausibility. Beckett's profound engagement with Yeats justifies the assumption that not only his formal sense but also his visual imagination might have been shaped in part by his deep absorption in specific works. So much is this so, indeed, that the images that he offers as prototypical in his review of MacGreevy seem indeed to foreshadow the scenarios of later dramas and prose texts, even if they are not directly applicable to the visual effects of *Godot* itself. Yeats's later paintings are, moreover, notoriously dramatic, often seeming to present stills or tableaus of enigmatic moments of encounter or dialogue or scenes of imminent or accomplished violence. By the same token, given how celebrated the relationship between the young writer and the older painter is, it is perhaps difficult to look back at Yeats's paintings and not see them as in a certain respect 'Beckettian', if only on account of their shared interest in the marginal, vagrant or 'antinomian' figure.

Such associations, however, establish little more than an iconographic affinity, more or less casual, between painter and dramatist. They do little to help us understand the significance of Beckett's visual imagination or to clarify the intellectual and aesthetic work that the theatre as a visual medium performs. Nor do they explain why it is for *Godot* alone that such strong connections can be made, rightly or wrongly, to quite specific paintings. In his early prose work, in particular, Beckett himself frequently invoked specific paintings in order to anchor the appearance of a specific character or to delineate a gesture, while critics have sought to identify the visual sources of the later works. Fionnuala Croke, for example, has ingeniously located May's folded arms in *Footfalls* in Gherarducci's *Assumption of St Mary Magdalene* and the set of *Ohio Impromptu* in ter Borch's *Four Franciscan Monks* (both in the National Gallery of Ireland).[44] But these and similar identifications never bear the immediate conviction that the sources proposed for *Godot* seem to do. The reason for this may lie in the kind of visual work that *Godot* and the formally closely related *Endgame* perform, a work that may also indicate the grounds of dissatisfaction that drove Beckett to the restless and often astonishing visual experimentation of the later drama.

Even the most casual reader of Beckett will be acquainted with the numerous attempts to interpret *Godot*, usually efforts to understand it by establishing some ulterior message. The interpretative urge began even before its first production, as its director, Roger Blin, and the actors sought explanations from Beckett as to the play's meaning, or the identity of Godot, or the motivations of its characters. Beckett's steadfast refusal to answer such questions and the play's own resistance to definitive interpretation are equally well known: for him, 'the critics and public were busy interpreting in allegorical or symbolic terms a play which "strove at all costs to avoid definition"'.[45] Similarly, he would remark of *Godot* to its first American director, Alan Schneider, 'My work is a matter of fundamental sounds (no joke intended) made as fully as possible, and I accept responsibility for nothing else. If people want to have headaches among the overtones, let them. And provide their own aspirin.'[46]

And yet it is hard to fault either critics or audiences for seeing in both *Godot* and *Endgame* plays that both suggest and demand interpretation. Both are plays that tease us into thought, so to speak: they offer innumerable symbolic possibilities, from Godot's name, with its apparent allusions to both God and the French *pierrot*, or clown, to the tree that has been held to allude variously to the Cross, Yggdrasil or Buddha's tree of enlightenment. They are replete with literary allusions: to St Augustine and the thieves at the crucifixion; to Shakespeare's *Tempest* when Hamm remarks 'Our revels now are ended' and casts aside his pole or gaff; to T. S. Eliot's 'In my end is my beginning'; and to Yeats's 'The Wind among the Reeds'. Such randomly cited instances can be multiplied indefinitely and the temptations they proffer to the interpretative impulse are only reinforced by the apparently symbolic sets and visual tableaus that each play presents. *Godot*'s action turns around the tree and the stone between which Didi and Gogo circulate in motion and rest; *Endgame*, with its characters that allude in their names to the crucifixion and in their relations to generations of an archetypal family, with its two-windowed set, and with its apparently post-catastrophic landscape, has been seen at different times to be set in Golgotha (the Hill of the Skull), inside a human skull in which ego, id and superego play out their drama, and in a post-nuclear bomb shelter. This tissue or debris of allusion and citation, what Theodor Adorno called, in his virtually definitive essay on the latter play, 'cultural trash' or 'the reified residues of culture', at once invites and repulses interpretation, summoning it both by its very manifestation and by its evocation of the traditional modernist function of quotation while repelling it by the caustically sardonic context and relentless irony or bathos that frames it.[47]

Nor is Beckett innocent of permitting such interpretative lures. As Leo Bersani and Ulysse Dutoit tersely comment, 'With remarkable perversity, Beckett appears to have done everything to encourage just that kind of symbolic interpretation he was inclined to reject. Given the guide they are so trustfully following, it is hard not to sympathize with all the readers who organize their understanding of the play around the notion of God's absence or non-existence.'[48] It is not only that Beckett at times confirmed such symbolic associations, as in affirming the significance of *Godot*'s tree as vertical and vegetal and of the stone as mineral and horizontal or in clarifying the associations of the names in *Endgame*, thus leaving all other associations equally viable.[49] He was also tantalisingly ambiguous about the symbolic dimensions of these works. 'No symbols where none intended', as the end of the novel *Watt* declared, refusing to specify to what degree any apparent symbols in that work may indeed have been intended.[50] Writing to the German director of *Godot*, Carlheinz Caspari, Beckett remarked with no less tantalising ambiguity:

> If my play contains expressionist elements, it is without my knowledge. Nor is it, for me, a symbolist play, I cannot stress that too much. First and foremost it is a question of something that happens, almost a routine, and it is this dailiness and this materiality, in my view, that need to be brought out. That at any moment Symbols, Ideas, Forms, might show up, this is for me secondary – is there anything they do not show up behind?[51]

Whether intended or not, even if secondary rather than primary, symbols there seem inevitably to be, and we are open to interpret Godot as 'heavenly' or as Thanatos. Indeed, as Daniel Albright puts it, Beckett's teasing reticence results in 'a stage vocabulary of pseudosymbols around which a large cluster of pseudomeanings gathered'.[52] The problem is that every effort at a systematic or coherent interpretation meets with frustration as it comes to be contradicted by other networks of allusion or apparent symbolic value that cut across it. To draw on yet another available allusion in the title of *Endgame*, the effort at interpretation is drawn into a futile pursuit of a clinching move that again and again meets not with a checkmate but with *échec*, repulse or failure. Yet the two plays differ profoundly from dramatic work with which they are often associated under the rubric of the 'theatre of the absurd': these are not nonsense plays like Ionesco's *La Cantatrice chauve* or *La Leçon*, but ones that integrate as part of their effect the tension between a potential coherence and its immanent dissolution.

The point here, however, is not to seize on Beckett's ambiguity to permit yet further interpretations of either play – without doubt, there are more than enough and probably little could be added by way of original contributions. It is, rather, to suggest how Beckett's evident determination to evacuate these plays of any potentially consolatory layer of meaning is frustrated not only by the ineluctable condition of any text that is made, as The Unnamable has it, of 'others' words', and therefore incapable of not suggesting meaning, but also by certain formal constraints and effects that constitute the visual rather than the textual dimension of the plays. These in turn present the temporary limit to Beckett's experiments in theatre as, indeed, *The Unnamable* and *Texts for Nothing* brought him to a similar impasse in prose.

The history of critical interpretations of *Godot* and *Endgame* testifies, in its insights as in its failures, to the close relation between the tissue of verbal allusions, images and partial narratives that constitute the text of the plays and the set and action or gestures that make up what we might call the visual image of the plays. Both are as remarkable for the unity and the coherence of the scene they establish as they are for the singularity and integrity of the action they stage. In this respect, they constitute theatrical *images* in the sense that Rémi Labrusse argues that term was theorised by Georges Duthuit, the art critic with whom Beckett was most engaged at least during this period and with whom he shared for a while related theoretical concerns. For Duthuit, the image as exemplified by both the fauvists and the artists of the Byzantine mosaics that he studied represented something other than the mimetic tradition that had dominated the West since the Renaissance with its 'carnivorous possession of appearances'. It furnished rather a space in which the emotional and intellectual state of the viewer, rather than the illusionist representation of the external world, was invoked and incarnated. This 'faith in the incarnate image', according to Labrusse, was one that Beckett shared and which, 'in the manner of lightning flashes, never ceased to rip through his work'.[53] As we have seen, Beckett had indeed argued in his 1938 review of Denis Devlin's volume of poetry, *Intercessions*, 'It is naturally in the image that this profound and abstruse self-consciousness first emerges with the least loss of integrity.'[54]

By the same token, Beckett's contemporaneous interest in Yeats was hard to divorce from the latter's presentation of images which, if not subsumable for the writer to any nationalist agenda, nonetheless spoke to the 'issueless predicament of existence'. It is, after all, a list of images that Beckett furnishes precisely in the attempt both to illustrate this commitment to 'bring light' or 'reduce the dark' and to emancipate Yeats from his nationalist admirers. And yet, as we have seen, Beckett cannot have been insensitive to the extraordinary tension that persists in Yeats's work between the production of such images and the material from which, with such difficulty, they emerge. It is, thus, in the formal energies of Yeats's painting as opposed to what he depicts that we may find some analogue through which to delineate the potentialities and the limits of Beckett's own theatrical images.[55]

Beckett's own comments on the formal qualities of his work – comments that seem to go primarily to his plays – push to an extreme degree Adorno's remark that 'the unmediated identity of form and content would annul the idea of art', shattering even the residual dialectical organicism of that theorist by implying an absolute separation of the rigorous forms of the works and the 'mess' that they contain. Form, for Beckett, at least in the sparse and rare public comments he has made on his own work, does not emerge from the material, but seems distinct from it: whereas in Kafka 'the consternation is in the form', in his own work 'there is consternation behind the form, not in the form'. Later, he emphasised the same point to Tom Driver:

> The form and the chaos remain separate. The latter is not reduced to the former. That is why the form itself becomes a preoccupation, because it exists as a problem separate from the material it accommodates. To find a form that accommodates the mess, that is the task of the artist now.[56]

This radical separation of the form and the content is far more evident in Beckett's plays than in the major prose works at least through to *How It Is*, whose forms still seem to be determined and integrated by the idea of the speaking or at least dictating voice. Contrarily, from first to last the plays are singular for their formal perfection, including the feature that Adorno is one of the few to have remarked on: their absolute fidelity to the Aristotelian unities.[57] They know only a single action (though Hamm fears that the arrival of a child outside in the desolate landscape of *Endgame* might betoken an 'underplot'[58]) and are set without exception in a single and unchanging space. The only exceptions to the unity of time are in *Godot*, where nothing famously happens twice over, *Happy Days* and *Play*, but in each case repetition of the action seems to betoken less the representation of the passage of real time than the force of entropy or of a time reduced to an unbearable sameness. The intent and effect of this adherence to the unities is not, however, as it was for Aristotle and the classical theatrical tradition, the maintenance of verisimilitude as a means to facilitate identification, pity or catharsis. On the contrary, the rigorous and formally perfect unity of the plays becomes a kind of carapace that contains a material that is in a state of continuous and radical dis integration. Rather than affirming any kind of naturalistic illusion by means of their integration, form and material remain in a state of vital tension that is allegorised in the early plays by the figure of the clown whose apparently clumsy antics are always enabled by an acrobatic skill that often outshines the graceful motions of the acrobats themselves. Decayed remnants of Chaplinesque clowns, Didi and Gogo, Hamm and Clov, Pozzo and Lucky play out routines whose repetitions within the tight framework of the plays retain, as formal elements, a mathematical and choreographic precision belied by the inanity of their content. It was precisely such elements that Beckett as both director and consultant to directors of his works sought to emphasise increasingly as he grew more confident in his own sense of theatrical space and rhythm, interspersing the slapstick routines or the recurring gestures of the characters in *Godot*, for example, with moments of arrest that produced tableaus through which formal repetitions could be highlighted.[59] The apprehension of the formal perfection of the plays, whether in terms of such repetitive set-pieces or in terms of the overall rhythm and timing of their emotional curves, stands for any attentive audience in almost unbearable tension with the spectacle of entrapped and decaying human beings playing out their bickering or plangent routines in the face of darkness. This is perhaps one reason why Beckett always insisted on maintaining the 'very closed box' of the theatre and rejected performance in the round that would have shattered the frame of the theatrical space.[60] The very artificiality of the theatre's architecture reinforced the formal structure of the plays themselves, while at the same time allowing the disintegration of dramatic illusion by foregrounding the characters' frequent allusions to the stage – as in Didi's exits offstage in his efforts to urinate – or to the audience itself, as in Clov's comment on peering though his telescope: 'I see . . . a multitude . . . in transports of joy. . . . That's what I call a magnifier.'[61]

Such frequently noted moments of self-referentiality in Beckett's early theatre, moments that are rare if not entirely absent in the later plays, coincide with the relation specific to these plays between their marked formal integrity and the disintegrating content that is deliberately separated from it. This is the dramatic correlative of the tension that Beckett noted in Yeats's paintings between human figure and inhuman landscape, or between their form and their imagistic content. Beyond any common concern with the figure of the derelict and the outsider, with the circus clown or the tramp, one may descry in each artist an insistent sense of the tension between the human image and the materials that condition and constrain the work, whether the space of the stage or the literal materials of oil and brush. The effect is that of an image that emerges and is held in suspension with all that it stands out against and that threatens to dissolve its integrity. In theatrical terms, that effect is perhaps best registered precisely in the very frustration that arises from the tension between the formal perfection of *Godot* or *Endgame*, perfection that seems to promise to yield meaning and coherence, and the inner dissolution that defies that promise and is repeatedly marked by a self-conscious theatricality: 'We're not beginning to . . . to . . . mean something?' as Hamm asks of Clov, merely to inaugurate another round of verbal repartee.[62]

And yet what does remain, as critical responses to the plays testify, is the figure and the image of the human that seems in turn to defy and survive its own disintegration. It is as if the dissolution of the human that these plays seem to propose is arrested in the form of their insistent couples, separated into 'two entities that will never mingle' as they may be, or into manifestations of distinct aspects or psychic dispositions, as many critics have asserted and even Beckett on occasion suggested. The temptation to derive from *Godot*, and even from *Endgame*, a kind of heroic pathos, a moral vision of reduced humanity surviving with mordant wit or

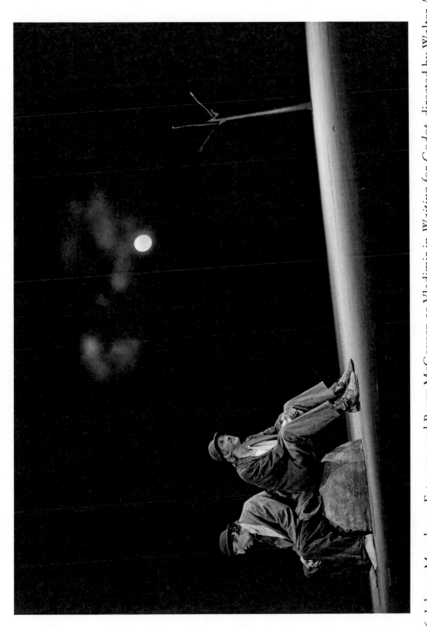

Fig. 1.16 Johnny Murphy as Estragon and Barry McGovern as Vladimir in *Waiting for Godot*, directed by Walter Asmus, Gate Theatre (Dublin) production at the Barbican, London, 1999. Photo © John Haynes/Lebrecht Music & Arts.

defiant play in face of its loss of all significance, clearly remains powerful. 'But at this place, at this moment of time, all mankind is us, whether we like it or not,' declares Vladimir, sententiously enough.[63] The inevitable appeal to humanity is of a piece with the desire to anchor these scenarios in specific visual images, and neither impulse is entirely at odds with the aesthetic mode of the plays themselves. For they do indeed turn insistently around striking visual images which seem to leave the human subject in its integrity and to offer at least the vestige of some kind of symbolic framework within which it might 'mean something', even if that something offers scant reason for consolation. *Godot*, with its tree and stone, *Endgame*, with its skull, shelter or ark, even *Happy Days*, with the figure of Winnie subsiding act by act into her burial mound, continue to operate visually with emphatic theatrical images that inevitably suggest a symbolic import and at the same time unify the space of the stage around the human figures that they frame or project.

Such a deployment of the theatrical image could scarcely be surprising in a writer who had once declared that self-consciousness first emerges in the image and for whom, indeed, painting, like music, was in advance of literature in its capacity to 'tear the veil' over Nothingness. But already, as Rémi Labrusse has argued, Beckett's discussions with Duthuit and his fascination with the work of Bram van Velde were leading him to turn away from the image as the privileged vehicle for expression, remarking that 'the fact is that the question does not interest me'.[64] In a subsequent letter, it was specifically a painting without images that Beckett imagines, anticipating the 'Three Dialogues' that we will discuss more fully in the next chapter. Speaking of the Breton painter Tal-Coat, who will figure in those dialogues, Beckett remarks:

What it all amounts to is the wish to save a form of expression which is not viable. To want it to be, to work at making it be, to give it the appearance of being, is to fall back into the same old plethora, the same play-acting. Apoplectic, bursting at the arteries, like Cézanne, like Van Gogh, that is what he is about, the pale Tal-Coat, and what [André] Masson would be about, if he could. No point in talking about details. Does there exist, can there exist, or not, a painting that is poor, undisguisedly useless, incapable of any image whatever, a painting whose necessity does not seek to justify itself?[65]

Here, only months after he had completed *Godot*, and before it had seen its first production, Beckett is already beginning to grasp the limits of the image as a mode of expression – as, indeed, a form of 'play-acting'. It is clear that that apprehension continued to haunt him even as he considered the set and the total visual aspects of the play, leading him to use terms that anticipate Jerzy Grotowski's concept of 'poor theatre' by a decade or more.[66] In a remarkable passage of another letter to Duthuit, Beckett distances himself from a specific form of painterliness, precisely that which would seek to make of the play a total or integral image, and commits himself to a kind of iconoclasm that he ironically refers to his own Irish Protestant background:

> Frankly I'm totally opposed to Staël's ideas for the set, maybe wrongly. He sees the whole thing with a painter's eye. For me, that is aestheticism. They have turned ballet and theatre into branches of painting, and done them a great deal of harm, I think. It is Wagnerism. I do not believe in collaboration between the arts, I want a theatre reduced to its own means, speech and acting, without painting, without music, without embellishments. That is Protestantism if you like, we are what we are.[67]

Though Nicolas de Staël's designs are no longer available, it is clear that Beckett already feels an anxiety about the way in which the theatrical image might lead towards the repleteness of a 'Wagnerian' total art, bearing with it a specific mode of expression and a practice and a vision of the possessive rather than the dispossessed human subject. But literature continues to lag behind even painting, or at least a 'poor painting' such as – we shall see further – Bram van Velde has come to represent for Beckett: 'One drives in vain towards figurelessness.'[68] What Jack B. Yeats's work had enabled Beckett literally to envision, a world in which the breakdown of the subject and the object and a 'rupture of the lines of communication' between them had occurred, was no longer an adequate description of the disintegration that – perhaps in the wake of his post-war apprehension of 'humanity in ruins' – the writer had begun to aim at. That breakdown, now perceived as internal to the human subject or object, would no longer sustain even as radical a theatre as *Godot* or *Endgame* appeared to be. Though the implications of what Beckett came to see in van Velde's work took another decade to absorb into a theatre adequate to such an apprehension, it was through his intense encounter with his painting that Beckett worked his way towards another possible modality of dramatic work, one more visual, more independent of even the vestiges of linguistic virtuosity and literary allusion, even as it is stripped of action, narrative or dialogue. For all its visuality, what will emerge is a theatre radically suspicious of the total theatrical image and of what Beckett had come to see as the literary or figurative remnants of the symbol the image preserves. Bram van Velde's painterly impasses are, as we shall now see, the occasion of Beckett's first formulations of his own way beyond the theatrical image.

Notes

1. See Hilary Pyle, *Yeats: Portrait of an Artistic Family*. The epithets are selected more or less at random from her descriptions of the paintings.
2. Bruce Arnold, *Jack Yeats*, chapters 6 to 8.
3. 'The Man Who Tried to Get the Hang of a Jack Yeats Picture', *Dublin Opinion*, 8 (May 1929), p. 73.
4. Arnold, *Jack Yeats*, p. 234.
5. Anthony Cronin's dismissive comments on the relationship between the two are especially egregious in this respect. Finding Yeats's work Romantic, he is surprised at Beckett's admiration and attributes it to personal needs: 'conceived as it was at a time in Beckett's life when he sadly needed someone to admire or look up to, it is a triumph of personal affection over critical or aesthetic considerations.' See Cronin, *Samuel Beckett: The Last Modernist*, p. 140.
6. For Yeats's relation to Joyce and to Kokoschka, see Arnold, *Jack Yeats*, pp. 235–6 and 220–1 respectively.
7. Samuel Beckett, *Disjecta*, p. 96; apart from adding a couple of commas, Beckett's citation substitutes 'a nation's painter' for MacGreevy's 'a national painter'. See Thomas MacGreevy, *Jack B. Yeats*, p. 10. Beckett's *Disjecta* is hereafter cited as *D* and MacGreevy's *Jack B. Yeats* as *JBY*.
8. On representation in relation to the cultural nationalist aesthetic, see David Lloyd, *Nationalism and Minor Literature: James Clarence Mangan and the Emergence of Irish Cultural Nationalism*, pp. 95–8.
9. Though one might be tempted in each case to echo Gabriel Conroy's perplexed query, 'Of what was it a symbol?' See James Joyce, 'The Dead', in *Dubliners*, p. 207.

10. Beckett to MacGreevy, 14 August 1937, in *The Letters of Samuel Beckett, Volume I: 1929–1940*, p. 540.

11. Beckett, *Letters, Vol. I*, p. 540.

12. Beckett, *Letters, Vol. I*, p. 540.

13. On this episode, see Mike Cronin, *Sport and Nationalism in Ireland: Gaelic Games, Soccer and Irish Identity since 1884*, pp. 87–8.

14. Recent work has established the clear intersection of aesthetic modernism with 'advanced' political republicanism in post-independence Ireland. See Nicholas Allen, *Modernism, Ireland and Civil War*, and Mark Quigley, *Empire's Wake: Postcolonial Irish Writing and the Politics of Modern Literary Form*.

15. On the alternative national Marxist tradition in Ireland, see Gregory Dobbins, 'Whenever Green Is Red: James Connolly and Postcolonial Theory', and David Lloyd, 'Rethinking National Marxism: James Connolly and "Celtic Communism"'.

16. See Philip Pettit, *Republicanism: A Theory of Freedom and Government*, pp. 80–109.

17. See David Lloyd, 'Adulteration and the Nation', in *Anomalous States: Irish Writing and the Post-Colonial Moment*, pp. 88–124.

18. *JBY*, p. 17, cites O'Malley's *On Another Man's Wound*, published in 1936. Beckett also seems to have known O'Malley by mid-1937: a letter to MacGreevy, 26 April 1937, mentions his aunt Cissie Sinclair meeting and liking him. See *Letters, Vol. I*, pp. 490 and 494 n. 27.

19. Terence De Vere White remarks: 'Most people by then [1920s] knew a drawing of a donkey by Jack Yeats. It was printed by the Cuala Press, which his sisters managed. The people who were disapproving of Bohemians would have wished that one Yeats should continue to reproduce that pretty little donkey, and the other the lake-isle of Innisfree, over and over again.' See 'The Personality of Jack B. Yeats', in Roger McHugh (ed.), *Jack B. Yeats: A Centenary Gathering*, p. 23.

20. For example, Luke Gibbons, 'Synge, Country and Western: The Myth of the West in Irish and American Culture', in *Transformations in Irish Culture*, p. 23: 'The equation of rural life with all that is truly Irish has dominated the work of many modern Irish painters, but is particularly evident in the work of Jack Yeats, Paul Henry and Sean Keating.' Gibbons associates this with 'the idealization of the west', though his essay does much to complicate that equation in the case of Synge. Yeats's difference from either Henry or Keating will be suggested later in the present chapter.

21. Travellers in Ireland, like Thomas Croker and Mrs S. C. Hall, who

witnessed keening and wakes in the nineteenth century, generally regarded them as probable sites of sedition, political talk and general impropriety. See David Lloyd, *Irish Culture and Colonial Modernity, 1800–2000*, pp. 53–61.

22. See John Barrell, *The Dark Side of the Landscape: The Rural Poor in English Painting 1730–1840*.

23. For Daniel Corkery's use of such a scene as an instance of the 'life of this people', see his classic *Synge and Anglo-Irish Literature*, p. 22. I have commented on Corkery's cultural nationalism and on Beckett's distance from it in 'Writing in the Shit: Beckett, Nationalism and the Colonial Subject', in *Anomalous States*, pp. 43–4.

24. Gibbons, 'Synge, Country and Western', p. 27, in the context of the American homesteader, cites this famous formula of Marx's *Eighteenth Brumaire*. All this suggests that, for Yeats, to be outside representation, in the position of the 'subaltern', is in no unambiguous way to occupy a position of disempowerment.

25. Arnold, *Jack Yeats*, p. 180. See also pp. 198 and 229–30 for further remarks on the transition in Yeats's work away from line and on the later oil technique that emerges with that break.

26. Pyle, *Yeats*, p. 204, comments nicely on a number of these features in the painting.

27. Arnold, *Jack Yeats*, p. 191.

28. Ernie O'Malley, 'The Painting of Jack B. Yeats', in McHugh (ed.), *Centenary Gathering*, p. 68; John Rothenstein, director of the Tate Gallery, quoted in Arnold, *Jack Yeats*, p. 231.

29. See, for example, James Knowlson, *Damned to Fame: The Life of Samuel Beckett*, pp. 378–9. It is equally possible that this painting lies behind Molloy's very painterly description of the 'two wayfaring strangers' on a road in the country, 'halted face to face', at the opening of that novel. See Beckett, *Molloy*, pp. 4–5.

30. Brian O'Doherty, 'Jack B. Yeats: Promise and Regret', in McHugh (ed.), *Centenary Gathering*, pp. 80–1 and passim.

31. This is precisely the effort that the *Dublin Opinion* cartoon captures; see Fig. 1.1.

32. Theodor W. Adorno, 'Music and Technique', in *Sound Figures*, pp. 197–8.

33. Shotaro Oshima, 'An Interview with Jack Butler Yeats', in McHugh (ed.), *Centenary Gathering*, pp. 52–3.

34. This may be especially true of *A Silence* (1944), which has been seen as an assembly of dead and living friends, including, in the foreground, J. M. Synge.

35. See Louis Marin, *To Destroy Painting*, p. 47.
36. Cited by Tom Driver, 'Beckett by the Madeleine', in Dougald McMillan and Martha Fehsenfeld, *Beckett in the Theatre: The Author as Practical Playwright and Director, Vol. 1*, p. 14.
37. Beckett, 'Dante . . . Bruno. Vico . . . Joyce', in *Disjecta*, p. 27.
38. The phrase comes from Beckett's essay *Proust*, p. 540.
39. Pyle, *Yeats*, p. 24, quotes a letter of Yeats to Joseph Hone: 'No one creates . . . The artist assembles memories.' She also remarks on the collection of small notebooks in which he kept sketches from which later paintings could be 'assembled'; see *Yeats*, p. 26.
40. Pettit, *Republicanism*, pp. 45–50.
41. For a historical account of the emergence of this cultural and political formation, see David Lloyd and Paul Thomas, *Culture and the State*. For the Irish context, I have elaborated some of these terms in the introduction to *Nationalism and Minor Literature*.
42. See Pettit, *Republicanism*, p. 101.
43. See Knowlson, *Damned to Fame*, p. 342, and Peggy Phelan, 'Lessons in Blindness from Samuel Beckett', pp. 1280–1.
44. See Fionnuala Croke, 'Introduction to the Exhibition, Part 1', in Croke (ed.), *Samuel Beckett: A Passion for Paintings*, pp. 14 and 18.
45. McMillan and Fehsenfeld, *Beckett in the Theatre*, p. 59. See also Tom Bishop's interview with Roger Blin, 'Blin on Beckett', in S. E. Gontarski (ed.), *On Beckett: Essays and Criticism*, p. 228, where Blin remarks of Beckett that 'All he knew was that they wore bowler hats'.
46. Cited in McMillan and Fehsenfeld, *Beckett in the Theatre*, p. 15.
47. Adorno, 'Trying to Understand *Endgame*', pp. 241 and 243.
48. Leo Bersani and Ulysse Dutoit, *Arts of Impoverishment: Beckett, Rothko, Resnais*, pp. 27–8.
49. McMillan and Fehsenfeld, *Beckett in the Theatre*, pp. 83 and 89; Walter Asmus, 'Beckett Directs *Godot*', in Gontarski (ed.), *On Beckett*, p. 282; Anne Atik, *How It Was: A Memoir of Samuel Beckett*, p. 40.
50. Beckett, *Watt*, p. 379.
51. Beckett to Carlheinz Caspari, 25 July 1953, in *The Letters of Samuel Beckett, Volume II: 1941–1956*, p. 391.
52. Daniel Albright, *Beckett and Aesthetics*, p. 52.
53. Rémi Labrusse, 'Beckett et la peinture', pp. 670–1. My translations.
54. Beckett, '*Intercessions* by Denis Devlin', in *Disjecta*, p. 94.
55. The idea of Beckett's theatre as a theatre of images has been prevalent in the criticism. See for example Martin Esslin's comment that 'from

his very earliest *dramatic* experiments Beckett was already striving for a poetry of concretized images', in his 'A Poetry of Moving Images', p. 66; see also Rosemary Pountney, *Theatre of Shadows: Samuel Beckett's Drama, 1956–76*, p. 165: 'Beckett's visual images become increasingly startling, in settings that have no pretensions to be representational, except in so far as they are dramatic metaphors, accurately reflecting the human predicament.'

56. Both these remarks on form are cited in McMillan and Fehsenfeld, *Beckett in the Theatre*, p. 14.

57. Adorno, 'Trying to Understand *Endgame*', p. 259.

58. Beckett, *Endgame*, p. 148.

59. McMillan and Fehsenfeld, *Beckett in the Theatre*, pp. 89–91.

60. For Beckett's comments to Alan Schneider, and his preference for the proscenium arch theatre, see McMillan and Fehsenfeld, *Beckett in the Theatre*, p. 80.

61. Beckett, *Endgame*, p. 112.

62. Beckett, *Endgame*, p. 114.

63. Beckett, *Waiting for Godot*, p. 72.

64. Beckett to Duthuit, 26 May 1949, *Letters, Vol. II*, p. 156, previously cited by Labrusse, 'Beckett et la peinture', p. 672. It is not in fact clear in context that Beckett refers specifically to the question of images rather than the larger debates they were having about the status of Bram van Velde's work and the future of painting. Labrusse's larger point holds, nonetheless.

65. Beckett to Duthuit, 9 June 1949, *Letters, Vol. II*, p. 166.

66. See Jerzy Grotowski, *Towards a Poor Theatre*.

67. Beckett to Duthuit, 3 January 1951, *Letters, Vol. II*, p. 218, previously cited by Labrusse, 'Beckett et la peinture', p. 676.

68. Beckett to Duthuit, 12 August 1948, *Letters, Vol. II*, p. 104.

2

Beckett's Thing:
Bram van Velde and the Gaze

Above all, let Bram not get the idea that I'm moving away from him.
The very reverse. The farther I sink down, the more I feel right beside
him, feel how much, in spite of the differences, our ventures come
together in the unthought and the harrowing. And if there had to be
for me a soul-mate, I make bold to say that it would be his soul and no
other. . . . Bram is my great familiar. In work and in the impossibility
of working. That's how it will always be.[1]

I

No consideration of the peculiar version of republicanism that
finds its articulation in Jack B. Yeats's painting, and which, as we
have seen, Beckett seems to approach in his understanding of that
work, can ignore the embeddedness of the notion of the thing in the
term 'republic' itself. The *res publica* is the people's thing, *la chose
du peuple*, its matter or affair, what concerns it or that around
which it gathers.[2] But in the deontological version of republicanism that Yeats and Beckett seem to have embraced as the resistant
residue of a disappointed nationalism, the thing of the republic
is no longer a question of representation or expression. Their
emphasis falls instead on the recalcitrance of both the human and
the thingly to representation, a recalcitrance that Beckett finds set
forth in Yeats's insistence on the absolute separation both between
humans and between the human and the natural. That insistence
would seem to imply, moreover, that what we call the human
is itself also a dimension of the thingly once the 'old relation'
between subject and object that establishes the subject in its relation to its objects has been dissolved. Unimaginable from the perspective of Ireland's post-colonial nationalism, such a dissolution
is the very ground of Beckett's aesthetic as he articulates it in the

1930s. It entails at once the abolition of the subject of expression, a term that assumes an a priori interiority that issues in utterances that are consubstantial with it, and the subsumption of the object in whose representation by or for the subject that subject is established in its formal anteriority. The object that is *for* the subject, as opposed to being for itself, is, indissociably from the subject that posits it, no less the object *of* the subject, object of an act of possession that forms, for Beckett, the counterpart of the act of expression. Possession and expression in turn entail that the subject is the subject of representation, persisting in and through its representations by virtue of its representative capacity. These post-Kantian reflections constitute the fundamental tenets that link Beckett's emerging aesthetic values, tenuous and tentative as they remain, to his response to post-war debates on politics and culture and to his earlier engagement with the wake of Irish decolonisation. At the core of both lies the question of the thing that remains beyond the overarching framework of representation, in both its aesthetic and its political dimensions, once that has succumbed to ruination in the pervasive violences of decolonisation and total war.

Nowhere is the link between the expression of the subject and its possession of the object in representation more clearly articulated than in Beckett's archly ironic post-war text 'Three Dialogues with Georges Duthuit', which appeared in the latter's journal *Transition* in 1949.[3] The 'Three Dialogues' are best known to readers of Beckett by virtue of the passage that is so often cited as the touchstone of Beckett's artistic project, as a kind of writerly credo:

> The expression that there is nothing to express, nothing with which to express, nothing from which to express, no power to express, no desire to express, together with the obligation to express. (Tr, 98; D, 139)

Abstracted from its context in these dialogues on visual art, this – along with other aphorisms from the text, such as 'to be an artist is to fail, as none other dare fail' – has generally been taken as a statement of Beckett's own *literary* principles and elaborated in that context. This is, of course, not in itself wrong. Certainly, what Beckett remarks, however ironically and agonistically, both in the 'Three Dialogues' and in other art-critical writings of the time to which we will return, is not inapplicable to the writerly dilemmas that he was engaging with at the same time. It is well known that at least since the 'German letter' to Axel Kaun of 1937, Beckett had been thinking his way through the problems of the late-modernist literary artist by way of the other arts, specifically music and painting. And, as I shall suggest later, it may be that to think the literary through painting was one important way in which he was able to find the terms through which to take his distance from Joyce's massively mythical method and rhetorical repleteness. The problem is that so direct a reduction of Beckett's very deliberately 'allegorical' mode of approach to the literary by way of the painterly is simply too hasty. It short-circuits the detour through which he passes, thus failing to grasp exactly what this allegory that speaks through another medium uncovers for this most expressly anti-symbolist of writers. Above all, too hasty a transfer from visual art to writing overlooks the work of the painters to whom he paid such notoriously close attention. It also fails to grasp the remarkable situatedness of Beckett's post-war writings on painting, their engagement with an intense political and cultural debate that was ongoing at the time, thus lending credit to the myth of Beckett's abstraction from mundane questions such as the political significance of art.

'Three Dialogues with Georges Duthuit' is structured around three painters, each one of whom represents for Beckett, and indeed for his friend and interlocutor Duthuit, a possible direction for French painting and for the resurgence of the 'School of Paris' in the post-war moment. While the Dutch painter Bram van Velde is, so to speak, the anti-hero of the story the dialogues tell, the other painters, Pierre Tal-Coat and André Masson, form an aesthetically and critically indispensable foil to the former's work and its foregrounding in the text. Though neither remains a prominent figure in the contemporary canon of modern art, they were not only significant painters in their moment, but also ones whom Beckett and Duthuit indubitably held in high regard, even if Beckett views the paths taken by each as dead ends. What is less easy to understand, once one begins to engage with the work of each that Beckett might have been familiar with at the time, is why – despite their 'prodigious value' – he would finally reject their example and dismiss their 'tendency and accomplishment' as being 'fundamentally those of previous painting, straining to enlarge the statement of a compromise' (Tr, 97; D, 138). To approach this question is to open the way into grasping just how radical for their time the claims of Beckett's aesthetic writings were.

Pierre Tal-Coat (1905–85) was a Breton artist who, having spent most of the war and the occupation in Aix-en-Provence, returned in 1946 to Paris, where he became acquainted with Duthuit and his circle, including the poet André du Bouchet and fellow painter André Masson. He held a retrospective of his work at the Galerie de France in 1949 and it is presumably there that Beckett became acquainted with his work, since he does not appear to have exhibited in Paris in the late 1930s. Like most of the artists in whom Beckett was interested, Tal-Coat was an 'independent', and it is hard to assign his work to any school of painting. Indeed, his career is marked by rapid shifts in style and manner, as if, as one critic has put it, 'the painter felt the need sometimes to shake off his chains, to pass from one register to another without transition, out of the pure passion for painting'.[4] He is perhaps best known for his monumental portrait of Gertrude Stein (or his portrait of Stein as monumental) of 1935, which belongs with a series of related portraits and self-portraits that seem to synthesise the manner of Fernand Léger with the post-cubist neoclassicism of Picasso. Such works seem to draw on his early training as a sculptor, deploying painted surfaces as if they were sculptural forms flattened into the two dimensions of the canvas (see Fig. 2.1, *Femme au Bol* [*Woman with a Bowl*], 1933). Conceivably this sculptural sense of pictorial

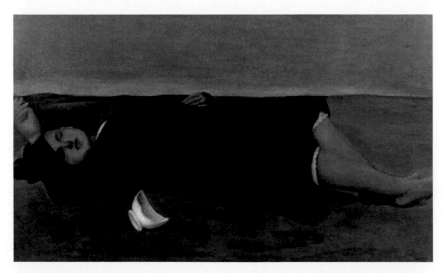

Fig. 2.1 Pierre Tal-Coat, *Femme au Bol* [*Woman with a Bowl*] (oil on canvas, 90 × 150 cm, 1933), © Artists Rights Society (ARS), New York/ ADAGP, Paris, 2016.

space prepared him to absorb what he described as the 'shock' of seeing the medieval illuminations of the *Apocalypse* of Saint-Sever with its violent images dispassionately disposed in non-perspectival space and which, according to Tal-Coat, influenced his powerful series of paintings on the Spanish Civil War, *Les Massacres* (1936–7; Figs 2.2 and 2.3: *Le Déluge* [*The Flood*], from Saint-Sever; Tal-Coat, *Massacres*).[5] This direction in Tal-Coat's work seems, however, to have stalled during the war. Critics note a shift in the mode of his painting across this period that is generally understood as his turning from the expression of violence and aggression to a more passive relation to the world. This turn may have begun after his demobilisation and settlement in Le Tholonet, near Aix-en-Provence and Cézanne's famous Mont Sainte-Victoire.[6] Paintings from the wartime period in fact suggest that formally Tal-Coat was seeking to come to terms with the work of his major French antecedents. A painting like *Paysage du Tholonet* [*Landscape at Le Tholonet*] (1941; Fig. 2.4) betrays his engagement with Cézanne's explorations of the deep geometrical structure of the landscape, whereas others, like *Maternity* (1943) or the large canvas *Still Life (On the Table)* (1944), seem to attempt a synthesis of post-cubist Picasso and the almost decorative, flattened perspectives and bold colorific rhythms of Matisse. The paintings reproduced in black and white from the Galerie de France exhibition in *Transition Forty-Nine*, where the 'Three Dialogues' also appeared, suggest that what Beckett would have been most aware of was Tal-Coat's continuing attempt to forge an almost minimalist synthesis of Cézanne and Matisse that would culminate in the spare works of the series *Rochers, Failles et Lignes* (*Rocks, Cracks and Lines*) of a few years later (see Fig. 2.5: *Failles dans les Rochers* [*Faults in the Rocks*], 1950). Where the focus of the latter is intense and close up, often depicting a few square inches of the aleatory geometry of a rockface, the paintings reproduced in *Transition* seem to reduce the structural preoccupations of Cézanne to the barest outlines of mountain or river bed, while taking over from Matisse's interiors the sinuous and suggestive brushstrokes that designate foliage or biomorphic forms (Tr, 113–14). (Compare Fig. 2.6: Tal-Coat, *Pluie sur la Sainte-Victoire* [*Rain on Mount Sainte-Victoire*], 1952.)

Considering this trajectory of Tal-Coat's work in the 1940s, it is possible to grasp why Duthuit might have been impressed – as are his contemporary critics – by Tal-Coat's intimate

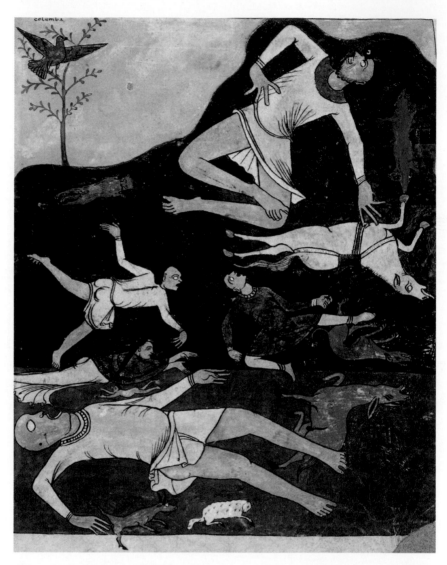

Fig. 2.2 *Le Déluge* [*The Flood*], miniature from the *Apocalypse* of the Saint-Sever (Saint-Sever Beatus), Latin manuscript, folio 193 (France, 11th century).

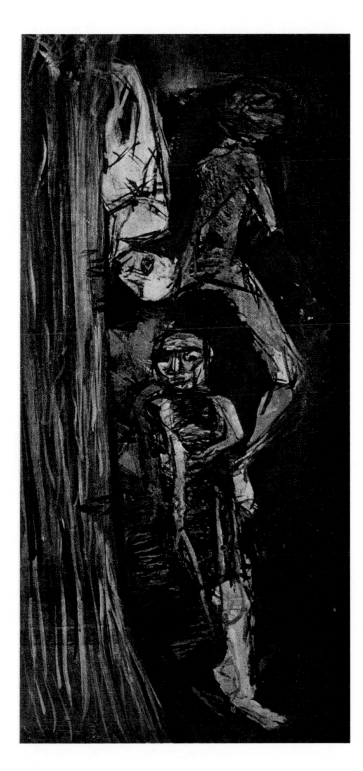

Fig. 2.3 Pierre Tal-Coat, from *Massacres* (oil on card, 25×52 cm, 1936–7), © Artists Rights Society (ARS), New York/ADAGP, Paris, 2016.

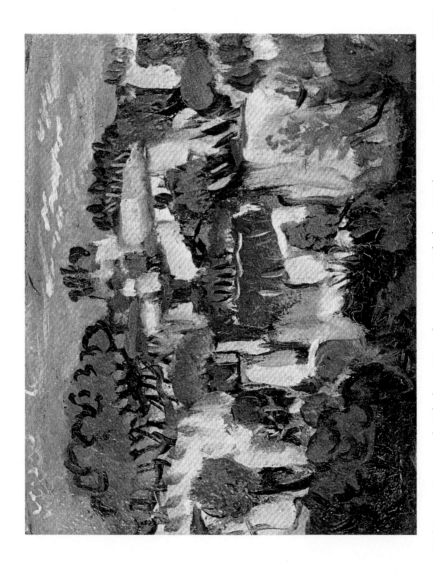

Fig. 2.4 Pierre Tal-Coat, *Paysage du Tholonet* [*Landscape at Le Tholonet*] (oil on canvas, 19×24 cm, 1941), © Artists Rights Society (ARS), New York/ADAGP, Paris, 2016.

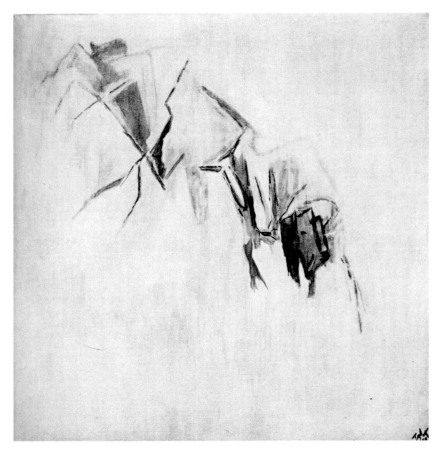

Fig. 2.5 Pierre Tal-Coat, *Failles dans les Rochers* [*Faults in the Rocks*] (oil on canvas, 143.5 × 143.5 cm, 1950), © Artists Rights Society (ARS), New York/ADAGP, Paris, 2016.

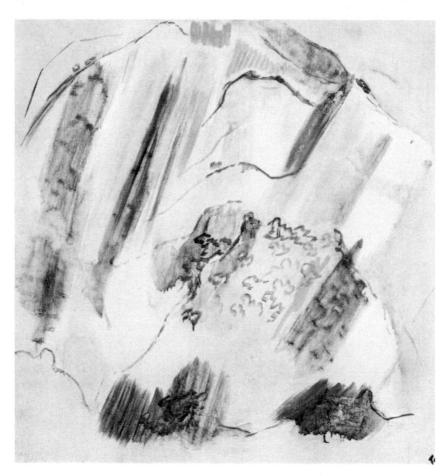

Fig. 2.6 Pierre Tal-Coat, *Pluie sur la Sainte-Victoire* [*Rain on Mount Sainte-Victoire*] (oil on canvas, 80×81 cm, 1952), © Artists Rights Society (ARS), New York/ADAGP, Paris, 2016.

phenomenological focus: 'The world a flux of movements partaking of living time, that of effort, creation, liberation, the painting, the painter. The fleeting instant of sensation given back, given forth, with context of the continuum it nourished' (Tr, 97; D, 138). Rather than seek the representation of a totality through the illusion of its spatial capture, Tal-Coat's increasingly restricted focus might allow for the 'passive' apprehension of minimal objects in a manner Duthuit hails – surely with full cognisance of its aesthetic heritage – with the word 'disinterested' (Tr, 97; D, 138). Beckett's response is more caustic: 'Total object, complete with missing parts, instead of partial object. Question of degree' (Tr, 97; D, 138). However much his intensity of focus or reduction of representational ambitions seems to disavow the desire for mastery, Tal-Coat has merely inverted the relation of whole to part. What Duthuit celebrates as the intuition of the whole in the part, redolent of its total context, Beckett sardonically renders as merely a kind of amputation. Despite their 'prodigious value' (Tr, 98; D, 139), Tal-Coat's 'tendency and accomplishment' – perhaps precisely in light of his extension of Cézanne and Matisse – are 'fundamentally those of previous painting, straining to enlarge the statement of a compromise' (Tr, 97; D, 138). Even if Tal-Coat's painting represents 'a composite of perceiver and perceived', process rather than 'datum', it remains a 'gain in nature' (Tr, 97; D, 138). It is continuous with the work of Western art stretching back to the Renaissance Italian painters, of whom Beckett remarks acerbically that 'they surveyed the world with the eyes of building-contractors' (Tr, 98; D, 139). And if Tal-Coat – and indeed Matisse – are able to disturb only 'a certain order on the plane of the feasible' (Tr, 98; D, 139), it is because they seek 'a more adequate expression of natural experience, as revealed to the vigilant coenaesthesia' (Tr, 97; D, 138). Even the most submissive phenomenology remains a pretext for the desire for expression which, in this dialogue, Beckett so famously rejects. Indeed, as we have seen, it is precisely this expression of the subject through a relation to its objects in the natural world that Beckett had insisted that Jack B. Yeats refused, echoing that breakdown of the subject-object relation he had already defined in the early 1930s as 'the new thing that has happened'.[7]

Both the fuller stakes of Beckett's reservations regarding Tal-Coat and the relation between expression and possession become clearer in the second and longer dialogue on André Masson. As we have already seen in relation to Beckett's response to the 'expressive' spirit of nationalism, expression assumes the prior existence of the subject in an interior domain to be *ex*pressed – outered or uttered – and an external object that becomes the vehicle or correlative of the thing that is to be expressed. Expression thus becomes a possessive claim on the object as the instrument of the subject, its function being to serve as a means or vehicle for the subject in its self-representation. Presented as the exemplar of an insuperable drive to both expression and possession, Masson presents a more formidable object to Beckett's critique than Tal-Coat. For one thing, Masson was the far more prominent and established painter, an independent fellow-traveller of the surrealists through the 1920s and 1930s, friend of André Breton, Michel Leiris and Georges Bataille, and a technically masterful, stylistically restless artist. His work had moved formally from a post-cubist symbolism through a surrealist period that drew on myth and metamorphosis in ways more technically jagged and less academic than Salvador Dali, to a body of work, composed during his exile in the Caribbean and New England during the war, that seemed to draw on indigenous art and mythology in ways doubtless stimulated by his friendships with Breton and Claude Lévi-Strauss.[8] Moreover – at least in Duthuit's rendering of him – Masson was already grappling with the issues that preoccupied Beckett in the dialogue on Tal-Coat. For Duthuit, Masson is already one who 'aspires to be rid of the servitude of space' (Tr, 99; D, 140) and who rejects the possessive relation to the object that Beckett had suggested is emblematised in Western perspective. Duthuit:

> Masson himself, having remarked that western perspective is no more than a series of traps for the capture of objects, declares that their possession does not interest him. He congratulates [Pierre] Bonnard for having, in his last works, 'gone beyond possessive space in every shape and form, far from surveys and bounds, to the point where all possession is dissolved'. (Tr, 100; D, 141)

We can track Masson's experiments with the representation of space and with the space of representation most economically through a somewhat arbitrary alignment of work from the decade prior to Beckett and Duthuit's dialogue. Like Tal-Coat, Masson assumed a variety of painterly modes, from Cézannian landscapes in the 1910s, through post-cubist allegories, to the metamorphic dreamscapes of the 1930s. Like Tal-Coat, he had been influenced by the *Apocalypse* of Saint-Sever to paint a series of *Massacres*. It is perhaps the legacy of that work, rather than his surrealist dreamscapes, that influenced his *Vue Emblématique de Tolède* [*Emblematic View of Toledo*] (1936; Fig. 2.7), painted at the onset of the Spanish Civil War. In expressly allegorical manner, a bent-shouldered human figure and spread-eagled bull, which presumably represents the Spanish people, both threatened by the flaming, projectile-like head of a tiger descending from the upper right, surmount an emblematic image of Toledo, depicted from above in the iconic style of late-medieval battle scenes. Beneath them lies a reclining biomorphic figure whose twisted, embryonic form presumably contains the painful seeds of the future.[9] Spatially, the canvas is distributed into five or six more or less discrete areas that refuse any perspectival depth and simply hold in tension the distinct allegorical elements of the whole. It enacts a sense of temporal suspension as if, perhaps, in anticipation of the oncoming violence of the civil war. A slightly later canvas, *Le Peintre et le Temps* [*The Painter and his Time*] (1938; Fig. 2.8) differently allegorises the relation of painter and painting to the world they represent. Here a painter's hand at the bottom of the canvas is in the act of composing a distraught female head whose features are – as in so many of his surrealist paintings of the 1930s – made up of fragments of biological and geological landscape. These features are continuous with those glimpsed through the window that, in the absence of perspectival depth, seems to fuse with the canvas and easel themselves. Interior and exterior, represented and representation appear to collapse into one another as if what is presented as an allegory of the relation of the painter to his *time* is transformed into a reflection on the spatial continuity of representation and the world. In the terms of Beckett's remarks on Tal-Coat, it presents a classic painterly meditation on the painting as 'partial object' for which the peculiarly detached hand stands as the metonymic index.

Referring to what is almost certainly this painting in a review of Masson's 1949 exhibition that immediately precedes 'Three Dialogues' in *Transition Forty-Nine*, André du Bouchet comments:

There is a canvas of his, painted in 1938, in which he makes an effort to get beyond the yawning sea-shell and the blazing plumage and up to the very hand that holds the brush – a storm in a sealed vase. He does not go further than that hand, which, cut off by the frame and

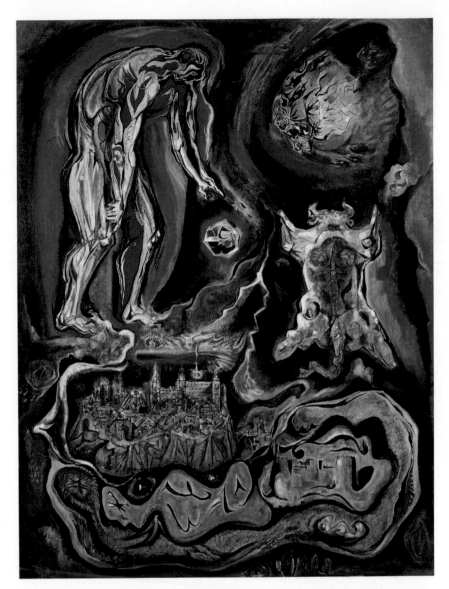

Fig. 2.7 André Masson, *Vue Emblématique de Tolède* [*Emblematic View of Toledo*] (oil on canvas, 162 × 122 cm, 1936), © Artists Rights Society (ARS), New York/ADAGP, Paris, 2016.

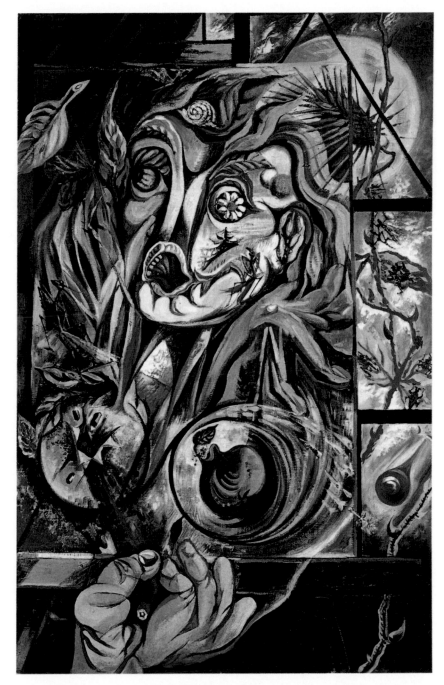

Fig. 2.8 André Masson, *Le Peintre et le Temps* [*The Painter and his Time*] (oil on canvas, 116 × 73 cm, 1938), © Artists Rights Society (ARS), New York/ADAGP, Paris, 2016.

left lying there, seems like a token of that open world whither he has just returned. His art, which then seemed to be seeking its substance in mythology, must henceforward be counted among the signs which today point to the decline of mythologies.[10]

Certainly, throughout the war years, Masson's painting had continued to be intensely mythological, ranging from canvases apparently inspired by Native American iconographies like *The Seeded Earth* (1942) to ones that pursue further his preoccupation with surrealist metamorphoses of human, biological and geological forms. The recent paintings from his 1949 exhibition reproduced in *Transition*, however, indeed indicate a move back to the more or less Cézannian mode of his youth. All three – *La Carrière de Bibemus* [*The Bibemus Quarry*] (1948; Fig. 2.9), *The Little Falls* (1949) and *Pine-Trees in the Rain* (1949) – represent to an even greater extent than Tal-Coat's gentler studies a vigorous, even virtuosic attempt to reappropriate and extend a mode of painting that had to a considerable degree marked the specificity of French

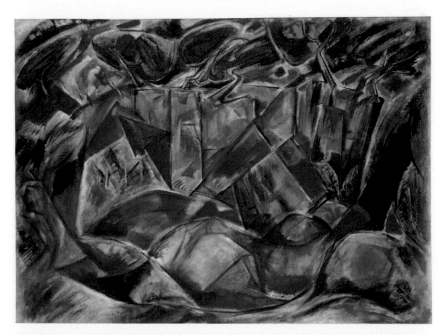

Fig. 2.9 André Masson, *La Carrière de Bibemus* [*The Bibemus Quarry*] (oil on canvas, 97×130 cm, 1948), © Artists Rights Society (ARS), New York/ADAGP, Paris, 2016.

painting before the war.[11] Devoid of any mythological or allegorical reference, and stepping back from any apparently surrealist
motivations, they seem at once to return urgently to the task of the
representation of the real and, in ways whose significance we will
explore further, to resuscitate the interrupted lineage of French
painting. And yet these paintings are not fully representative of
Masson's immediate post-war work. Another instance of his restless stylistic shifts from the same year, *L'Extase II* [*Ecstasy II*]
(1949; Fig. 2.10), one of his various experiments in sand and oil,
is certainly no less imbued with a richly mythological apprehension of the natural world and its metamorphoses than, say, *The
Seeded Earth* (1942) or the earlier *Metamorphosis of the Lovers*
(1938). Its frenetic lines and fusion of figure and ground justify,
perhaps, Duthuit's invocation of Masson's eye frolicking 'among
the focusless fields, tumultuous with incessant creation' (Tr, 99;
D, 140). Certainly, the existence of such works alongside the work
Transition actually reproduced testifies not only to what Duthuit
sees as Masson's 'technical gifts' and 'great technical variety' and
Beckett as 'the scars of a competence that must be most painful to
him' (Tr, 99; D, 140), but also to the very dilemma that Beckett
recognises such competence creates for him: Masson's very capacities as an artist lead him over and over again to a restless stylistic
experimentation whose poles are those of realism and surrealism,
representation and allegory. Neither mode frees him from either
expression or possession and his very competence seems doomed
to prevent him from the acts of radical dispossession that Beckett
was already envisaging for himself and, perhaps, projecting on to
van Velde. As Beckett concludes:

> With such preoccupations, it seems to me impossible that he should
> ever do anything different from that which the best, including himself,
> have done already. . . . His so extremely intelligent remarks on space
> breathe the same possessiveness as the notebooks of Leonardo who,
> when he speaks of *disfazione*, knows that for him not one fragment
> will be lost. (Tr, 100; D, 141)

And it is here that Beckett returns to his dream 'of an art unresent-
ful of its insuperable indigence'.

The juxtaposition of Masson's 'possessive' competence and his
'ferocious dilemma of expression' (Tr, 99; D, 140) with their
antithesis in a dream of indigence suggests what precisely is at

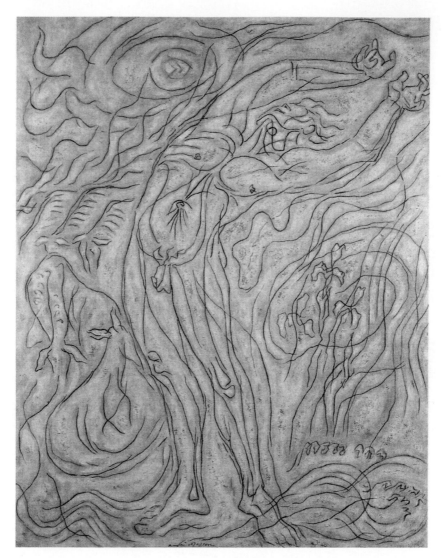

Fig. 2.10 André Masson, *L'Extase II* [*Ecstasy II*] (oil and sand on canvas, 128 × 100 cm, 1949), © Artists Rights Society (ARS), New York/ADAGP, Paris, 2016.

stake for Beckett in his rejection of Masson and the uncomfortable degree of identification or insight that may have impelled it. His own work had oscillated wildly between the mannered excesses of poems written under the influence of Joyce, like 'Enueg' I and II, or of the wartime novel *Watt*, and the spare, *avant-la-lettre* minimalism of the 'Three Poems' published in *Transition Forty-Eight* or of the short post-war stories that were the first of his works to be written in French.[12] Like Joyce, of whom Beckett notoriously remarked that 'the more he knew, the more he could',[13] Masson's work suffers not only from an excess of technical competence but also from a repleteness of meanings. From the paintings of the 1920s, like *Man Holding a Rope* (1924), through to his surrealist metamorphoses, Masson is a painter who seems unable to resist the temptation of a certain 'literariness'. The escape from that redundance of meaning lies in the turn to modes of representation that were already, at least in Beckett's view, exhausted, and so to another mode of mannerist excess. Hence Beckett's suspicion of Masson's competence, precisely because it enables such a virtuosic performance of apparent alternatives that are really repetitions.

Beckett himself was not entirely free yet of such temptations. As we have seen, in the work that he was producing at this very moment, the trilogy of novels and *Waiting for Godot*, he was still seeking to break with his own abundant capacity for allusion, allegory, symbolism. These works' mode may be parodic, eliciting the reader's allegorical desire only to disappoint it time and again, but it is still a mode unthinkable without a self-conscious exploitation of that desire for an apparatus of symbolic interpretation, instituted on the basis of the high modernist work of Eliot and Joyce, Rilke, Yeats and Valéry, even as it excoriated them. Such a mode of working clearly continued to represent an as yet ineluctable framework for the literary. What Duthuit calls Beckett's 'violently extreme and personal point of view' (Tr, 98; D, 139) on both Tal-Coat and Masson is doubtless the index of a force of attraction with which he still sought to break. Moreover, as Rémi Labrusse insightfully suggests, he had yet to break with precisely that possible way forward which his correspondence with Duthuit in the post-war years seemed to propose: the *image* thought as an alternative to the West's post-Renaissance mimetic desire.[14] The work of Bram van Velde, approached in the third dialogue, was one of the means through which he was able, gradually and with difficulty, as it appears, to break with even that 'issue' from his predicament.

Before abandoning his advocacy of Masson, however, Duthuit makes one more effort to convince us of his value:

> But must we really deplore the painting that admits 'the things and creatures of spring, resplendent with desire and affirmation, ephemeral no doubt, but immortally reiterant', not in order to benefit by them, not in order to enjoy them, but in order that what is tolerable and radiant in the world may continue? Are we really to deplore the painting that is a rallying, among the things of time that pass and hurry us away, towards a time that endures and gives increase?
> B. – (Exit weeping). (Tr, 100; D, 142)

Beckett's histrionic response serves as a reminder that these dialogues, which he composed in their entirety on the basis of actual conversations or letters with Duthuit, are in fact among his dramatic works. The dialogues are generally read as a parodic response to Duthuit's fervent appeal to humane values as the foundation for art. That they certainly are, and throughout Duthuit is given the unenviable role of the fall guy in this highbrow slapstick routine. What is less apparent, on account of the routine excision of the dialogues from their intensely intertextual relation to the cultural debates that *Transition* staged and participated in, is that it is not only Duthuit who is being parodied, but a set of cultural precepts everywhere on display in *Transition* and in post-war French culture at large.

As Serge Guilbaut has pointed out, post-war French culture was preoccupied with the question of how to reconstruct a civilisation on the ruins of a catastrophe that was as much ideological in the largest sense as it was a question of 'bricks and mortar'. Not just the physical destruction and economic ruin but, more importantly, the manifestation of barbarism at the heart of civilisation to which Walter Benjamin was so keenly attuned had issued in a crisis of culture that was particularly intense in Paris, the former capital of modernism and the vanguard of art. 'Art and the image of France were crucial in this scheme, but what kind of image was really needed or effective? This would be at the center of French reconstruction and at the core of the debate, which would be quite violent and complex.'[15] That debate was pursued across the political spectrum, ranging from nostalgic attempts to reconstruct

pre-war French modernism and reassert its prestige to the promotion of socialist realism in place of the discredited languages of
modernism and the avant-garde. It was also pursued in debates
that sought to come to grips 'with the history of modern painting, with old theoretical models and with the new cultural and
political situation at a time of intense scrutiny of self and national
identity'.[16] These debates had material effects in both private and
official endeavours to reassert – or rebuild on a new basis – the
prestige of the 'School of Paris' through exhibitions of French art
in New York and elsewhere – endeavours that notoriously failed
to prevent New York from becoming the new centre of gravity of
modern art and which critics like Clement Greenberg and others
would greet as marking the demise of Paris's monopoly on the
avant-garde.[17]

Transition was an important organ of post-war reconstruction,
both as a participant in these debates and in its role as a kind of
cultural ambassador, representing contemporary French cultural
production to an English-speaking, primarily American public.
Under the editorship of Eugene Jolas, its previous incarnation,
transition, had gained renown in the 1920s and 1930s, primarily as the publisher of Joyce's *Work in Progress*, before folding in
1938. With Jolas's permission, Duthuit re-established the journal
in 1946, managing to include Jolas, along with Jean-Paul Sartre,
Georges Bataille, René Char and Joyce scholar Stuart Gilbert,
prominently on its masthead. Beckett was closely involved with
the new journal – as he had been when Jolas was editor – and for
Transition Forty-Nine alone he translated essays by René Char,
Paul Eluard and Francis Ponge.[18]

Beckett would thus have been thoroughly familiar with the type
and tone of reflections on art and politics that appeared in the
pages of *Transition*. He would have been no less aware that in
its new incarnation the journal, although it published a range
of younger French writers and artists whose work had emerged
during the relative isolation of the war years (Ponge being a prime
example), was considerably less concerned with promoting the
Parisian-based international avant-garde than its predecessor had
been. Duthuit seems rather to have dedicated it to re-establishing
the continuity of contemporary art with what had become the
'tradition' of the School of Paris and affirming the vital role of
art in the reconstitution of a humanist culture. In that context,
Beckett's parodic presentation of Duthuit in the dialogues ceases

to seem a personal jibe. Rather, it grasps the editor's redemptive and utopian demands on art in relation to statements that are to be found everywhere throughout the journal. Similarly, his larger scepticism regarding the representative and public role of art takes its meaning in relation to historically specific debates well encapsulated in a forum published in the same issue, with contributions by Braque, Matisse and Masson, among others, 'A pre-war and post-war questionnaire: Art and the Public'. Beckett's disgust for the notion of 'the public' presented in that forum, a public represented as the judge of art's 'utility' or as the guardian of a cultural patrimony, is palpable in the dialogues. What further drives Beckett's 'violently extreme' rejection is a specific tone and aesthetic attitude in *Transition* that the words he puts in Duthuit's mouth typify with only slight exaggeration.[19]

In his review of Tal-Coat, the young poet André du Bouchet writes with an effusiveness that sharpens the point of Beckett's jab at the painter's 'Franciscan orgies' (Tr, 98; D, 139):

> His pictures well up like springs and he creates an object which is endowed with as much radiance and limpidity as a fountain, but which is placed for the nonce in a room and submitted to the restrictions of the canvas, of the wall, of the cube of air which arrests it. We can see some of his pictures capturing the gleams of the passing hour and following the changes of the day as if they were living organisms.
> . . .
>
> He puts the horizon back as far as that prehistoric region in which nature has not yet suffered the assaults of language and is therefore at the entire disposal of all and sundry. The substance of the fish has not yet been disentangled from that of water and weed.
>
> It is to this troublous and essential enjoyment that Tal Coat summons us at a time when the multiplicity of techniques has resulted in an increased dessication of substances and words; instead of isolating and outlining forms in order to give them their values, he invites us to a kind of vital communion, of which we were beginning to lose even the memory.[20]

Du Bouchet's projection on to Tal-Coat of a primordial 'essential enjoyment', reaching back into a nature unsullied by language, eagerly endows art with a socially restorative function, one that proffers a 'vital communion' lost to memory as it is to language. The willed nostalgia of this high lyrical effusion betrays what

Beckett might have dubbed its 'possessive' drive in the peculiarly instrumental locution with which du Bouchet indicates just what is to be restored: a nature that will be 'at the entire disposal of all and sundry'. Beneath the rhapsodic enjoyment of an art that is a 'living organism' persists a functional, moralising appropriation of both art and nature, no less possessive for being proposed in the form of a compensatory aesthetic commons.[21]

Duthuit's own essay in the same volume of *Transition* is similarly devoted to restoring the socially restorative function of art and to affirming the aesthetic foundations of community. It participates expressly in ongoing French debates on the social function of art, opening with the observation that:

> It is singular that the work of our best painters should have ignored more or less completely the overwhelming drama of modern existence, a drama that has assumed the proportions of a universal cataclysm. Europe is falling apart but painting continues to thrive.[22]

The 'harmony' and 'grace' of the best art, its 'resplendent surfaces', is counterpointed by that of the painters 'who have acknowledged the impact of the battle' but have done so 'at the cost of distorting the very essence of the conflict they seek to portray'. Duthuit continues:

> This failure to create a true type of communal art, which is merely more blatant among the adepts of 'socialist realism' because of the sudden widening of the gap between capacity and purpose, has become something of a tradition and even of an aesthetic requirement in our civilization. (20)

Rather than explore further the contradiction he is outlining between the most advanced artistic techniques – those of Matisse, presumably – and the alienation of the individual artist from society, Duthuit instead turns 'towards an ancient type of institutional art . . . where society as a whole seemed to express itself at its peak of intensity' (20). In line with his pre-war preoccupations, he proposes the model of Byzantine representations of space as if a reorientation of spatial relations could figure and even produce a reconstitution of art's own relation to community.[23] Byzantine space 'is the unseen, interacting extension of persons and things and the air in which they are steeped' (30); unlike post-Renaissance perspectival or 'fictitious space' (33), it does not impose a boundary between the work and the world. It is this space that Matisse and the fauvists sought to recreate, 'a space in which measuring instruments are not involved' and which 'is not limited . . . by such and such an object placed in the foreground of a design' (33). In this space, 'objects extend far beyond their appearances. There is no such thing as an isolated object. Nor is there such a thing as an isolated picture. The picture cannot be isolated from the material universe in which the work is born' (34).

Duthuit's concerns in this essay hence permit us to grasp better what was at stake in Beckett's scepticism regarding Tal-Coat's and Matisse's achievement and, more generally, regarding the relation of post-war art to spatial and, consequently, social relations. Commencing with the most intimate subject-object relations, the painter's representation of space becomes for Duthuit an analogue for social relations:

> A direct, spontaneous fusion of the *I* with the *NOT I* is sought – one so intimate that the painter ends by painting himself, by putting himself into the composition. What he grasps, is an ensemble to which we can fix no limits. Nor are the images produced in this way to be itemized. They do not spring from a vision that is incomplete or partial.[24]

The expressive representation of space – 'Expression is in the whole arrangement of my painting', according to Matisse (35) – thus becomes continuous with its social implications:

> Matisse regards space as a gathering of force or energy everywhere present, surrounding us, penetrating us, going through us with all its vibrations: my own body, moreover, being part of these vibrations. . . . Space is everywhere, it is the universe around me, it is myself, my flesh, and the consciousness I have of it; it is part of my creation. (35)

For Duthuit, Matisse accordingly expresses – in a phrase with remarkable resonances of W. B. Yeats – 'the unity of beings and the light in which they move' (36). And yet this 'elusive painting' still remains no more than an 'intimation' of 'the world of unity': it requires still 'to be deepened, humanized, rooted in the earth where we are struggling' (36). Returning to the social as well as aesthetic example of Byzantium for 'an artistic structure capable of containing the individual and of supporting him in his effort toward freedom', Duthuit calls for an art that 'would claim as its own the space which separates the tentative spectator from itself as fully as the fictitious space which is alluded to within its frame' and in this dissolution of spatial distinction 'foster a communal climate':

> As in Byzantium, there would be no element in the individual which would not be persuaded into unison with the community that expresses itself by a monument, by solemn imagery and sacred language. We must continue to search and remember the fact that however dark and difficult the circumstances to-day, an order of things did exist in which man and the matter he organizes put an end to the rages and conflicts of individualism in a way that did not imperil the powers of the individual. (37)

There is, in the wake of the destructive triumph of Nazi ideology, something by turns inane and disturbing about Duthuit's and du Bouchet's pronouncements, a wishful drive to overcome alienation at the risk of coercive 'communion' or prelapsarian fantasies of a paganism without content that are equally inadequate to the 'universal cataclysm' whose effects were still all too evident in 1949. In the face of such rhetorics of reconciliation, driven as they were by the urge to achieve a cultural as well as material reconstruction of post-war France, Beckett's 'extremism' may come to seem both intellectually and ethically judicious. It stands as his rejection of what must have seemed the most fervent denial of what he had, even before the war, grasped as 'the new thing that has happened', a thing that he had forcefully apprehended in the Irish hospital in Saint-Lô as 'the conception of humanity in ruins'.[25] In the third dialogue he notoriously turns to an artist who, rather than seeking in art a means to reconciliation, remarks tersely enough in *Transition Forty-Nine* that 'Painting is man face to face with his débâcle'.[26] Bram van Velde is, for Beckett, 'the first to submit wholly to the incoercible absence of relation' between represents and representee, or who confronts as no other 'the acute and increasing anxiety of the relation itself, as though shadowed more and more darkly by a sense of invalidity, of inadequacy, of existence at the expense of all that it excludes, all that it blinds to' (Tr, 103; D, 145). The question remains as to what justifies Beckett's high estimation of van Velde's work.

II

Bram, or Abraham, van Velde, whom Beckett befriended in the late
1930s when both had settled in Paris, was born in Zouterwoude,
Holland, in 1895. After the death of his father when he was thir-
teen, he found employment with a manufacturer of house paints
in The Hague. The latter, recognising the young painter's talent,
offered him a scholarship to study painting that allowed van Velde
to stay at the German expressionists' colony of Worpswede in the
1920s.[27] The influence of expressionism on his work is evident
from paintings of the period, like *Dorf* [*Village*] (1923; Fig. 2.11)
or the small, almost schematic *Three Masks* (c. 1925). Despite that
influence, however, van Velde was by no means an expressionist
in any very full sense of the word. He lacks, as his curator Franz
Meyer points out, 'that specific arousal of subjectivity that matters
to Kirchner, Kokoschka, Soutine, Nolde or even the COBRA
group'.[28] But rather than the 'objectivity' or 'hardness' that Meyer
attributes to his painting of this period, one finds in a painting
like *Dorf* a peculiar and quite precise hesitation: not a hesitation
to express, so much as a hesitation to settle on a particular line
of perspective or focal centre for the painting. The eye hesitates
among the figures, unsure which to endow with visual primacy,
and between the figures in the foreground and the titular village
that ought to be the perspectival focal point in the background.
The gaze remains in an early painting like this – as it so markedly does in that other painter whose work Beckett admired at
the same period, Jack B. Yeats – in a state of radical uncertainty
as to where to settle, as to where its gaze should fix. It *circulates*,
as van Velde remarked of his painting at a much later date.[29]
There is nothing here of the strident, highly focalised power of a
painting like Munch's famous *Scream*. If it is an expressionism,
it is one already convinced, as Beckett would later say, that there
is 'nothing to express, nothing with which to express, nothing
from which to express, no power to express, no desire to express,
together with the obligation to express' (Tr, 98; D, 139).

Liberation from the 'obligation to express' may have come to
van Velde through his encounter with Matisse in the late 1920s.
Certainly his principal critic and curator, Rainer Michael Mason,
records van Velde's viewing of paintings from Matisse's experi-
mental period of the mid-1910s, and in particular *La Leçon de
Piano* [*The Piano Lesson*] of 1916 (Fig. 2.12), as having had a

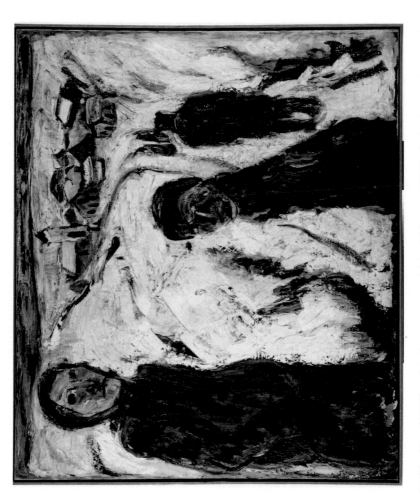

Fig. 2.11 Bram van Velde, *Dorf* [*Village*] (oil on canvas, 111 × 130 cm, 1923), © Artists Rights Society (ARS), New York/ADAGP, Paris, 2016.

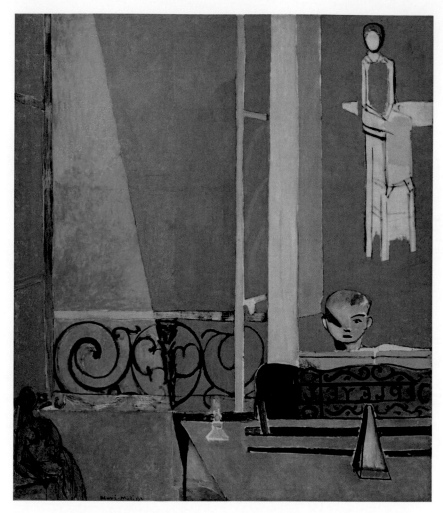

Fig. 2.12 Henri Matisse, *La Leçon de Piano* [*The Piano Lesson*] (oil on canvas, 245×212 cm, 1916), © Succession H. Matisse, Artists Rights Society (ARS), New York. Digital image © The Museum of Modern Art/Licensed by Scala/Art Resource, New York.

formidable effect. The latter painting constituted '*une véritable révélation*' for the young Dutch painter, whose work undergoes henceforth a remarkable process of perspectival flattening, complemented by an increasing emphasis on the rhythmic distribution of colour and of largely two-dimensional forms repeated and distributed across the surface of the canvas.[30] Van Velde's experiments with pictorial space, at first so evidently modelled on those of Cézanne and Matisse, begin by holding in tension the still vestigially representational forms of conventional still life – the citruses of *Nature Morte, Corse* [*Still Life, Corsica*] (1930; Fig. 2.13), for example – with an increasingly flattened pictorial space that remains, for a while at least, 'background space'. One can still read in *Nature Morte, Corse* the allusions to Matisse's *Leçon de Piano*: in both paintings, the stylised frame of a window abolishes perspectival depth, pushing the 'background' forwards into the foreground of the pictorial space. In place of the representation of volume, whose remainder persists in the fruits and bowl of the still life, the rhythms of colorific movement across the canvas dominate. In *Nature Morte*, the strong visual diagonal that runs from upper right to lower left through the abstract yellow brushwork and the lemons in the bowl counterpoints the march of black and grey verticals across the picture. What remains of representational space is demarcated by these verticals, which compose an ambiguous reminiscence of both the window frame and the frame of the picture in a visual pun on the capture of three-dimensional space through the aperture of the window or on the flatness of the canvas. They construct what Pierre Alechinsky would come to call the *crypto-fenêtres* that proliferate in his mature painting.[31] Indeed, van Velde's paintings of this period are haunted by the memory of the ironwork balustrade that figures so prominently as a marker of space and of the border between inner and outer in *La Leçon de Piano*. Its tracing hovers along the lower edge of *Nature Morte*, marking – as Jan Greshoff presciently noted in an early review of van Velde – the barrier or hindrance (*empêchement*, a term Beckett would echo in an early essay on the van Velde brothers) to vision or to the appropriation of the natural world by the painter.[32] The gaze is, as it were, arrested at the frame or in the very aperture of vision.

Simultaneously a motif that had already fascinated van Velde in his 'expressionist' period, that of the mask, takes on a new form. In an early painting like *Three Masks* (1925), the masks

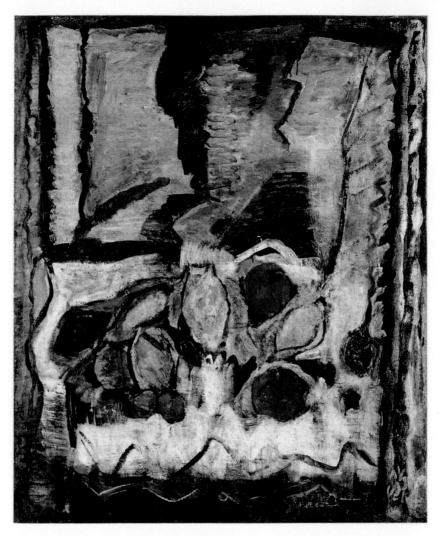

Fig. 2.13 Bram van Velde, *Nature Morte, Corse* [*Still Life, Corsica*] (oil on canvas, 98.5 × 81.1 cm, 1930), © Artists Rights Society (ARS), New York/ADAGP, Paris, 2016.

are those of an actor, allegories of the subject's inauthenticity. By 1930 they have become reminiscent of the primitivist masks of the cubist Picasso.[33] Already in *Nature Morte* there looms a vague and shadowy form that would, were the painting under glass, appear to be the reflection of the viewer. Framed as it is by the zig-zag vertical lines on right and left of the painting, it may occupy the space exterior to that which contains the represented still life. It is a residue of the inside/outside distinction that continues to haunt painting as a model of the subject-object relation.

In a somewhat later painting, *Masques* [*Masks*] (1933; Fig. 2.14), these pictorial motifs undergo a striking process of condensation. The gridwork that appeared to recall a balustrade is now configured with the masks that face outwards to demarcate the upper portion of the painting, while on the right the zig-zag framing lines now appear to form the leafy or feathered fringes of another mask that stares out of the painting. What might at one point have been fruits in a still life have been reduced to coloured lozenges and triangles that proffer to the eye multiple possible trajectories and rhythmic pathways through or across the canvas. Already this painting manifests all the traits of van Velde's mature style. Confronted with *Masques*, or with a somewhat later painting like *Sans Titre* [*Untitled*] (*Montrouge*) (1939; Fig. 2.15), the viewer finds it impossible to stabilise a position in relation to pictorial space, to identify any perspectival foreground or background. In one of his rare remarks on his own work, van Velde homed in on this quality of constant movement: 'Ma toile est une circulation. C'est comme l'être, la vie. Ils sont toujours en mouvement. Si ma toile était statique, elle serait fausse . . .'[34] As Franz Meyer has pointed out, this effect of circulation or of constant, restless movement is generated more by the colours than by any forms depicted in the paintings, colours being 'the true actors in the painting, and thus the vectors of its movement'.[35] Without the anchor of any figurative representations, we confront tumbling and mobile forms that generate peculiarly uncertain spatial relations. The paintings have an effect that one can only term a strangely assured hesitancy. And yet these are not quite abstract paintings: they occupy the shifting borderland between figuration and abstraction where, observing this incessant and restless motion of pictorial forms, the viewer cannot help being captivated by the possibility of discerning a vestigial figure, the figure, if you like, of figure itself, of the face or mask that is the prototype of all figuration. As Avigdor

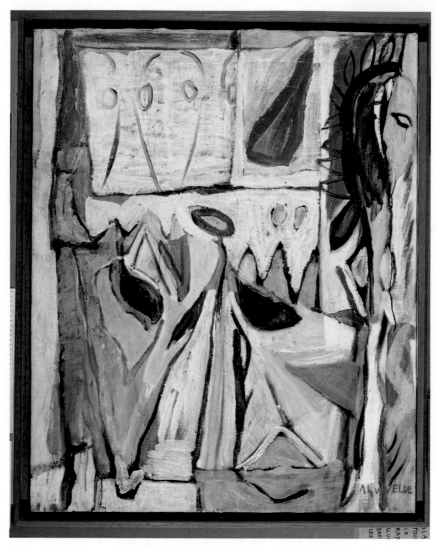

Fig. 2.14 Bram van Velde, *Masques* [*Masks*] (oil on canvas, 100 × 80 cm, 1933), © Artists Rights Society (ARS), New York/ADAGP, Paris, 2016.

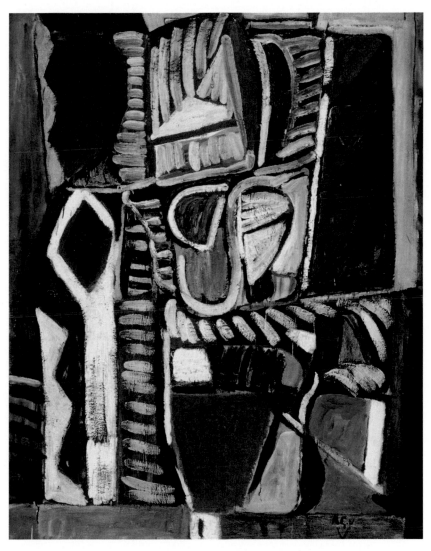

Fig. 2.15 Bram van Velde, *Sans Titre* [*Untitled*] (*Montrouge*) (oil on canvas, 98.3×74 cm, 1939), © Artists Rights Society (ARS), New York/ADAGP, Paris, 2016.

Arikha remarked, 'in each of his canvases, "a head" was hidden.
. . . But Bram decomposed the figure into formal, chromatic and
rhythmic variations.'[36] It is as if the paintings stage the difficulty
of seeing: 'decomposing' or dismantling any perceptible depth or
surface, seeming to erase what remains of their figures with layers
and layers painted over them, they produce an effect of disfigura-
tion without entire erasure. As in Balzac's story Le Chef d'oeuvre
inconnu, to which van Velde alluded in the title of one of his paintings, Le Chef d'ouevre indifférent, the figure is buried, hidden,
layer on layer, or dispersed across the canvas, not entirely consigned to oblivion.[37]

Out of these canvases, the remains or the ruins of a face seem to
stare. From the start, Beckett observed these canvases with peculiar acuity. In a letter to van Velde's wife on the eve of the German
occupation of Paris, Beckett wrote of the painting that he himself
owned (Sans Titre [Untitled], 1937; Fig. 2.16):

> Under the blue glass Bram's painting gives off a dark flame. Yesterday
> evening I could see in it Neary at the Chinese restaurant, 'huddled in
> the tod of his troubles like an owl in ivy.' Today it will be something
> different, and it is always yourself that you choose; a self that you did
> not know, if you are lucky.[38]

What is this non-figurative work in which one sees one's own face,
one's figure, or, to put it another way, this painting which returns
one's gaze with a difference? In a sense, it was to this question
that Beckett's surprisingly copious writings on van Velde were
persistently devoted, aligning the question as to what one sees
in the painting with the crisis in the subject-object relation that
his criticism of all the arts continually homed in on. That crisis
is, of course, inseparable from a general crisis of representation
whose intimate dimensions Beckett's work stubbornly measures.
In the earliest of several essays on van Velde, 'La peinture des van
Velde', Beckett homes in on the fundamental issue of the arts, that
of representation: 'To what', he asks, 'have the representative arts
so obstinately devoted themselves, since forever? To the desire to
arrest time, in representing it.'[39] Around this simple observation
as to the dilemma of an art that seeks to capture life in motion on
the immobile surface of the canvas hover the paradoxical locutions 'still life' and its French equivalent, nature morte, oxymorons
whose correlative is the representation of three-dimensional space

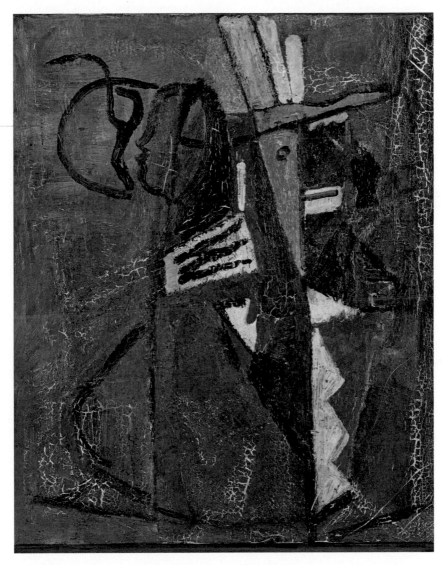

Fig. 2.16 Bram van Velde, *Sans Titre* [*Untitled*] (oil on canvas, 126×75 cm, 1937), © Artists Rights Society (ARS), New York/ADAGP, Paris, 2016.

on two-dimensional surfaces. Both constitute the eternal dilemma of Western painting whose trajectory Beckett came to describe in the second essay on van Velde, 'Peintres de l'empêchement', as 'the history of its relations with its object, the latter evolving, necessarily, at first in the sense of extension, then in that of penetration. What renews painting is first that there are more and more things to paint, then a more and more possessive mode of painting them.'[40]

For Beckett, the obsession and the power of Western painting lie in this perpetual and possessive effort to appropriate the object, and van Velde at first seems to him to address the dilemma by suspending the object as object:

> The painting of A. van Velde would then be in the first place a painting of the thing in suspension, I would willingly say of the dead thing, if the term didn't have such troublesome associations [i.e. with *nature morte*]. That's to say that the thing one sees there is not only represented as suspended, but strictly such as it is, really fixed [in space]. It is the thing alone, isolated by the need to see it, by the need to see. The thing immobile in the void, there at last is the visible thing, the pure object. (D, 126; my translation)

Beckett's precise phrasing begins to open here a distinction between the object of representation and the 'thing' or 'pure object'. This distinction shapes the terms of his quite extensive claims for van Velde's achievement. 'Peintres de l'empêchement' pushes the argument further: here, it is not only that the medium of painting contingently fails to represent objects, *it is the essence of the object to elude representation*. 'What remains to be represented if the essence of the object is to elude [*se dérober*] representation?' (SBV, 166; D, 136).[41] Moreover, it is not just that the object is difficult to represent, but that it actually *resists* representation: 'The object of representation always resists representation' (SBV, 166; D, 135). In the quasi-Heideggerian terms that Beckett's argument approaches but, as we shall see, significantly deviates from, the object could be described as 'Gegen-stand', as a thing that is not only *entgegen*, opposite, or coming to meet one, but one that actively opposes the subject that seeks to appropriate it: 'Der Gegenstand ist Widerstand', as Beckett might have punned in German.

And this resistant object of painting – 'that in which Christ, a potato, and a square of red are one' – culminates in one thing, 'that they are things, the thing, thingliness' (SBV, 166; D, 135–6). What van Velde paints, then, is this thing or thingliness. Post-Kantian that Beckett appears to have been in the later 1930s, he is not naïve enough to conclude that van Velde paints the 'thing in itself'. Rather, he paints 'la chose qui cache la chose', the thing that hides or conceals the thing – a phrase that markedly echoes a similar formulation of van Velde reported by Cäsar Menz: 'I seek to see, above all in this world, what hinders us from seeing.'[42] Ironically, the processes of erasure and layering, of perpetual, cir-culatory movement across unstable surfaces, that characterise van Velde's paintings at this period and that *hinder* the gaze appear also to Beckett as the process of *unveiling* the thing, in a ceaseless pursuit: 'An endless unveiling, veil behind veil, plane after plane of imperfect transparencies, light and space themselves veils, an unveiling towards the unveilable, the nothing, the thing again' (SBV, 167; D, 136).[43] Beckett's insight here registers something that accounts for the peculiar, and for some viewers repellent, quality of van Velde's paintings of these years, the murky dense-ness of their surfaces, the thickness of the muddy impastos that he seems to favour, their obdurate obscurity. Van Velde does not paint light, or the appearance of the object in the play of light that falls on it, nor does he seek to render, as Cézanne or the cubists might be said to have done, the inner structure of phenomena. His painting is neither the light that plays on the surface of things nor the light that penetrates their interiors. It is, rather, the trace of a continuous and paradoxical effort to see what obscures the vision of the thing, a trace that only ends up, as Beckett sees, depositing a further layer or obscuring veil.

But this endless veiling-unveiling is also 'burial in the unique, in a place of impenetrable nearnesses, cell painted on the stone of [the] cell, art of confinement [*art de l'incarcération*]' (SBV, 167; D, 136). This was not the only occasion on which Beckett used this image of rigorous incarceration to characterise the artist's confrontation with the void that has opened where representation was. At almost the same moment, he wrote of Jack B. Yeats as one who 'brings light, as only the great dare bring light, to the issue-less predicament of existence, reduces the dark where there might have been, mathematically at least, a door'.[44] At this post-war moment, Beckett descries in both painters – who resembled one another in their silences and intensity – not an easy and effusive escape from the predicament of a ruined humanity ('a vocable . . . reserved for times of great massacres'),[45] but a closing in on a state of dispossession whose most powerful image is that of the cell. The prevalence of this image – 'the man, alone in his box, thinking (thinking!)'[46] – has given rise to the assumption that Beckett is an advocate of philosophical solipsism, an assumption that is all too hasty. Rather, the cell – an enclosure from whose utter dispossession the idea of the mastery of 'possessive space' could not be more remote – becomes a passage, aporetic perhaps, through which a more rigorous thinking of the subject can be engaged, in which the human is reduced to a thing without objects, or a thing among things.[47]

In light of his preoccupation with the condition of thingliness, it is striking how closely, if unsystematically, Beckett's formulations correspond with those that his German contemporary Martin Heidegger elaborated across precisely the same period in a series of lectures and essays between 1936 and 1950: *What Is a Thing?*, 'The Origin of the Work of Art' and 'The Thing'. It remains uncertain how well Beckett knew Heidegger's work, and it seems probable that the convergence of some of their thinking derives from their close engagement with Kantian epistemology in the pre-war years.[48] But given Beckett's concerns, it is not surprising that that convergence, independently arrived at or not, should turn around a comparable critique of representation. Heidegger's approach to the thing seeks to dismantle the constitutive assumption of Western philosophy of a subject-object polarity much as Beckett sought to interrogate 'the new thing that had happened' in light of post-Renaissance art's positing of a relation with its objects secured in place by the punctual positioning of the subject in perspectival space. While Heidegger's 1936 lectures, collected as *What Is a Thing?*, remained substantially tied to the Kantian propositions that they sought to displace, 'The Origin of the Work of Art' (1936) already began to establish the distinct thingliness of things. This thingliness is opposed to mere materiality, which remains embedded in a form-matter distinction that merely rewrites the subject-object polarity in 'a conceptual mechanism that nothing can resist'.[49] The thing, we might say, is the excess of the real over the object as which it appears.

In this respect, the thing cannot be the object of a representation, whose terms are given not by the substance of the thing itself but by its appearance for a subject whose own faculties determine a priori the form of its possible apprehension. As Heidegger clarifies in the later essay 'The Thing' (1950):

> An independent, self-supporting thing may become an object if we place it before us, whether in immediate perception or by bringing it to mind in a recollective re-presentation [*Vor-stellung*]. However, the thingly character of the thing does not consist in being a represented object, nor can it be defined in any way in terms of the objectness, the over-againstness of the object [*Gegenstand*].[50]

For Kant, the object, understood as the 'unity of the manifold' in sensory perception or 'presentation' (*Darstellung*), becomes the object of a concept (*Begriff*) though the act of re-presentation (*Vorstellung*), a reflective or reflexive act that consciously posits (*stellt*) or places the object before the subject in relation to other objects of cognition. In this way the immediate sensory perception is generalised and grasped (*begreifen*) by the subject in a moment of repetition through which the object is possessed. As Kant was at pains to stress, the object thus conceived as an object for our cognitive faculties is by no means the 'thing in itself' (*noumenon*), but a phenomenon whose appearance is determined by the a priori constitution of our faculties. Hence Heidegger's consistent insistence on the distinction between the object and the thing.

The question remains, however, as to how this Kantian metaphysics – which evidently stands in for Western metaphysics in general – could be displaced without the most naïve realist reduction. If the moment of re-presentation, *Vorstellung*, determines the object at the expense of its thingliness and is yet the very condition of any possible cognition, how would it be possible to approach the world of things without the appropriative or possessive gesture that seems to define the human subject? Heidegger's response is to propose in place of subjective representation or *Vorstellung* the notion of *Vor-stehen* that he describes as 'the more precise expression "what stands forth"'.[51] *Vorstehen* is a modality of the thing rather than a disposition of the subject; it clearly displaces not only the representative moment of *Vorstellung* but also the *gegenstehen* (standing against or 'over-againstness') of the object (*Gegenstand*) that always implicitly opposes it to the subject on which it depends. Where the object stands over against the subject, the thing 'stands forth' in the world that is its support or ground. It is therefore aligned with another term by which Heidegger displaces the

Kantian vocabulary and whose implications he had already begun to trace in *What Is a Thing?*. That term is *vorgreifen*, literally, to anticipate, a disposition of the subject that allows for another relation to things than their capture as objects, as implicit in the term *begreifen*, or conceptual 'grasping'. *Vorgreifen* is a capacity of the human to anticipate, to be readied for, what will stand forth to it as a thing: 'The *what*-character of what can be sensed must be presented before hand and anticipated in advance within the scope and as the scope of what can be received.'[52]

Vorgreifen is the apprehension of the thing before it is grasped and subsumed under a concept. It is thus distinct from the act of *Vorstellung*: thingliness is irreducible to the object that is bound to the subject over against which it is necessarily posited. The moment of *Vorstellung* is not only the appropriative act of the subject that subsumes the manifold of perception into the unity of a concept, reducing the raw data of sensation to the general form of a cognition; it is also the moment in which the formal unity of all human subjects, the identity of the Subject in the identity of their modes of representation, is manifested. Kant's critiques thus succeed in knitting together the distinct strands of the notion of representation, the political and aesthetic as well as the epistemological, and in tying what he poses as the fundamental forms of human faculties to the universal forms of human 'common sense'.[53] As we have already seen in Chapter 1, the critique of the aesthetics of representation is at one and the same time the critique of the political sphere of public sense whose formal presupposition is the possibility of subjects meeting in and through their formal identity with one another. The thing as it is thought in convergent ways, though from very different perspectives, by both Beckett and Heidegger thus becomes the vehicle for a simultaneously aesthetic and political dismantling of a Western, liberal system of representation and of the understanding of the human and of political community that it sustains. Here the recalcitrant 'thing' of the *res-publica* that defied the political formation of the nation emerges in the aesthetic domain as the thing that resists representation itself.

If, for Beckett, the 'pure object', *la chose*, is that which resists representation, for Heidegger the thing not only resists representation, it *is* resistance:

> The thing in the sense of a natural body is, however, not only what is movable in space, what simply occupies space . . . but what fills space,

keeping it occupied, extending, dividing, and maintaining itself in this occupying: it is resistance, i.e., force.[54]

Or, as he puts it in the more tentative unfolding of 'thingliness' in *Origin of the Work of Art*, in a way that brings out the relation between thingliness and the resistance to instrumentality:

> The inconspicuous thing withdraws itself from thought in the most stubborn of ways. Or is it rather that this self-refusal of the mere thing, this self-contained refusal to be pushed around, belongs precisely to the essential nature of the thing?[55]

Elusive of definition, the thing cannot be equated with 'formed matter', the assumption of both aesthetics and metaphysics, an equation that would for Heidegger reduce the thing to the status of 'equipment'.[56] Not to be conceived as a 'unity of the manifold' or as a bearer of properties, the thing is also not to be understood as a product of technology. Furthermore, even consideration of the thingly as that which is 'left over' once the equipmental or commodity character of the made object is set aside does not serve to define the thing: 'It remains questionable whether the process of stripping away everything equipmental will ever disclose the thingness of the thing.'[57] What begins here as a negative critique of philosophical modes of representation and definition that Heidegger traces back through their Aristotelian roots will rapidly become a 'step back', back not only from what he terms 'the thinking that merely represents', but even from the historical implications of the instrumentality with which 'The Thing' commences and whose effect is universal equivalence, 'the countless objects everywhere of equal value'.[58] In face of the commodification of both humans and objects, Heidegger turns for an instance of the thing to the hand-crafted jug, things being 'inconspicuously compliant', 'compliant and modest in number'.[59] That the artisanal appeal of the earthenware jug derives its charge only from the condition of universal commodification against which it is posed does not come under consideration. Removing things from their historical condition (*Bedingung*) thus allows their role to become that of restoring 'nearness', what he denominates 'the simple onehood [*Einheit*] of the world', such that condition is freed of historical limits to become the abstract condition of being 'be-thinged'.[60] Stepping back from the actual historical circumstance that he pretended to address, Heidegger evacuates the thing at once of its obdurate resistance and of its uncanny capacity to unsettle the subject. The anticipation in which the thing 'stood forth' becomes the suspension in which the thing appears only in so far as it is abstracted from its condition.[61]

Despite the initial appearance of convergence, then, nothing could be further from Beckett's apprehension of the condition of thingliness or of the anticipation that meets it. Both his responses to van Velde and van Velde's own relation to the act and engagement of painting at the time are haunted by a sense of suspension or anticipation that can perhaps best be captured by the word 'dread'. The notion of anticipation is intrinsically shadowed by an affective ambiguity, condensing both excitement and openness to what is to come and a fear of the not yet fully apprehended – precisely what we refer to as *apprehension*. Beckett speaks of van Velde in his 'Three Dialogues with Georges Duthuit' as confronting 'the acute and increasing anxiety of the relation' (Tr, 103; D, 145), while van Velde himself remarks on more than one occasion on the fear that for him attends and motivates the approach to painting: 'La peinture me fait peur. Et pourtant il me faut peindre'; 'La peur a été le moteur de tout ce que j'ai fait.'[62] This sense of dread is one of pure anticipation, unmotivated by any specific object or cause of anxiety. It is the apprehension of the subject's suspension in relation to the thing that only through a constitutive movement of negation will become an object for it. The trace of that splitting effect for the subject is what Beckett calls, in a precise and haunting phrase, 'fear – followed by no genitive'.[63]

In his essay on the van Velde brothers, Beckett has another term for this inexpungible trace of negation and splitting that nicely captures the negative reciprocity of the breakdown of relation: *le deuil de l'objet* (D, 135). Once again, the phrase stages the ambiguity of the relation. It can be translated on the one hand as the mourning of the subject for the object that eludes it (*qui se dérobe*). On the other, it can signify the mourning that is that of the object itself in its separation from the subject and the trace of a relation that this painting refuses: 'refusal to accept as given the old subject-object relation' (SBV, 167; D, 137).[64] It is, at all events, the doleful effect of a painting of mourning that refuses to accomplish either the incorporation of the object or the subject's identification through and with the object. What remains is the painful trace of a painting that refuses to perform the possessive work of the gaze that

Beckett had identified as the drive of Western painting, the work of the gaze that seeks to redeem the knowledge of its own alienation from the world of objects in acts of totalising appropriation, 'a series of traps for the capture of objects' (Tr, 100; D, 141). It is what stands forth, as one might say, in a painting that abnegates expression, possession and representation.

Indeed, looking at Bram van Velde's paintings, our gaze seems haunted not merely by the memory of a figure that eludes us, but by a gaze that is not ours, by the figure of a blind gaze that peers back at us out of the canvases.[65] It is perhaps what Beckett himself glimpsed looking back at him from van Velde's painting, the self that is not-self, a different self, but it is also the gaze of the gaze itself. Often in van Velde's paintings of the late 1930s and 1940s, a peculiar transformation has taken place of those coloured lozenges and ovals that were the traces of the fruits of the still lifes: they have become lenses, protruding, from one or other perspective, from the canvas, on the ends of scope-like stalks or projections, or, perhaps, spotlights that fix on us from within the canvas. (See *Sans Titre* [*Untitled*] (*Montrouge*), 1947; Fig. 2.17.) It is as if the gaze has materialised and been momentarily, ambiguously fixed within the canvas that is the object of our gaze. In these figurations that are at once the trace of looking and figures for the prostheses of looking, one encounters the uncanny sensation of seeing one's own gaze given back from the figure in which it is suspended. This uncanny registering of the gaze in or of the object van Velde traced late in his life in one of his earliest canvases, *Dorf*. Looking at it in 1980, he remarked:

> Years later, I saw that this person was myself. Years later, I said: I see my own gaze.[66]

It is not simply that he sees himself – or a former self – seeing or looking back; rather, he sees his own gaze. Van Velde's remark is the unsettling recognition that the gaze is a thing – a thing that looks back and intervenes in the subject's otherwise 'possessive' relation to the visible. The various figures in *Dorf* – who may in fact all be 'turnings' of the same figure – interpose between the perceiving subject, the painter or viewer, and the line of flight of the perspective that should lead us uninterruptedly to the village that is the ostensible 'subject' or object as well as the focal point of the painting. It would occupy, in classical perspective, that point where the lines of sight converge to furnish the locus from which

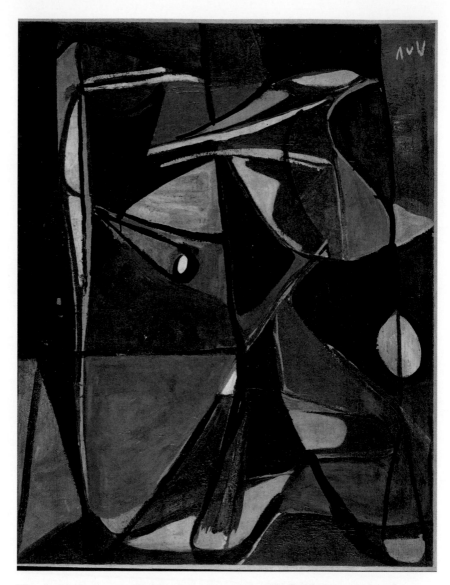

Fig. 2.17 Bram van Velde, *Sans Titre* [*Untitled*] (*Montrouge*) (oil on canvas, 144.5 × 113 cm, 1947), © Artists Rights Society (ARS), New York/ADAGP, Paris, 2016.

the Subject is reflected back in its secure sovereignty. Here, in *Dorf*, the 'thing in the void' is the figure – the *figura* or face – that looks back, constituting the subject *not* in its wholeness or sovereignty, but in the moment of alienation that underlies the primal *dis*-figuration of its image into distinct and disparate subject-object relations. Van Velde may have acknowledged in it the prototype of what Antonio Saura describes so well as the characteristic of the later painting, in which, for all its dissolution of any representative aim, 'the face appears . . . consciously or unconsciously, but present, in its inevitable and ancestral enclosure':

> And always, as if a reminder, there appears the sign of the revelatory eye, the eye of an indefinite divinity that always presides at the feast, the eye at times painfully detached from any form, the eye as a clumsy and vain wink, the eye that begins to suggest the unfinished mask.[67]

In this respect, Bram van Velde's later painting is in no simple way 'abstract painting', however much it refuses the representation of objects. It furnishes rather a 'matrix' in which the gaze and a set of partial, implicit, even 'archaic' figures appear and dissolve, exerting the unsettling fascination that Beckett confronts as the enigma of 'this thing in the void'.[68]

We can go some way towards an understanding of this complex play of gaze and figure and its relation to the thinking of the thing that is not an object through Jacques Lacan's careful unfolding of the distinction between the eye and the gaze. His seminars on this topic, though fifteen or more years later than Beckett's writings on van Velde, resume to a striking degree the same set of preoccupations with perspective, the subject's relation to space and the painting, and, above all, the function of the gaze. Lacan insists on a 'split' between the eye and the gaze, the latter of which escapes the subject's visual and representational field, and may be said both to 'pre-exist' and to elude it:

> In our relation to things, in so far as this relation is constituted by way of vision, and ordered in the figures of representation, something slips, passes, is transmitted, from stage to stage, and is always to some degree eluded in it – that is what we call the gaze.[69]

On one side of this split, it appears that the function of the eye, in rendering visible, is to secure the subject in its place and its certainty. Hence the absolute distinction, on which Lacan insists, between the effectively Cartesian 'I see myself seeing myself' and 'I see my own gaze'. The former 'grounds [the subject's] certainty', establishing for the subject a reciprocity of mirrored seeing that functions much as the 'geometral point' of perspectival space secures the position of the viewing subject outside the frame of the picture. Indeed, Lacan emphasises this relation between 'the geometral laws of perspective' and 'the institution of the Cartesian subject, which is itself a sort of geometral point, a point of perspective'.[70] In so far as painting respects the laws of perspective, one might say, it remains in the domain of the eye and the visible, disabling the unsettling function of the gaze: '[The painter] gives something for the eye to feed on, but he invites the person to whom this picture is presented to lay down his gaze there as one lays down one's weapons. This is the pacifying, Apollonian effect of painting.'[71] Fixing in place what Beckett called the 'relations between representer and representee' (Tr, 103; D, 145), painting performs the work of a representation for which the philosophical problem of the 'thing-in-itself' that cannot be apprehended by the subject ceases to cause trouble – 'everything works out for the best'.[72]

And yet, 'it is not in this dialectic between the surface and that which is beyond that things are suspended.'[73] For the gaze is not identical with the viewer's capacity to look, with the punctiform eye that is the instrument and metaphor of the sovereign subject. The gaze does not belong to the subject but, being 'imagined in the field of the other', is 'the gaze by which I am surprised' and, ultimately, primordially, split and 'mutilated'. The gaze is 'the object on which depends the phantasy from which the subject is suspended in an essential vacillation'.[74] But it is not, as Lacan emphasises throughout, an object in the Kantian sense, an object conformed to the representative faculties of a subject; it is, rather, one of those 'things' that simultaneously constitute and suspend the subject to the point that it even annihilates it, symbolising its lack in being, not its acts of possession or appropriation. In his 'algebra' Lacan designates such an object the 'objet petit a', that is, 'a privileged object, which has emerged from some primal separation, from some self-mutilation induced by the very approach of the real'.[75] These objets petit a would include those things on which, as is familiar from Freud's essays on sexuality, the infant fixates or cathects, such as the breast, the turd or the penis, and

which institute the different psychic economies of the develop-
ing ego. They are virtually inseparable from the functions of the
body's orifices and from the topology of openings, lips and rims
through which the subject and its libidinal flows connect with
the world and around which it forges the map of its desires and the
contours of its body-image. To these, Lacan adds those immaterial
things, the voice and the gaze, which emanate from eye and mouth
and by which the subject is no less captured, at once determined
and split.[76]

The gaze is not the eye, nor the organ of sight. It has to do less
with the visual mastery of space and the order of representations
than with 'a play of light and opacity'. By the same token, the
subject ceases to be 'that punctiform being located at the geometral point from which the perspective is grasped':

> That which is light looks at me, and by means of that light in the
> depths of my eye, something is painted – something that is not simply a
> constructed relation, the object on which the philosopher lingers – but
> something that is an impression, the shimmering of a surface that is
> not, in advance, situated for me in its distance.[77]

In its opacity, in the opacity of its annihilating light, the gaze functions as if through a screen or, more precisely, through a *mask*,
'beyond which there is the gaze'.[78]

A peculiar oscillation links the mask and the figure, an oscillation that is both the source of uncanny effects of misrecognition
and embedded in the history of the term 'figure' itself. In van
Velde's work, as we have seen, the mask is one of a handful of vestiges of figuration, a vestige which in a peculiar fashion expands
to become the painting itself, endowed as it is with the eye-like
objects and other traces of orifices – the circles, lozenges, moons
and so forth that proliferate across the rhythmic circulations that
lure the viewer's gaze, or those *crypto-fenêtres* that survive in the
inner frames of the canvases. They function in the painting much
as what Lacan calls *points-de-capiton*, nodes in which the subject's
desire, in this case in the form of the gaze, are captured.[79] As so
many critics have noted, they draw the viewer to read in them the
remnants of figures even as they refuse to be totalised into a system
of 'figurative' representation. In that respect, they mobilise the
gamut of transformations that the notion of the figure itself historically underwent and which it continues to condense. Initially the

word for any 'plastic form', *figura* assumes gradually the meanings of face (*le figure* in French) or physical form and of appearance as well as those of 'figure – or turn – of speech' and, eventually, of 'veil', in the sense of the veiled meaning which reveals a deeper truth or reality.[80] Much like the mask or *persona* – the mask through which the actor's voice sounds (*per-sonare*)[81] – the notion of the figure condenses all the ambiguities of the dialectics of appearance. Figuration is the mask and the mask that at once gazes and conceals, capturing the gaze of the subject. If the gaze is a thing, it is the thing that veils the thing, as Beckett recognised in seeking to render the perplexing layers of van Velde's painting: 'An unveiling without end, veil behind veil, plane on plane of imperfect transparencies, an unveiling towards the unveilable, towards nothing, towards the thing once more' (D, 136).

Van Velde's non-figurative art, or his painting that occupies the threshold where the figure oscillates between appearance and disappearance, has little to do then with the forms of abstraction that gave rise to abstract expressionism, coeval as their emergence may have been. It is not, anti-literary as it may have been, a painting in which the logic and traditions of the aesthetic culminate in order to produce what can be comprehended as the most Kantian of appearances, representations for the aesthetic judgement that please by means of form alone and not by virtue of what they depict or signify. Beyond deconstructing painting in the traditions of Matisse and Picasso, as Guilbaut and others contend, van Velde's work dismantles the subject-object relation that grounds the aesthetic judgement in the first place, suspending the subject in its fragmentary object relations as a thing among other things. In face of van Velde's canvases, confronting the unmasterable ambiguity of their depths and surfaces, 'plane on plane of imperfect transparencies', the subject is captured in a ceaseless circulation that denies it a fixed position from which to exercise its sovereignty. Perspectival space is dissolved in the peculiarly precise yet mobile geometry that vertiginously superimposes multiple states and dimensions.[82] The effect, as van Velde so often acknowledged, is annihilating – annihilation, however, not of any trace of the subject, but of the sovereign subject of representation so masterfully reinstated in the major work of abstract expressionism with its optimistic sublimity and arrogant assumption of a historical destiny.[83]

Together with representation and the subject of representation, van Velde's work also dissolves the image into the figure. We may recall Beckett's fascination with the image in which, as he claimed of the poet Denis Devlin, 'self-consciousness first emerges'. The image was the core to which, in his review of MacGreevy, he reduced Jack B. Yeats's painting and the image remained, as we have seen, the visual core of his early theatrical work. Rémi Labrusse claims that it was around this time that Beckett's interest in the image, one he shared with Duthuit, began to wane. It is, indeed, hard to see how it could long have survived his engagement with van Velde if, indeed, we understand by the image what Labrusse calls *l'image incarnée*, a visual correlative of some state of being or meaning.[84] It is not merely that van Velde dismantles what remained of the image in the late painting of Cézanne, Matisse or Picasso, dissolving it into the ambiguities of figure and mask. It is, rather, that what remains in the thinking of the image as the vehicle of self-consciousness and of the work as that of the subject, however dispossessed and reduced, is shattered, dispersed into the endless circulation of things. Dramatic as van Velde's work is, it offers no visual correlative, no theatrical image around which one could imagine a play cohering, as *Godot* and *Endgame* do around the powerfully reduced images of tree and road or of a bare interior. The drama is rather that of a subject constantly displaced by the gaze that meets it as a thing that eludes it, fixes and unfixes it, and that itself fractures and disperses across the surface of the canvas. Far from the Heideggerian thing that nestles and restores the subject to 'nearness' and oneness, this unsettling gaze is a thing that registers the fate of the subject in a world relentlessly subjected to circulation, reification, possession and dispossession. The question that arises, in face of the severity with which this work, in Beckett's eyes, confronts the catastrophe, is what writing could be adequate to its vision? What writing – fiction or drama – could find its analogue in a work so rigorously defiant of any image, any representation, any shelter for the subject?

III

Beckett's plays are full of things, things of all kinds with which his characters play, fiddle and even fight. Didi and Gogo play with hats and boots to while away the time. Hamm clings to his toy dog, to his gaff or handkerchief, Winnie to the contents of her handbag – brush, spectacles or magnifying glass – till these too must be relinquished. These are the relations of humans to their objects, to those things that are the prostheses of the subject, extending it into its world or anchoring it there. Such objects fail in that function, over and over again, and in failing call the subject and its certainties into question. But they do not fundamentally displace the subject from its centrality in the world arrayed around it, nor do they shatter the image of the human in its world, however much the subject's hold on the world has decayed.[85] Many critics locate the beginnings of Beckett's 'late theatre' in *Play*, seeing that as the point beyond which 'Beckett's stage images would grow increasingly dehumanized, reified, and metonymic, featuring dismembered or incorporeal creatures as Beckett's became a theatre of body parts and spectres, a theatre striving for transparency rather than solidity, a theatre, finally, trying to undo itself.'[86] But we can already see the first shift in Beckett's conception of the human subject's relation to its things in *Krapp's Last Tape*, where Krapp appears not so much extended into his world by things as suspended among them. Moments of this kind appear within the text and actions of the play, as the younger Krapp relates his play with 'a small, old, black, hard, solid rubber ball' or fixates on the eyes of a nursemaid or of past lovers: 'The face she had! The eyes!'[87] But things also dominate the scenario itself. The tape recorder, which may have commenced as the prosthesis of Krapp's memory, has become a thing that displaces him. Not only does he hang above it, listening to his own past voice split him between past and present, but increasingly the tape recorder with its turning, mesmeric spool vies with him for the attention of the audience. His voice, separated from him on the tape, has become a thing for our ear and for his, even as individual words have become material sounds around which his lips form: 'Spool! [Pause.] Spooool!'[88] Beckett, indeed, notes with some excitement the discovery of 'the kind of personal relationship that developed between Krapp and the machine' and which he had not foreseen before working on the first Royal Court production with Donald McWhinnie and Patrick Magee. It 'arose quite naturally and was extraordinarily effective', he writes to his American director, Alan Schneider, clearly intending this effect to be incorporated into future productions of the play.[89] In McWhinnie's later production of the play for BBC television in 1972, that effect is made all the more prominent through the series of slow close-ups of Krapp as he listens, head inclined, to the tape of his own voice, to the

point that at several moments throughout the play the rectangle of
the reel recorder's box seems to push Krapp's disembodied head
to the very margin of the screen (see Fig. 2.18). In collaborating
with McWhinnie on the first production, Beckett had also noted,
in the final fade-out, 'the quite unexpected and marvellous effect
of recorder's red light burning up as the dark gathered.'[90] In the
BBC production, it is not the light but the turning spool that plays
on, exerting a hypnotic fascination, as Krapp's head and his hand,
inert around the box, seem to become separate things captured in
suspended animation.

It is clear from Beckett's correspondence with Schneider that the
potentials secreted in *Krapp* took some time to become apparent
and emerged in the space of rehearsal and performance itself. The
play offers, nonetheless, a first trial ground for those features of his
later theatre that will become the hallmark of his later drama and
for which the idea of 'a theatre of images' seems strikingly misleading.[91] Where the image suggests the concentration and focali-
sation of the visual into a single condensed point, 'one that might
compress all of experience into a single, all-embracing metaphor',
Beckett's theatrical effects are increasingly those of dispersion,

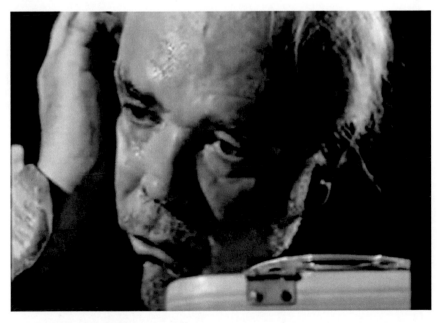

Fig. 2.18 Patrick Magee as Krapp in *Krapp's Last Tape*, BBC television
production directed by Donald McWhinnie, 1972.

both of 'character' (as Gontarski remarks) and of the total sensory impact.[92] While the plays indeed become increasingly visual, it is a visuality that has absorbed to the full the example of van Velde's destruction of pictorial space and of the image. Where in *Krapp's Last Tape* the subject becomes displaced and split by his own voice emanating from the technological prosthesis of the tape recorder, Beckett's subsequent theatre will more and more break apart the elements of the theatre, and with them all that remains of the human character. In the years that follow *Krapp*, Beckett produced *Play* (1962–3), *Film* (1963–4) and *Eh Joe* (1965), all of which experimented, in the distinct media of stage, film and television, with the function of camera or spotlight as *active* personae in the drama of perception and, indeed, of interrogation. These works participate not only in the visual scene but – as *Play* and *Eh Joe* remind us – in a general 'sundering' of gaze, figure or subject, and voice. This involves more than his 'frequent separation of body and voice', which so many critics have rightly emphasised.[93] Beckett's interest is not only in the speaking or moving, gesturing person, nor only in the perceiving subject and the perceived or 'fixed' object, but in the distribution or dispersal of the subject into the multiple things, technical and corporeal, that constitute it and its relations with objects, effects of which the eye of the perceiver or the voice of the speaker are but several corresponding instances.

Play marks the first moment in which that sundering of elements and the transformation of the technical apparatus of the theatre into a full protagonist of the drama becomes deliberate and fundamental to the conception of the work. As is well known, the three human figures appear on stage up to their necks in burial urns, inhabiting what most critics compare to a purgatorial space. Lit turn by turn by a single spot, each character – a man and two women, apparently his wife and mistress – babbles at high speed some fragment of a self-consciously banal tale of adultery.[94] The narrative, indeed, is often virtually unintelligible, constituting another version of the 'cultural trash' that furnishes the contents of Beckett's theatre, and the impact of the play lies rather in its relentless and repeated scenario of interrogation. It is a scenario that reduces the characters to 'voices, instruments, or things, part of the funeral urns which appear to have swallowed – like some leviathan – all but their protruding heads'.[95] As they turn into things, the spotlight that interrogates or 'invests' them (to use the word that Beckett will use of the camera in *Film*) becomes a protagonist, to the extent that in the second cycle of the play, its action seems to become weaker, more hesitant, as if in frustration at being unable to extract from these vestigial figures whatever statement it is that would put an end to this unceasing mutual torture.[96] The human things and this animated thing are thus joined by yet another 'thing', that unnamable core that remains to be uttered or extracted: the woman W1's invocations to the light make clear that both the spotlight and the matter it seeks are the things of the play: 'but it will come, the time will come, the thing is there, you'll see it, get off me, keep off me' and 'Yes, and the whole thing there, all there, staring you in the face'.[97] This thing is at once the externalised light that interrogates, object of her perception as much as she is of it, and at the same time the elusive thing it seeks 'within' her or, rather, in the words she is obliged to speak.

Dispersed as agency is among reified humans and animated things, part of the uncanny effect of *Play* is that the audience finds itself situated in line with the gaze of this interrogating spotlight. It is implied that our gaze as spectators is what traps these characters in their endless cycles of interrogation, the thing that impels the interrogation and, by the same token, captures us in the darkened space, obliged to hear this unintelligible babble over and over again. That single source of light on which Beckett insisted consequently constitutes the last vestige of a theatrical space in which the spectator occupies the same space in relation to the stage as the viewer of a painting occupies in relation to what Beckett had defined as the 'possessive' space of Western painting. Indeed, Beckett's own diagrams for the German production of *Spiel* that he directed in 1978 map that relation perfectly: they are like horizontal visual pyramids, three lines leading from the single spot to the three heads on stage.[98] Just as the separate individuals that make up the audience are united in the same focus on the stage, so each of those individuals finds in itself the locus of the Subject whose gaze seeks to secure it in the world and through its objects. In *Play*, that gaze is troubled by the inability of the characters to vocalise the 'thing' that it seeks in order to establish its certainty and the ensuing silence that would be the identity of subject and object. But the relation of subject to object itself is still in place, secured precisely by that spot that emplaces us before the space of the stage.[99]

In the dramatic work, for screen and for stage, that follows *Play*, Beckett will seek the means to disrupt and dismantle that space to a greater and greater degree. *Godot* and *Endgame* had, as we have seen, played with the separation of actor and audience, turning the spectators into the actors' objects or gesturing towards the rupture of the fourth wall, but such disruptions were never fundamental. Paradoxically, perhaps, Beckett with rare exceptions refused 'theatre in the round', with its gesture towards rupturing the border between audience and actors, and insisted on retaining 'a very closed box'.[100] It gave him initially, one may surmise, the means to deconstruct rather than simply to disavow the subject-object structure implicit in spectatorship in the theatre, as later it would give him a kind of black box or arcanum on which the increasingly foregrounded frieze of the later plays would be 'painted'. The latter effect we will discuss in the following chapter; here, it is crucial to stress how Beckett's dismantling of theatrical space involved neither the reduction of the drama to an integral, lyrical or poetic image, nor the all too easy dissolution of the proscenium arch, but rather the deep disruption of theatrical space and the perceptual relations it implied through the disassemblage of the elements of the play and their dispersal within the 'closed box', or cell, that increasingly embraced both spectator and spectacle. That would involve in the first place a further interrogation of the gaze and its putatively constitutive relation to the subject.

Of all Beckett's dramatic works – few of which are oblivious to watching, surveillance, or simply being visible – none is more notoriously devoted to the question of the gaze than *Film*, the only work that he produced in the medium of cinema. Yet, like the oblique gaze of the camera that pursues its protagonist, critical approach to this work always seems tantalisingly snagged in indirection. Beckett notoriously prefaced his screenplay with a set of notes that he almost immediately and mischievously retracts as lacking in 'truth value' and as being of merely 'structural and dramatic convenience'.[101] Yet the film has generally been understood thematically, and not merely structurally, as a dramatisation of Bishop Berkeley's dictum with which Beckett commences: *esse est percipi* (to be is to be perceived). Interpretation continues to draw on the framework supplied by an idealist philosophy for which the subject, though 'sundered' between self and self-perception (F, 163), is in the end secured in place even when its world is evacuated of all other objects. In a peculiar way, the painful solipsism that appears to be the organising stance of Beckett's work would safeguard the subject in face of what he had elsewhere described as 'the new thing that has happened', the breakdown of the subject-object relation. As Lacan remarked, Berkeley's own formulation does not escape precisely what Beckett sought to leave behind, 'namely, this *belong to me* aspect of representations, so reminiscent of property'.[102]

Reading *Film* in relation to Beckett's ostentatious citation of his compatriot gains force from the apparent coherence of Berkeley's aphorism with the larger Cartesian framework for subject-object relations within which – at least since Hugh Kenner – his work has often been read. It sunders it, nonetheless, from Beckett's larger dramatic project and from his long-standing and very critical relation both to post-Cartesian idealism and to the phenomenon of the gaze or – as the slightly later *Eh Joe* dramatises – of the voice.[103] The voice and the gaze, registered not as media of expression or of seeing, but as things in which the subject is dispersed, constitute discrete elements of Beckett's later theatre. In *Eh Joe*, the woman's voice that speaks emanates ambiguously from some unidentified and unanchored space that is at once within and without the silent protagonist: space disintegrates between an inner and an outer that have become undecidable. As each close-up moves further and further in to isolate Joe's face, we may seem to approximate more and more the interior that his motionless face betrays. Yet it is the voice resounding from some indeterminate space outside that seems to indicate the audible content of that interior, its ceaseless, nagging murmur like that of some Kantian inner moral law. In *Film* we see yet another dimension of that disintegration of the subject that takes place in the visual domain, its separation out into a subject that is an object for a gaze that is its object.

Reading back into *Film* from Beckett's extended engagement with van Velde, then, our attention may be less caught up in the idealist framework with which the screenplay opens than with the peculiar tableau in which the subject – Object or, rather, O, as Beckett is at pains to dub him – for a moment exchanges the realm of highbrow slapstick for what might be taken as a remnant of biographical narrative. Having finally expelled the animals from the room and destroyed all other possible traces of the gaze – animate or, significantly, inanimate – that might disturb him, O begins to review a set of photographs. Their sequence, from infancy to mature manhood, implies that they represent the various stages of his life. But given how schematic that sequence is – and how indifferent the drama of *Film* is to biographical content – what is clearly of more significance is the form they reveal: virtually every one of the photographs is a representation of the gaze. As Beckett wrote to the film's director, Alan Schneider, they 'represent O (with possible exception of last) in percipi'.[104] The sequence opens with a male infant of six months in his mother's arms, staring out at the camera. The mother looks down, 'Her severe eyes devouring him'. The second, at age four, repeats the mother's gaze, 'head bowed towards him, severe eyes'. This act of gazing is repeated in the third or fourth almost parodically by a dog begging, 'looking up at him', and by a graduation-day public watching. In photo six, the gaze is reversed as a little girl 'looks into his face, exploring it with finger' (F, 381–2).

Taken together, those photos stage the triangulated structure of the gaze as it simultaneously constitutes and alienates the subject, fixing (or 'devouring') him even as it leaves him suspended in the status of object for another and – all too clearly here – for himself. They prepare the way for what the screenplay describes as O's 'investment proper' by E (F, 376), where what is dramatised is the subject's apprehension of 'E's gaze' as it twice 'pierces' O's sleep (F, 377). Despite the final shots, where a figure of O standing (in the position formerly occupied by the image of God-the-Father) gazes with 'acute *intentness*' at the seated O, the logic of the drama cannot be reduced any longer to an idealist scenario of self-perception (F, 377). The latter supplies, as Beckett emphasises, the *structure* rather than the meaning of *Film*. Were we to take the figure of O gazing at O to be the final *meaning* of the drama, we could revert to the closed self-identity of the Cartesian *cogito* in which, in a world voided of objects, the subject returns to its unmediated sovereignty. By the same token, the assumption that we are meant to identify our own gaze as viewers with that of E as Subject too easily restores us to our location as unitary spectators of *Film*. That is not, I think, the odd sensation of watching this work, whose uncanniness survives multiple viewings.[105]

Beckett's screenplay is at pains to displace the primacy and unity of E's gaze as the final instance of the subject. Not only is it parodied in the 'minor' gazes of humans, animals and images, it is powerfully figured in an inanimate thing that Beckett repeatedly returns to in the screenplay: the 'curiously carved headrest' of O's rocking chair (F, 375). The screenplay explains this 'insistence on headrest' as a convenience for locating the various perspectives of O and E. In the film itself, the supplementary function of the headrest is more apparent as its 'curious' carving resembles eyes that gaze out at us: the headrest is a thing that looks back (see Fig. 2.19). Rosemary Pountney, indeed, reminds us that 'Alan Schneider has described how "eyes" began to proliferate in the studio once the film crew became alive to the possibilities of pairs of holes, such as the folder in which O's photographs were kept.'[106] Eyes proliferate as things, things as eyes. *Film* becomes for us less about the interiority of self-perception than it is about the materiality of the gaze and the *multiple* things through which the subject is distributed in relation to its objects.

This reading of *Film* helps us to understand Beckett's deliberate choice of silent film as the medium for the work and his no less deliberate drawing attention to that medium and its apparent obsolescence by insisting that silent-movie star Buster Keaton incongruously take the lead in a metaphysical drama.[107] In a letter to Thomas MacGreevy in 1936, Beckett had remarked on the as yet unexhausted potentials of silent film, as opposed to the 'naturalistic colour and sound of "industrial" film', and hoped 'that a back water may be created for the two-dimensional silent film that had barely emerged from its rudiments when it was swamped'.[108] For all his diffident remarks in the screenplay of *Film* about his inadequate technical knowledge, this would-be student of Eisenstein and Pudovkin was remarkably acute about the specific capacities of his media. Just as the medium of the radio play allowed him to separate out voice and music as emphatic characters, or TV would allow him to differentiate voice and image as distinct prostheses of the subject, so the fact that silent film was obliged to distribute the functions of visual image and act, quasi-allegorical or deictic text, and musical accompaniment implies a technical memory of a moment in which film was characterised by the *assemblage* of its discrete functions rather than by the unitary totality of its effects that we have become accustomed to in the wake of Hollywood sound film.[109] The evident obsolescence of the medium becomes the means to a critical meditation on the production of the subject as a material thing suspended among its things. Here the attenuated remnants of slapstick, embodied in Keaton's physical performance, find their proper place.

The role played by the gaze, prosthetically embodied in the camera, is cognate with that played by the tape-recorded voice in *Krapp's Last Tape* or the disembodied female voice of *Eh Joe*. Like the gaze, the voice appears in the disintegrated technoscapes of

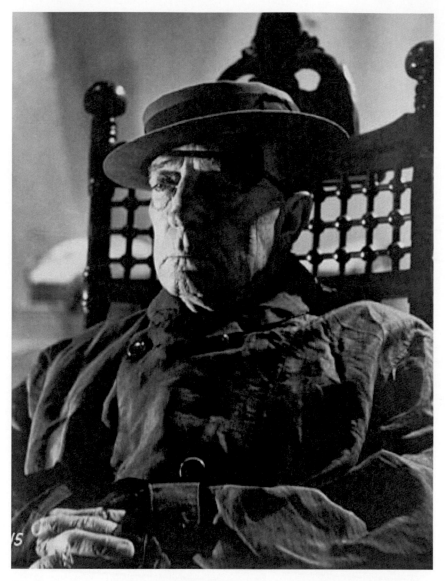

Fig. 2.19 Buster Keaton in *Film*, directed by Alan Schneider, 1961.

Beckett's dramatic work, not as the validating sign of an authentic inner life, but as one of the 'things' among which the subject is distributed in its constitutive self-alienation. In this respect, we may read Beckett's work not as a replay of eighteenth-century idealism, but as an allegory for the fate of things, including human things, in the era of late capitalism. The technological obsolescence of *Film* becomes the index of wasted human life, where even a star like Keaton can become the remaindered techno-trash of superannuated forms of image production. It marks an era when the subject has become the sum of its prosthetic function in relation to the technologies through which it produces itself and dwells among its imaginary, troubled relations to its part-objects as an appendage of the machines. It took him all of a decade, a decade of restless theatrical experimentation and of failed sketches, those 'roughs' for theatre that he never had produced and which seem like 'fizzles' or dead ends in his trajectory, to achieve the radical dismantling of the unity of the theatrical space and of the theatrical subject or 'character' into the dispersed elements of voice, music, lighting or lens, gesture and movement that characterise the later plays from *Krapp's Last Tape*, through *Play* and *Eh Joe*, down to *What Where*. These plays, for which the human has become a thing among its things, suspended in its relation to technologies and part-objects, in its painful annihilation into being by voice and gaze, function in Beckett's work as the dramatic correlative of Bram van Velde's painting with its ceaseless circulation of gaze and figure and its abolition of any stable place for the sovereign subject to maintain.

Notes

1. Samuel Beckett to Marthe Arnaud and Bram van Velde, 25 March 1952, in *The Letters of Samuel Beckett, Volume II: 1941–1956*, p. 305.

2. On these multiple meanings of the word 'thing', see Martin Heidegger, 'The Thing', pp. 174–5.

3. Samuel Beckett and Georges Duthuit, 'Three Dialogues', *Transition Forty-Nine*, 5 (1949): 97–103. This dialogue, familiar to most readers of Beckett in the version reprinted by Ruby Cohn in *Disjecta* or in its earlier Grove Press printing along with the essay *Proust*, is cited in the text hereafter as Tr. 'Three Dialogues' is reprinted in Beckett, *Disjecta*, pp. 138–45, cited in the text hereafter as D.

4. Raoul-Jean Moulin, 'Aussi loin que l'on remonte le cours . . .', in *Tal-Coat*, catalogue of the exhibition at the Grand Palais, Paris, 1976, p. 14. My translation.

5. See Moulin, *Tal-Coat*, pp. 15–16. Interestingly, Tal-Coat was preceded both in his encounter with the *Apocalypse* of Saint-Sever and in his *Massacres* series by Masson, who produced a series of the same title in 1932. See Laurie Monahan, 'Violence in Paradise: André Masson's *Massacres*'.

6. See Henri Maldiney, 'Présence et absence dans l'art de Tal-Coat', in *Tal-Coat*, pp. 6 and 8.

7. In a letter to Duthuit, 9 June 1949, Beckett expresses succinctly the same sentiment regarding Tal-Coat: 'What all that amounts to is the wish to save a form of expression that is not viable'; *Letters, Vol. II*, p. 166. In a slightly earlier letter to Duthuit, 2 March 1949, Beckett explicitly recalls 'an angry article on modern Irish poets' (i.e. 'Recent Irish Poetry') in which he had defined that 'new thing that has happened' and directly connects it to reading Duthuit 'on the Aix School' – the circle of Tal-Coat and Masson; *Letters, Vol. II*, p. 131.

8. For an excellent overview of Masson's life and work, see Dawn Ades, 'Introduction' and 'Chronology', in *André Masson*, pp. 7–30.

9. A later version of this painting, reworked in 1942, is much darker, as if irradiated and charred, with the city exposed and illuminated as if to aerial bombing; it seems to have absorbed both the catastrophe of the Civil War and the dark first years of the Second World War to which it was a prelude. The 1936 version of the painting may owe its depiction of Toledo to El Greco's *View of Toledo* (1596–1600) in the Metropolitan Museum of Art, New York.

10. André du Bouchet, 'Three Exhibitions: Tal Coat – Masson – Miró', p. 89. Beckett had apparently reworked Bussy's translations; see *Letters, Vol. II*, p. 150, n. 2.

11. Like Mount Sainte-Victoire, the Bibemus Quarry in the same region was in fact one of Cézanne's recurrent objects. See for example *Bibemus Quarry* (c. 1895) and *La Montagne de Saint-Victoire* (c. 1897), both reproduced in Nina Maria Athanassoglou-Kallmyer, *Cézanne and Provence*.

12. Beckett published, in French and with his own English translations, the poems 'je suis ce cours de sable qui glisse', 'que ferais-je sans ce monde sans visages sans questions' and 'je voudrais que mon amour meure' in *Transition Forty-Eight*. It must be said that the English translations of the first two are still haunted by Beckett's

own competence, the linguistic range and energetic virtuosity that pushed his earlier poems to expressive, even expressionist excess. No better evidence could be found for his remark that it is easier to write without style in French.

13. Beckett, cited in Dougald McMillan and Martha Fehsenfeld, *Beckett in the Theatre: The Author as Practical Playwright and Director, Vol. 1*, p. 14.

14. Rémi Labrusse, 'Beckett et la peinture', pp. 670–1.

15. Serge Guilbaut, 'Disdain for the Stain: Abstract Expressionism and Tachisme', p. 33.

16. Guilbaut, 'Disdain for the Stain', p. 31.

17. See Clement Greenberg, 'The School of Paris: 1946' and 'Contribution to a Symposium' (1953) in *Art and Culture: Critical Essays*, pp. 120–6. The full story that he summarises in 'Disdain for the Stain', Serge Guilbaut tells in his *How New York Stole the Idea of Modern Art: Abstract Expressionism, Freedom and the Cold War*.

18. On this history and Beckett's translations, see Labrusse, 'Beckett et la peinture', pp. 672–3, and Dougald McMillan, *transition: The History of a Literary Era, 1927–1938*, pp. 73–4. Beckett's letters to Duthuit provide a kind of running commentary on the contributions he is translating that serve as a prelude to the 'Three Dialogues'. See especially *Letters, Vol. II*, pp. 122–6, 129–34, 138–43, 148–51 and 164–6.

19. On Beckett's disgust for the all too crucial cultivation of the public in post-war France, see Labrusse, 'Beckett et la peinture', p. 673, citing letters to Duthuit.

20. Du Bouchet, 'Three Exhibitions', p. 92. These reviews immediately precede the 'Three Dialogues' in the journal issue.

21. Commenting that 'André warns me off any comment', Beckett remarks in a letter to Duthuit, undated but around May 1949, which clearly included the sheets of the corrected translations of du Bouchet's article, that 'there is no doubt a sizeable public for this kind of orgy'; *Letters, Vol. II*, p. 149.

22. Georges Duthuit, 'Matisse and Byzantine Space', p. 20.

23. On Duthuit's long-standing promotion of Byzantine art, see Labrusse, 'Beckett et la peinture', pp. 670–1.

24. Duthuit, 'Matisse and Byzantine Space', p. 34. Emphases in the original. It is perhaps a coincidence that Beckett's later play *Not I* dramatises as a *predicament*, not as a reconciliation, the condition of one who cannot erase herself from her representations.

25. Beckett, 'The Capital of the Ruins', p. 27.

26. Bram van Velde, 'Some Sayings of Bram van Velde', p. 104.

27. For an overview of van Velde's life and career, see Rainer Michael Mason (ed.), *Bram van Velde, 1895–1981: Rétrospective du Centenaire*, pp. 305–7.

28. Franz Meyer, 'Entre Matisse et Picasso; La Plénitude de l'Être', in Mason (ed.), *Rétrospective du Centenaire*, p. 244. My translation.

29. Cited in Roger Laporte, *Bram van Velde ou cette petite chose qui fascine*, p. 32: 'Ma toile, c'est une circulation.'

30. Rainer Michael Mason, 'Les Bram van Velde du Musée de Genève', in Mason (ed.), *Rétrospective du Centenaire*, p. 20.

31. Pierre Alechinsky, 'Deux Fenêtres', in Mason (ed.), *Rétrospective du Centenaire*, p. 237.

32. Jan Greshoff, 'Deux peintres hollandais à Paris: A. G. and Gérard van Velde', *La Revue de l'Art* 30 (January–June 1929), cited in Mason, 'Les Bram van Velde du Musée de Genève', p. 20.

33. According to Mason, these may in part have been inspired by African masks in the collection of his companion Marthe Arnaud, who had been a missionary in East Africa: Mason, 'Les Bram van Velde du Musée de Genève', p. 27.

34. 'My painting is a circulation. It's like being, life. They are always in motion. If my painting was static, it would be false . . .' My translation. Cited in Laporte, *Bram van Velde*, p. 32.

35. Franz Meyer, 'Préface', in Claire Stoullig (ed.), *Bram van Velde*, catalogue of the 1989 exhibition, Musée national d'art moderne, Centre Georges Pompidou, p. 191. My translation.

36. Avigdor Arikha, 'Le nuage rouge', in Mason (ed.), *Rétrospective du Centenaire*, p. 236. My translation.

37. Meyer notes the persistence of certain forms in the post-war paintings that may recall silhouettes, birds' heads or masks. These are, for him, less residues of figurative representation in the paintings than 'witnesses to the archaic quality of the image for Bram van Velde'. Meyer, 'Préface', in Stoullig (ed.), *Bram van Velde*, p. 191. My translation. See also Mason's observation that these forms seem to function as 'analogical signs' that integrate with the more abstract, quasi-geometric figures in the paintings to form an organic unity: Rainer Michael Mason, 'La croissance d'un arbre: Notes sur l'individuation du style de Bram van Velde', in Stoullig (ed.), *Bram van Velde*, p. 48. My translation.

38. Beckett to Marthe Arnaud, in *The Letters of Samuel Beckett, Volume I: 1929–1940*, pp. 683–4. The 'blue glass' refers to the

black-out coating on the window, rather than to any glass on the painting itself. The internal citation is to Beckett's own novel, *Murphy*, p. 72.

39. Beckett, 'La Peinture des van Velde, ou Le Monde et le Pantalon', in *Disjecta*, p. 126. My translation. The essay was originally published in *Cahiers d'Art* (1945–46), pp. 349–56, and was reprinted in *Disjecta*, pp. 118–32. This essay addresses the work of both Bram and his brother Geer.

40. Beckett, 'Peintres de l'empêchement', in *Disjecta*, p. 135. Part of this essay was reproduced in Beckett's own translation as 'the New Object' on the invitation card to the opening of Bram and Geer van Velde's exhibition at the Samuel M. Koontz gallery in New York, March 1948. The translation is reproduced in facsimile in Stoullig (ed.), *Bram van Velde*, pp. 166–7, and corresponds to pages 134–7 of the essay in *Disjecta*. Here, and where possible, I follow Beckett's own translation, indicated in the text as SBV, along with the original in *Disjecta*.

41. As van Velde was to put it, 'La chose échappe, on reste dehors.' Laporte, *Bram van Velde*, p. 21.

42. Van Velde: 'Je cherche à voir, alors que tout, dans ce monde, nous empêche de voir.' Cited in Cäsar Menz, 'Avant-Propos', in Mason (ed.), *Rétrospective du Centenaire*, p. 11.

43. The original French does not include the phrase 'light and space themselves veils'.

44. Beckett, 'MacGreevy on Yeats', in *Disjecta*, p. 97.

45. Beckett, 'La Peinture des van Velde', in *Disjecta*, p. 131. My translation.

46. Beckett, 'MacGreevy on Yeats', in *Disjecta*, p. 97.

47. For a profound and extensive investigation of the relation between the legacy of slavery, incarceration and the legal transformation of person into thing, see Colin Dayan, *The Law Is a White Dog: How Legal Rituals Make and Unmake Persons*. Bram van Velde himself experienced imprisonment once at least, in 1938, due to lacking proper identity papers: see his letter to his wife Marthe Arnaud, dated Bayonne, July 1938, in Mason (ed.), *Rétrospective du Centenaire*, p. 221.

48. Beckett's Cartesian interests have tended to occlude his engagement with Kant, which may in fact have been far more pervasive, especially in the Trilogy. The first books that Beckett ordered when he finally settled in Paris in 1938 were the collected works of Kant in German: a letter to MacGreevy, 5 January 1938, remarks that

'the entire works of Kant arrived from Munich ... two immense parcels that I could hardly carry from customs to taxi'; *Letters, Vol. I*, p. 581. Since subsequent letters refer to him reading and writing 'nothing, unless it is Kant (de nobis ipsis silemus)' (*Letters, Vol. I*, pp. 622 and 643), it is clear he intended a serious study of the philosopher, though the war and his refuge in Vichy France must have interrupted this project. His knowledge of Heidegger is harder to establish, though he moved among scholars and artists who were certainly engaged with that philosopher's work, like Jean Beaufret at the École Normale and possibly Brian Coffey, the Irish philosopher and poet. Coffey mentioned to me in conversation in 1981 that he and Beckett had discussed Heidegger in Paris cafés, though how seriously or soberly they did so it was hard to deduce. On Beaufret, see James Knowlson, *Damned to Fame: The Life of Samuel Beckett*, p. 104, and Rodney X. Sharkey, 'Heidegger, Beckett and Beaufret'. Sharkey indicates that both before and after the war, Beckett engaged quite extensively with Beaufret on Heidegger. In Hamburg Beckett also came to know well the Swiss artist Karl Ballmer (among those praised in the review of MacGreevy on Yeats), whose *Aber Herr Heidegger!* was one of the first critiques of the Nazi philosopher and his infamous Rectorial Address. See *Letters, Vol. I*, p. 480.

49. Martin Heidegger, 'The Origin of the Work of Art', p. 9.
50. Heidegger, 'The Thing', p. 167.
51. Heidegger, 'The Thing', p. 168.
52. Heidegger, *What Is a Thing?*, p. 220.
53. For a summary of Kant's complex of representation, see David Lloyd, 'Representation's Coup', pp. 11–15.
54. Heidegger, *What Is a Thing?*, p. 191.
55. Heidegger, 'The Origin of the Work of Art', p. 12.
56. Heidegger, 'The Origin of the Work of Art', pp. 8–11.
57. Heidegger, 'The Origin of the Work of Art', p. 11.
58. Heidegger, 'The Thing', pp. 181 and 182.
59. Heidegger, 'The Thing', p. 182.
60. Heidegger, 'The Thing', p. 181.
61. That Heideggerian phenomenology and its followers leads to 'accommodation, social compliance' is the burden of Theodor W. Adorno's critique of Heidegger throughout *The Jargon of Authenticity*, p. 142 and passim.
62. 'Painting frightens me. And yet I must paint' and 'Fear has been the motor of all I have done', cited in Laporte, *Bram van Velde*, pp. 25 and 27.

63. Beckett to MacGreevy, 11 March 1931, *Letters, Vol. I*, p. 73. Mark Nixon cites a clearly related passage from the 'Clare Street' Notebook, 11 August 1936: 'How translucent this mechanism seems to me now, the principle of which is: better to be afraid of *something* than of *nothing*. In the first case only a part, in the second case the whole is threatened, not to mention the monstrous quality which inseparably belongs to the incomprehensible, one could even say the boundless. . . . When such an anxiety begins to grow a reason must quickly be found, as no one has the ability to live with it in utter absence of reason.' See Nixon, *Samuel Beckett's German Diaries, 1936–1937*, p. 47.

64. In his own translation Beckett allows this ambiguity to evaporate, translating *deuil de l'objet* as simply 'the search for an object' (SBV, 166).

65. Marijo Kurz attributes to van Velde the remark that 'Painting is an eye, a blinded eye, which continues to see, which sees what blinds it'. See his untitled essay in Pierre Alechinsky et al., *Celui qui ne peut se servir des mots (pour Bram van Velde)*, p. 99. My translation.

66. Bram van Velde, cited in Mason (ed.), *Rétrospective du Centenaire*, p. 62.

67. Antonio Saura, 'L'infaisible miroir', in Mason (ed.), *Rétrospective du Centenaire*, p. 267. My translation. Jean Starobinski similarly remarks that in his painting 'an eye sometimes comes to signify to the painter and to the viewer together that the work, animated with its own life, faces them, looks at them and questions them in its turn.' My translation. See Starobinski, 'Le plein et le vide', in Alechinsky et al., *Celui que ne peut se servir des mots*, p. 142.

68. Pierre Schneider remarks of van Velde's post-war work: 'Neither figurative nor non-figurative, one might rather call it defigurative. . . . Bram van Velde buries himself in the painting in order to escape this gaze, but he never ceases to find it there again.' My translation. Cited in Mason (ed.), *Rétrospective du Centenaire*, p. 253.

69. Jacques Lacan, *The Four Fundamental Concepts of Psychoanalysis*, pp. 72–3. Lacan's metaphor for the 'pre-existent' gaze is that of a 'shoot' (*pousse*), a term that nicely corresponds to those stalk-like manifestations of the gaze in van Velde's paintings.

70. Lacan, *Four Fundamental Concepts*, pp. 80 and 86. See Michel Foucault's related reflections on Velázquez's *Las Meninas* and that 'point exterior to the picture' where the gaze of sovereign, artist and spectator converge, in *The Order of Things: An Archaeology of the*

Human Sciences, p. 15. Foucault's account has the advantage of emphasising the relation, which Lacan here passes over, between the perspectival positioning of the viewing subject and the commanding position of the imaginary sovereign.

71. Lacan, *Four Fundamental Concepts*, p. 101.
72. Lacan, *Four Fundamental Concepts*, p. 106.
73. Lacan, *Four Fundamental Concepts*, p. 106.
74. Lacan, *Four Fundamental Concepts*, pp. 83–4.
75. Lacan, *Four Fundamental Concepts*, p. 83.
76. On the relation of the *objet a* to orifices, see Jacques Lacan, 'The Subversion of the Subject and the Dialectic of Desire in the Freudian Unconscious'. On the gaze and the voice 'as the two paramount embodiments of the object *a*', see Mladen Dolar, 'The Object Voice', p. 13.
77. Lacan, *Four Fundamental Concepts*, p. 96.
78. Lacan, *Four Fundamental Concepts*, p. 107.
79. For this use of the term *point de capiton*, or 'anchoring point', see Lacan, 'The Subversion of the Subject and the Dialectic of Desire', p. 303.
80. On the history of the term *figura* and its shifting usage, see Erich Auerbach, 'Figura', in *Scenes from the Drama of European Literature*, pp. 11–76.
81. On the meaning of *persona*, complexly layered as those of *figura*, see F. Max Mueller, *Persona*.
82. See Kurz's eloquent remarks on this multiple geometry in Alechinsky et al., *Celui que ne peut se servir des mots*, p. 98.
83. Harold Rosenberg is perhaps most explicit in making the connection between abstract expressionism and a kind of imperial sublime: 'With the American, heir of the pioneer and the immigrant, the foundering of Art and Society was not experienced as a loss. On the contrary, the end of Art marked the beginning of an optimism regarding himself as an artist. The American vanguard painter took to the white expanse of the canvas as Melville's Ishmael took to the sea.' See Rosenberg, 'American Action Painters', cited in Joan Marter, 'Introduction: Internationalism and Abstract Expressionism', p. 2. On the relation between abstraction, painterly and otherwise, and US imperialism, see Sarita See, *The Decolonized Eye: Filipino American Art and Performance*, pp. xxv–xxvi, 65–7 and passim.
84. Labrusse, 'Beckett et la peinture', pp. 671–2.
85. Leo Bersani and Ulysse Dutoit comment similarly on Beckett's fic-

tional works through the Trilogy that they remain 'somewhat naive in their assumptions' and 'fail to fail' in the sense that they have not yet found a means to enact the critical insights sketched in the 'Three Dialogues' and elsewhere. See Bersani and Dutoit, *Arts of Impoverishment: Beckett, Rothko, Resnais*, p. 51.

86. S. E. Gontarski, 'Introduction', in *The Theatrical Notebooks of Samuel Beckett, Volume 4: The Shorter Plays*, p. xix. See also Anna McMullan, *Theatre on Trial: Samuel Beckett's Later Drama*, p. 13; McMullan begins her study of the later drama with *Play*.

87. Beckett, *Krapp's Last Tape*, p. 226.

88. Beckett, *Krapp's Last Tape*, p. 222. Later, in making his own recording, Krapp will emphasise this moment: 'Revelled in the word spool. [*With relish.*] Spooool! Happiest moment of the last half million' (p. 228).

89. Beckett to Schneider, 21 November 1958, in Maurice Harmon (ed.), *No Author Better Served: The Correspondence of Samuel Beckett and Alan Schneider*, p. 50.

90. Harmon (ed.), *No Author Better Served*, p. 51.

91. The phrase is Martin Esslin's in 'Towards the Zero of Language', p. 35. See also Gontarski, 'Introduction', in *The Theatrical Notebooks*, p. xv, where he claims that 'Beckett balanced a theatre of concrete visual images with a theatre of poetic images'.

92. Esslin, 'Towards the Zero of Language', p. 76; Gontarski, 'Introduction', in *The Theatrical Notebooks*, p. xvi.

93. McMullan, *Theatre on Trial*, p. 11. See also Daniel Albright, *Beckett and Aesthetics*, pp. 9, 64 and 129; Ruby Cohn, 'Beckett Directs *Endgame* and *Krapp's Last Tape*', in S. E. Gontarski (ed.), *On Beckett: Essays and Criticism*, p. 303; and Ulrika Maude, *Beckett, Technology and the Body*, pp. 114–15. For invaluable analysis of the technical aspects of both *Eh Joe* and *Play* in their TV and film versions, see Jonathan Bignell, *Beckett on Screen: The Television Plays*, pp. 19–28 and 31–7.

94. Gontarski's 'The Scoring of *Play*', in *The Intent of Undoing in Samuel Beckett's Dramatic Texts*, pp. 90–100, shows the extreme pains to which Beckett went to fragment and disperse this initial narrative. See also McMullan, *Theatre on Trial*, p. 23, on the dated conventions and extensive use of cliché in the text of the play.

95. Gontarski, 'Introduction', in *The Theatrical Notebooks*, p. xviii.

96. See Beckett's letter to director George Devine, commenting on the 1964 Paris production on which he assisted, cited in Rosemary

Pountney, *Theatre of Shadows: Samuel Beckett's Drama, 1956–76*, p. 35.

97. Beckett, *Play*, in *Dramatic Works*, pp. 356 and 365. Beckett's revision of the German translation emphasises his insistence on retaining the word 'thing' at precisely this juncture. Where the German translation had 'der Sinn ist da' ('the meaning is there'), Beckett amended it to 'das Ding ist da'. See Beckett, *Play*, in *The Theatrical Notebooks*, pp. 163 and 192.

98. Beckett, *Play*, in *The Theatrical Notebooks*, p. 189.

99. On this trapping of the spectator, see Graley Herren, *Samuel Beckett's Plays on Film and Television*, p. 173, and McMullan, *Theatre on Trial*, p. 25: 'While the audience perceives the heads' subjection to the mechanisms of the Light, indeed to the mechanisms of theatre itself, they also become aware of their own entrapment within their role as spectators.'

100. Beckett to Alan Schneider, 15 October 1956, in Harmon (ed.), *No Author Better Served*, p. 12.

101. Beckett, *Film*, in *Dramatic Works*, p. 372. Cited in the text hereafter as F.

102. Lacan, *Four Fundamental Concepts*, p. 81.

103. Over-adherence to the Berkeleyan reading of the play can also lead a critic so far as to fault Beckett with 'undermin[ing] his own stated premises': see Herren, *Samuel Beckett's Plays*, p. 43. 'Interesting failure' the play may have been for Beckett, but in terms rather different from those imposed by the 'structural convenience' of his citation of Bishop Berkeley.

104. Harmon (ed.), *No Author Better Served*, p. 159.

105. This appears to have been Beckett's own experience of watching *Film*. Writing to Alan Schneider, he remarked that 'it was really quite something. Not quite in the way intended, but as sheer beauty, power, and strangeness of image.' See Harmon (ed.), *No Author Better Served*, p. 166.

106. See Pountney, *Theatre of Shadows*, p. 190.

107. On the significance of Keaton's appearance in *Film* in the context of a European and especially French re-evaluation of his work, see Bignell, *Beckett on Screen*, pp. 136–7.

108. Beckett to MacGreevy, 6 February 1936, *Letters, Vol. I*, p. 312.

109. Albright sees silent film as a possible model for Beckett's separation of voice and gesture; see *Beckett and Aesthetics*, p. 64. Bignell, *Beckett on Screen*, pp. 137–8, emphasises the differences between watching *Film* and the actual experience of watching silent movies,

which would have been accompanied by the sound of music and the whir of the projector. This misses, I think, the way in which Beckett's disaggregation of the elements of the cinema repeats in a new way the dispersal of the elements in silent cinema.

3

'Siege laid again':
Arikha's Gaze, Beckett's Painted Stage

Siege laid again to the impregnable without. Eye and hand feverishly
after the unself. By the hand it unceasingly changes the eye unceasingly changed. Back and forth the gaze beating against unseeable and
unmakable. Truce for a space and the marks of what it is to be and to
be in face of. Those deep marks to show.

Samuel Beckett, 'For Avigdor Arikha'[1]

I

Beckett's relationships with Jack B. Yeats and Bram van Velde
were both the friendships of a younger man with an older artist
from whom he felt he learnt and to whom he paid homage. Close as
those friendships were, the circumstances of war and exile as well
as their shared reticence meant that meetings between the writer
and those artists were generally infrequent and, given their predilections, notoriously characterised by extended silences. Beckett's
deep reflections on their painting and the example he could draw
from it in a period when his own practice was still coming into
definition were thus in a certain sense monological, as he clarified the terms of his own aesthetic by way of a detour through
intense encounters with their work in a different medium. Indeed,
Beckett's sense, deeply felt if possibly misplaced, that his writings on van Velde had been to the detriment of the painter comes
through in various *pentimentos* addressed to Georges Duthuit and
Jacques Putnam as he responded with great reluctance to their
requests for further writings on the artist. Those regrets are not
always easy to separate from what becomes apparent in his letters
and in various remarks made to acquaintances: Beckett's feeling
that his and van Velde's aesthetic paths parted after a while, or

that he had exhausted what he had to learn from the painter. For whatever reasons, the intense friendship between Beckett and van Velde clearly subsided after the early 1950s, though the mutual respect endured, much as Beckett's friendship and correspondence with Duthuit himself virtually ceased after several intense years of dialogue.[2]

As I have remarked in the introduction, Beckett's relationship with the younger painter Avigdor Arikha was quite different, in its duration and its quality. Commencing after Arikha had attended a performance of *Waiting for Godot*, their friendship lasted until Beckett's death in 1989. Unlike the previous chapters, this one will explore the peculiar aesthetic convergences between two very different artists in different media, rather than focusing on exact correspondences or signs of influence. Once again, however, the intimacy with the artist has much to suggest about the development of the visual qualities of Beckett's theatre in the period of their long friendship.

Nearly twenty five years younger than Beckett, Avigdor Arikha was born in Rădăuţi in Bukovina, a northern province of Romania, in 1929. Like that other Romanian Jewish exile in Paris, Paul Celan, he grew up in the German-speaking Jewish community of Czernowitz, in the Ukrainian part of Bukovina, and then in Bucharest. At the onset of the Second World War, the family returned to the relative safety of Czernowitz, which had become a part of the Ukraine. But as German and Romanian troops invaded in 1941, he was deported along with his mother and sister – his father having died during their attempted flight – to a Romanian labour camp. The still unsettling and unsentimental drawings he made of the camp, in charcoal on butcher paper, were shown by the camp's commandant to Red Cross inspectors, who ensured Arikha's evacuation to Palestine along with his sister. There, after settling on a kibbutz and being gravely wounded in the 1948 Arab-Israeli war, Arikha continued his art studies at the Bezalel School of Arts and Crafts in Jerusalem, an institution founded on Bauhaus principles by Mordecai Ardon, a former Bauhaus student. There he studied drawing under Isidor Ascheim, whose striking aphorism 'Think that you may die in the middle of a line, therefore you must leave it perfect' continued to resonate powerfully in Arikha's graphic work as in his aesthetic principles.[3]

Arikha left Israel in 1950 for Europe, where, after some time travelling and viewing art in Italy, he settled in Paris. Apart from relatively short periods in New York and Jerusalem, he continued to live there till his death in 2010. Like Beckett, but in very different ways, Arikha had lived intensely through the traumatic and destructive events of the Second World War and its aftermaths. Apart from his early drawings of the labour camps, however, Arikha was no more drawn to the direct representation of those events than was Beckett. Throughout the 1950s and early 1960s, he was committed to abstract painting. As he put it to Barbara Rose:

> The second phase of abstraction began truly after World War II with a wave of mysticism. My own youth was filled with it, and abstraction was the aim I wished to achieve. I thought that painting could equal music in the sense that its real content was its own structure. The inner form being the 'song' from within, a sort of hidden pictorial melody. I believed in a sort of transcendental art.[4]

His gradual and growing dissatisfaction with abstraction as a painterly medium culminated in 1965 when, after viewing a show of Caravaggio and his Italian followers, Arikha committed himself once again to drawing from life, or from observation, as he preferred to put it, and spent the next seven years almost exclusively working in black and white, either drawing in charcoal or brush and ink or printmaking with various techniques. Having been 'taken by this hunger in the eye', he entered a period of intense experimentation, one that demanded starting 'from scratch, from the beginning' in order to learn to draw again.[5] For 'drawing from observation' is, as he has put it, 'a process of unlearning', unlearning accumulated skills in order to see afresh each time, and requiring 'intense feeling, acuity, high velocity, and instantaneous execution'.[6] Indeed, this deeply felt need to unlearn the skills he had developed as an abstract painter associates Arikha most closely with Beckett's notorious and continual effort to write without style, to become '*mal armé*', as he put it of his decision to write in French.[7] For Arikha, 'the act of drawing from observation is a dialectical one, supposing supreme mastery and the dismissal of mastery at the same time.' Or, as he elsewhere put it, in a thoroughly Beckettian paradox, 'Improving craft: by getting better one gets worse. The better you paint, the worse you get.'[8] Only in 1973 did he begin to paint again, and he remained committed to certain self-imposed constraints: all his paintings and other works were produced in a single sitting, without revision or retouching, and always directly from life. He consistently rejected terms such as representation, image, symbol or even figuration, in the sense of 'figurative painting', as implying acts of generalisation of the thing observed that were, for him, antithetical to the absolute particularity of the artwork. 'General experience', as he put it, 'has nothing to do with the particular experience of art.'[9]

After 1965, Arikha's work in every medium was driven by a quality of intense scrutiny, by 'a violent hunger in the eye', and by a no less relentless interrogation of what it is to see.[10] There have been few visual artists for whom the gaze was more obviously an obsessive and recurrent preoccupation than it was for Arikha. That gaze is, as Beckett's brief tribute to the painter so economically captures, the gaze of the artist seeking not merely to represent but to *see* the world, each time anew, and in seeing to interrogate what seeing is. But it is also a gaze that seeks to render, in the form of a questioning, the gaze of the artist himself. Arikha's oeuvre, in all its media – painting, graphics, drawing – returns over and over again to the self-portrait in which the subject is generally not the contemplative eye of the painter directed at himself, but the active gaze of the artist in the act of looking. 'Back and forth', that gaze and the act of depicting it are insistently, necessarily fleeting, necessarily because what Arikha seeks to capture is the ephemeral moment of the *unself*-conscious looking, the look in the moment before it becomes conscious of its act, the moment in which the subject is for itself a thing that stands forth rather than an object in representation, an object in itself, let us say, and not for itself. The condition of such an impossible task – how could the act of self-depiction not be self-conscious? – is speed, though not haste, and a phenomenal readiness that Arikha describes as the response to 'a "call", rather like a telephone ringing, which demands an immediate response'.[11]

The immediacy of innumerable self-portraits that register the moment when the artist catches himself looking, such as the brush and ink *Self-Portrait at Night* (1970; Fig. 3.1) or the aquatint *Self-Portrait with Open Mouth* (1973), obviates subjective preoccupations or psychological investigations. The look of the artist rests on a point somewhat oblique to the viewer's line of sight, preoccupied with something beyond either, which, especially in a work like *Self-Portrait at Night*, displaces the figure of the artist into the margins of the scene. There he sits framed by a dark column of

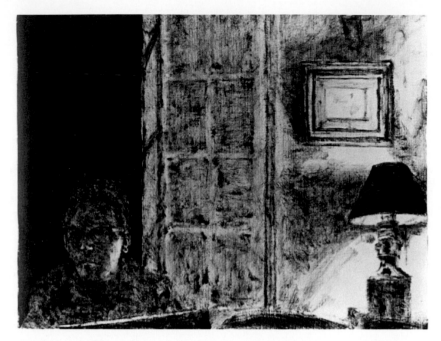

Fig. 3.1 Avigdor Arikha, *Self-Portrait at Night* (brush and sumi ink on coated paper, 27 × 35 cm, 1970), © Artists Rights Society (ARS), New York/DACS, London, 2016.

sumi ink out of which the image seems lifted by the drier brush-work, punctuated by clots of ink, that form his dark curls and lighter facial features. A single patch of light illuminating his left cheek connects him with the lamp on the far right whose glow cuts diagonally across the painting and whose deep black shade echoes the dark doorway behind the painter. The shadows it casts on the wall behind, seen in part through the glass panes of the door itself, are of the same substance as the artist's own features, brushed up off the paper with similar rapid, curling strokes and almost casually deposited clots of ink, as if in this single instant both human and objects were composed of brief flowers of smoke.[12] This is, no doubt, Arikha's depiction of 'what it is to be and to be in face of', the condition of what he variously describes as 'seeing' or observation, the activity to which, ethically and aesthetically, he devoted the greater part of his career.

Arikha's commitment, then, is to a kind of critical seeing, or to a re-seeing that opposes the habits of perception not only of the ordinary observer, but even of artists themselves: what he stresses in an essay on Giacometti's drawing is 'the difference there is between seeing "normally", which one has to understand, to my mind, as passive seeing, and active seeing, which would be perception through drawing'.[13] The artist's seeing is a mode of interrogation of the world, rather than an image or representation of it. As Barbara Rose put it in a remarkable early essay on his drawing, 'It is almost as if Arikha has inverted the statement of conventional realism: "This is what I see" becomes "Is this what I see?" Thus Arikha's drawings are not statements as much as questions.'[14] This conception of drawing as an investigation of the conditions of seeing is very precisely rendered in an apparently slight revision Beckett made at the very last minute to his brief tribute to Arikha. Beckett's frequently reproduced tribute to the artist, prepared for his 1967 show in Paris, is cited as the epigraph to this chapter. Brief as it is, it was the outcome of multiple drafts and revisions on Beckett's part, agonistic if not agonised, that are reproduced in Anne Atik's memoir of the couple's relationship with the writer, *How It Was*. There we can trace the evolution of the text, and in particular note the last-minute modification of the opening two sentences. In the 'final typed version' that Beckett presented to Arikha, these would have read as follows:

Recovered need of the impregnable without. Fever of hand and eye in a thirsting after the not-self.[15]

But in a letter sent from Lisbon on 25 December 1966, days before the exhibition was to open, Beckett requested Arikha change the first sentence to 'Siège remis devant le dehors imprenable', which is translated as 'Siege laid again to the impregnable without'.[16] It is not quite clear exactly when the no less important further modifications to the French and English texts were made, in particular the change from 'Fever of hand and eye in a thirsting after the notself' to 'Eye and hand feverishly after the unself'.

As always with Beckett, seemingly minor changes are fraught with precise significance. Beckett's replacement of 'need' with 'siege' crucially changes the terms of Arikha's engagement with the world of things, shifting the emphasis from the suggestion of an inner psychological insufficiency on the artist's part to the assertion of a methodical and systematic focus that is something other than psychological. Similarly, the emotive 'thirsting' is removed from the final version, allowing the 'feverishness' of eye and hand to refer not so much to an inner fever as to the notorious 'speed' of Arikha's drawing, its *vitesse*, the word Beckett used in his third revision. That word, indeed, echoes Arikha's own term 'high velocity', which he used in his essay 'On Drawing from Observation'.

Beckett's replacement of the phrase 'recovered need' with 'Siege laid *again* to the impregnable without' certainly highlights the repetitive process whereby Arikha's drawing continually interrogates what is seen, striving to render the visible on paper. But the phrase has further implications. It refers not only to Arikha's personal trajectory from abstract painting back to the draughtsmanship that marked his very early work, but also to his return over a terrain Beckett had already explored and departed from much earlier in his critical reflections on painting: that of the Italian Renaissance and its legacy. It seems probable that the source of Beckett's metaphor lay in Renaissance optics, a field in which he was well versed and which provides a common source for this metaphor and for his acerbic remark in the 'Three Dialogues with Georges Duthuit' about Renaissance painters 'surveying the world with the eyes of building contractors'.[17] Regarding sight as the effect of light rays emanating *from* the eye to grasp the object, sixteenth-century artist and architect Leon Battista Alberti remarked in his highly influential *On Painting*:

> As for the properties of the centric ray, it is of all rays undoubtedly the most keen and vigorous. It is also true that a quantity will never appear larger than when the centric ray rests upon it. A great deal could be said about the power and function of this ray. One thing should not go unsaid: this ray alone is supported in their midst, like a united assembly, by all the others, so that it rightly must be called the leader and prince of rays.[18]

Beckett's implicit allusion to this notion of seeing not as a passive reception of light reflected from an object but as an active process analogous to a kind of princely conquest or 'investment' of the world 'without' – what Arikha has referred to as a 'capture' or 'seizing' of the world[19] – suggests that Arikha's move is not an 'advance' in the progressive sense of art-historical development that dominates modernist criticism – a notion both would certainly have eschewed – but precisely a 'return'. Arikha's experiments in recommitting himself to drawing two years earlier appear to Beckett as a recursive and dialectical move from modernist

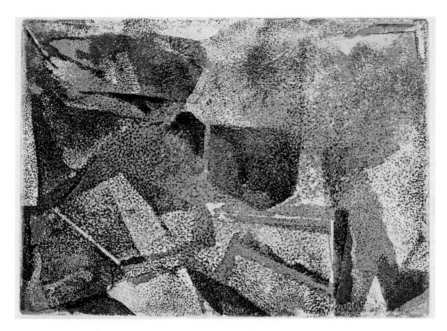

Fig. 3.2 Avigdor Arikha, *Composition* (etching on paper, 25.9 × 33.5 cm, 1959), collection of the Stedelijk Museum, Amsterdam, #8868, © Artists Rights Society (ARS), New York/DACS, London, 2016.

abstraction to the founding concerns of Renaissance painting that need to be re-envisaged, rethought. As Arikha was to put it himself somewhat later, 'what I would like to attain is to be nearer to the principles of Velázquez, through the twentieth century's experience. Of course, it's like going back through death, we cannot revert.'[20]

Arikha, indeed, always insisted that his painting is 'postabstract',[21] that is, informed both by his own training and discipline as an abstract painter and, more generally, by the history of abstract painting itself. His turn to drawing was not a disavowal or refusal of abstraction. On the contrary, he recognised the ways in which the tradition of abstraction had been crucial to freeing painting from its 'anecdotal' concerns, from what abstraction's champion, Clement Greenberg, would have described as its literariness. 'Modernist abstraction', Arikha once remarked, 'permitted the liberation of painting from the literary misunderstanding, from the anecdote (that virus of the eye) and gave the illusion that the old mimesis had vanished into oblivion.'[22] In a perpetual movement of return, of recommencing, that is embedded in the

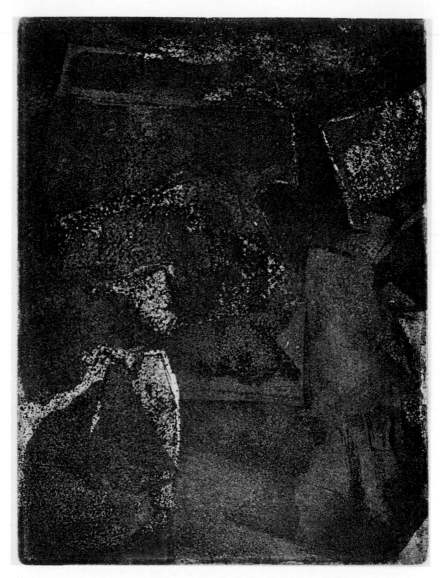

Fig. 3.3 Avigdor Arikha, *Composition* (etching on paper, 37.9×28.2 cm, 1959), collection of the Stedelijk Museum, Amsterdam, #8871, © Artists Rights Society (ARS), New York/DACS, London, 2016.

double sense of Beckett's 'again', Arikha's art represents at once a historical return to a founding moment in modern Western art from the vantage point of post-abstraction and a renewed commitment to the act of repetition that drawing from observation, according to Arikha, relies on: 'Drawing from observation is an endless recommencement.'[23]

To understand working directly from observation as recommencement helps us to grasp more precisely the genesis and terms of Arikha's eventual abandonment of abstract painting. As he conceived his goals in abstract painting quasi-musically, as 'a visual art of pure form, modulated like music and devoid of representation',[24] his focus was on the rhythm and orchestration of form and colour in a way that connects his work back through Mondrian to Kandinsky as well as to Matisse, whose use of colour fields Arikha came to understand both for its value to painting from observation (a point to which we will return) and as a decisive antecedent for post-war European abstraction.[25] In keeping with the history and theory of abstract painting across the Euro-American tradition, Arikha's practice involved the interrogation of the essence of painting as a medium, its reduction to the relations of form and colour across a two-dimensional plane. The impasse of such a painting would come increasingly to burden him, until eventually he came to see not only his own work, but even abstraction in general, as a form of mannerism, which he succinctly described as 'painting from painting'. The repetitiveness of abstraction was not a mode of 'recommencement', but a continual return over the same ground. As he put it to the critic Robert Hughes:

> It seemed to me then that all I had been doing was painting from painting; I had not linked the act of painting to the fact of seeing, and it struck me – a terrible blow – that our culture was manneristic, as Rome was before Caravaggio began to work there.[26]

The allusion to Caravaggio is, of course, deliberate and charged. As we know, Arikha attended the Louvre exhibition 'Le Caravage et la peinture italienne du xviie siècle' on 10 March 1965. The epiphanic nature of this event for him is perhaps best signalled by the precise insistence with which he recalls the date in virtually every interview as the moment at which his real artistic calling commenced, although it is clear that his dissatisfaction with abstract painting had had a longer gestation.[27] But it is from this moment that he always dated his dedication to what he came to call depiction and which remained his commitment throughout the next forty-five years of his career.

Arikha's emphatic choice of the word 'depiction' establishes an approach to painting that seeks to avoid the dichotomy between representation or figuration and abstraction. On the one hand, as he once remarked, 'all painting is abstraction', in so far as even the most representational painting is an abstraction from the visible world within the frame of a two-dimensional canvas, and even the finest line or most precise brushstroke is a kind of schematism of the thing seen. As Robert Hughes paraphrases Arikha:

> To draw with a line is to immerse oneself in abstraction; the more wiry and faint the trace, the more schematic it becomes. Our 'natural' tendency is apparently to see by patches of tone and colour rather than by contour; and for that reason the very nature of classical *disegno* was reductive, changing the tumultuous congestion of reality into comprehensible shape, measure, structure and proportion.[28]

Hence Arikha was never averse to retaining the lessons he had learnt from abstraction in painting.[29] On the other hand, neither representation nor figuration seemed to him adequate terms to render the kind of scrutiny of the visible in which he was engaged. Asked by Barbara Rose why he did not accept these terms, he responded: 'Because it presumes images. The image is not about restriction. It's about information. It designates more than it contains. It's a reminder of something it does not contain.'[30] Depiction seeks to render the thing seen without reducing it to a reference to something else for which it may be taken to stand. 'No symbols', as Beckett insisted, 'where none intended.'[31]

Depiction as a practice accordingly sets up an exceptional tension in Arikha's work between his awareness of the materiality of his technical and formal means and the constraint imposed upon him by the commitment to an accurate scrutiny of the world. In a certain sense, indeed, despite his emphasis on the rupture that occurred in 1965, many of the elements of his later work are already apparent in his abstracts even as they scrupulously resist the presentation of images of any kind. They operate typically through the dynamic interplay of geometric forms that, for all their gravity and apparent monumentality, hover and plunge through

ambiguous perspectival depths that are constituted by superim-
posed planes of colour which – as in some of Bram van Velde's
paintings – alternately appear to recede or stand forward from the
picture plane.[32] A set of small and intense graphic works of 1959
to 1960 in the collection of the Stedelijk Museum in Amsterdam
exhibit such tumbling forms that spin across uncertain perspectival fields constituted by overlapping visual triangles. Their ambiguous depths are created by the juxtapositions of black and white
of different intensities or by the apparently floating grey 'clouds'
that cover and unite them. Occasionally there emerge from these
abstract forms the hints or vestiges of figures – a human shape, a
boulder, or even an open book that might just be a pyramid (see
Figs 3.2 and 3.3). As so often with abstract work, these etchings
seem haunted by the remnants of a desire for figuration.

In the larger paintings, where colour fields play a crucial role in
the overall *disegno*, a similar 'tumultuous congestion' dominates.
In *Noire Basse* [*Deep Black*] (1959; Fig. 3.4), a large and sombre
painting from the same period as the Stedelijk Museum etchings,
the green, violet and indigo coloured form that dominates the
upper right quadrant of the painting seems at one moment to
emerge from the murkier browns and the heavy black shapes that
surround it; at another, it seems to open a tunnel that recedes into
the depths of the canvas. John Ashbery's description of Arikha's
work in this period seems particularly acute:

> abstractions whose shallow complex space is choked with shuttling
> planes, clouds of smoke, sudden bursts of light which are quickly extin-
> guished. Light is trying to seep through or around these dark shapes
> which seem to block the view but which are actually the subject.[33]

In the tonally much lighter *Noir et Blancheur* [*Black and Whiteness*]
(1965; Fig. 3.5) – one of Arikha's last abstractions – it remains
almost impossible to determine whether the cloudy whites and
greys form a background against which the black triangles and
rectangles emerge, or whether the latter establish an architectural
ground across which the whites and greys drift. Viewed, in so far
as possible, simply as a coloured plane, the whole is unified by the
rhythm of a broken or interrupted diagonal of red that rises from
bottom left towards the upper right and is met by a similarly dis-
continuous column of red along the right side, the whole alleviated
by momentary flashes of yellow.

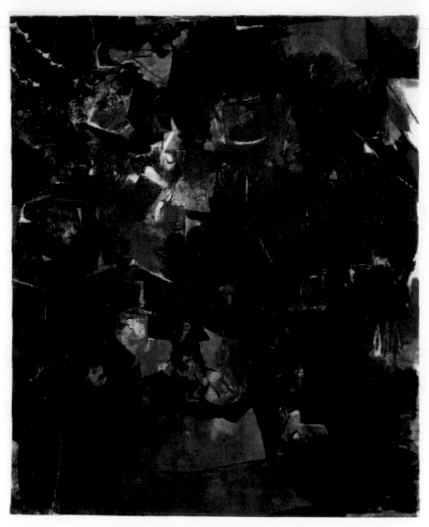

Fig. 3.4 Avigdor Arikha, *Noire Basse* [*Deep Black*] (oil on canvas, 195×160 cm, 1959), © Artists Rights Society (ARS), New York/DACS, London, 2016.

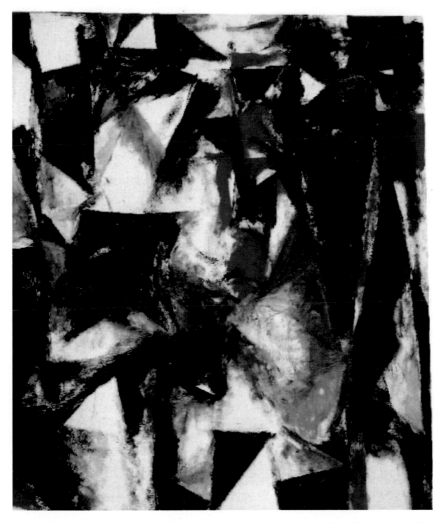

Fig. 3.5 Avigdor Arikha, *Noir et Blancheur* [*Black and Whiteness*] (oil on canvas, 162 × 130 cm, 1965), © Artists Rights Society (ARS), New York/DACS, London, 2016.

This painting already partakes of a simplification of palette and technical means that will be characteristic of Arikha's later work when he resumes painting some years later. But it also manifests the accuracy of Arikha's acknowledgement that in abstract painting he was still negotiating with a 'colour-grammar' derived from Cézannian principles. That grammar Arikha later defined as requiring 'no flat colour expanse, no sharp contrasts, no local colour, no sharp nor clear contours, no pure single lines; but instead, a process of short strokes (flat brush preferably), chiaroscuro by line and stain, equally distributed by reciprocal imbrication or overlapping. And, of course, no colour saturation.'[34] However much Cézanne's principles may have lent themselves to his intense investigations of the deep structures of landscape, for example, and however much they informed visual representation subsequently, they were, according to Arikha, no less influential on abstract painting. They laid the basis for the structural organisation of the painting, the underlying grid through which the disposition of colour and its rhythmic relations could be established even in the absence of any figure. This mode of organisation Arikha denominates the 'chequerboard':

> [In modernism] a new key form emerged, a new dominant: the *chequerboard*. It emanated from Cézanne's work. An imbrication of contrasts, the chequerboard came to dominate much of this century's art; to begin with, Cubism. The chequerboard illustrates perfectly the method which arose from the Cézannian heritage, being a quintessence of a vibrant screen, constituted of opposites, thus permitting the rationalization of all visual data and its distribution on a flat plane. The chequerboard is an optical trap, by holding the viewer's gaze within its imbrication, leading it back and forth from one point to the other. In this respect, the chequerboard is as much a conductor of sight as perspective, which it replaced.[35]

For Arikha, then, the break with abstract painting is not only a return to depiction, a re-engagement with the visible, but also a departure from what seemed to him the dominant organising principles of pictorial space. Crucially, that departure operated not through an attempt to restore the illusion of perspectival space as a means to recapture the terrain of visual realism, but through an engagement with colour and pictorial space that underlies the most vital tensions in Arikha's work, those that persist in the

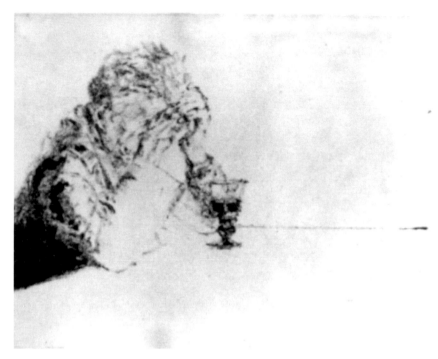

Fig. 3.6 Avigdor Arikha, *Samuel Beckett with a glass of wine* (brush and sumi ink on Japan paper, 26×33.7 cm, 1969), © Artists Rights Society (ARS), New York/DACS, London, 2016.

dynamic interplay of his formal or technical means with his visual acuity and that manifest in the very materiality of his works.

Paradoxically, perhaps, the experiments to which Arikha devoted himself throughout the seven-year period after his epiphany at the Caravaggio exhibition almost entirely excluded the use of colour. Working both in drawing, using pencil, charcoal and brush and ink, and in print media, principally etching and lithography, Arikha produced a large volume of work that was restricted to black and white and the intermediate shades of grey. As the Stedelijk Museum collection makes clear, neither these media nor the reduction to black and white were by any means new to Arikha, having offered him a vehicle for experimentation even when he was still working in abstraction. Comparing these black and white drawings and etchings to the earlier, abstract work suggests that what *was* new was not merely the return to depiction, but the whole spatial organisation of the work. Indeed, it seems probable that the abrupt and thorough impoverishment

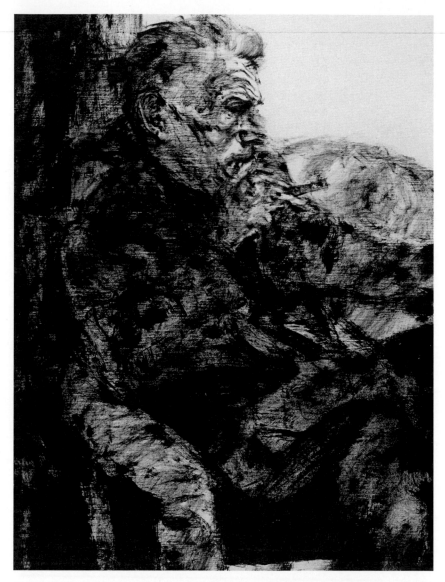

Fig. 3.7 Avigdor Arikha, *Samuel Beckett with cigar* (brush and sumi ink on gessoed paper, 35×27 cm, 1970), © Artists Rights Society (ARS), New York/DACS, London, 2016. Photo Georges Meguerditchian © CNAC/NMAM/Dist. RMN-Grand Palais/Art Resource, New York.

of his means was, given his illuminating remarks on Cézanne's colour-grammar, critical to the kind of break with the past – his own and that of the history of painting itself – which he sought to make. In that respect, it is not far-fetched to compare Arikha's stylistic and technical asceticism in this period to Beckett's decision to write in French: for both of them, such a deliberate reduction of means entailed a crucial break with a certain kind of facility that had resulted in impasse. Arikha's urgent need to destroy his 'craft' in order to escape the stylistic mannerism that he felt afflicted his abstract painting may be seen as the equivalent of Beckett's discovery that he needed to work 'with impotence, ignorance' in order to escape the compulsion to repeat what had become the excesses of a Joycean omnicompetence in language.

II

It is fitting that among the most powerful, as well as the most frequently reproduced, of Arikha's works from this period are a series of drawings of Beckett, whose extended visits to Arikha's home and studio and whose capacity for silent absorption must have made him an ideal subject. Two of these brush and ink drawings, *Samuel Beckett with a glass of wine* (1969) and *Samuel Beckett with cigar* (1970) (Figs 3.6 and 3.7), seem to be almost antithetical experiments with pictorial space even as they are extraordinary portraits of the writer. The earlier of the two is to a striking degree dominated by the white 'reserve' space of the paper, the table on which Beckett leans being demarcated horizontally by the sparest of grey brushstrokes and vertically by the dark flap of the writer's jacket into which it merges. The resultant expanse of whiteness seems to gain in gravity, weighing down on his lowered head and bent shoulders, which are, indeed, apparently teased out of the paper by dry and fragile brushstrokes whose grey outlines hardly diminish the sense of the emptiness out of which the figure emerges. Only the pitch black of the jacket and of the wine in the glass in the virtual dead centre of the paper form countervailing foci that prevent the whole from dissolving away into sheer vapour. It is as if the exact placement of the wine provides a pivot around which the figure and the whiteness from which he emerges can turn in a vital counterpoint while at the same time remaining an element in an immediately and, to judge by the rapidity of the brushstrokes, spontaneously observed and depicted instant.

Samuel Beckett with cigar presents a no less dynamic tension between a certain formal precision of execution and an apparently spontaneous image, though in an almost antithetical manner. Here, all but the upper right-hand quadrant of the drawing is dominated by Beckett's dark shape, relieved only by the arm of the chair that forms a diagonal with the chair's back where it fades into the white triangle of the upper right corner. That diagonal is crossed by the intersecting dark diagonal of the writer's body as he relaxes into the chair, forming roughly a right-angled triangle with the black column of the wall or door frame to the left. The dark patches and clots of ink out of which his suit is composed seem to generate the sure and rapid brushstrokes that sketch his facial features and wiry hair as if they emerged out of the dry remnants of unworked ink. At the same time, the highlights on fabric and chair appear to leak out of the whiteness of the paper into the drawing of the figure, incorporating the underlying material into the drawing itself in a kind of dialectic of paper and ink. It is, once again, as if the brushwork lifts the image out of the paper but is not made to vanish there. Rather, depending on the distance from which the drawing is observed or at which it is held, the viewer's attention is captured by the sheerly material quality of the drawing – its brushwork, its densities and transparencies of ink, the texture of the paper itself – such that it becomes possible to regard it almost as an abstract work. Or one may be drawn to contemplate the extraordinary vibrant acuity of the figure itself, an image of Beckett fixated on the empty gaze that emanates from the dark hollow of his eye. As are Arikha's self-portraits, this is a gaze at gazing itself. Formally, as in the texture of its execution, it shares much with the almost contemporary *Self-Portrait, shouting one morning* (1969; Fig. 3.8), where, as Robert Hughes has pointed out, in comments that can hardly be bettered, it is the mouth that holds the whole image from disintegrating under the force of its own 'high velocity' energies:

> Sometimes, as in *Self-Portrait Shouting One Morning*, the image is airy to the point of dissolution: the scrubby twists by which Arikha's corkscrew hair is rendered, the prodded, tentative line of the left cheek and pyjama stripes are only nailed on the page by one shape, the black shouting hole of a mouth; but for that, and a clot of black ink between the eyes, the brushmarks would fly apart.[36]

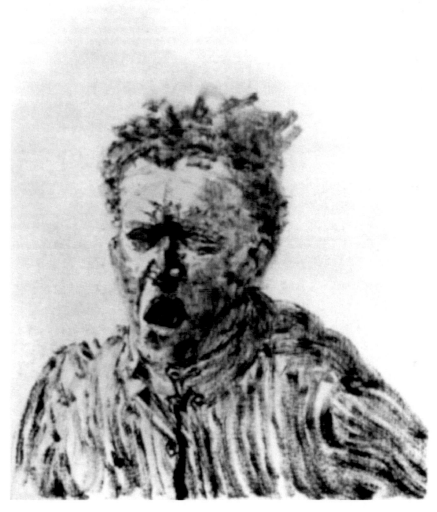

Fig. 3.8 Avigdor Arikha, *Self-Portrait, shouting one morning* (sugar aquatint on Mino paper, 46 × 38 cm, 1969), © Artists Rights Society (ARS), New York/DACS, London, 2016.

Looking again at *Samuel Beckett with cigar*, one may be struck not only by a similar 'airiness' of the brushwork, but also by how it succeeds in approximating the representation of the human figure to that of inanimate matter. The brushwork that demarcates Beckett's hair equally supplies the outline and textures of the chair itself, with similar clots and wisps of ink. It is as if the brushwork 'rhymes' across the drawing, to borrow a term from Arikha's painstaking formal analysis of Poussin's *Rape of the Sabines* in the Louvre, of which he remarks that 'Each point has its retort, each form its rhyme. As in a poem, everything in this painting rhymes.'[37] There, of course, Arikha is referring primarily to the formal and colorific correspondences across Poussin's masterpiece, to the echoes of postures or to the repetition of certain colourings. In an obvious sense, Arikha's work here, devoid as it is of any colouration at all, might seem to defy Poussin's dictum that 'Nothing is visible without colour' (*Il ne se donne point de visible sans Couleur*); but it may also propose that there is no depiction of the visible, even in black, white and greys, that does not imply or suggest colour.[38] In the essay, Arikha cites the deceptively simple definition of painting of the late-Renaissance Italian critic Raffaello Borghini: 'One can say that painting is a plane covered with various colours on a surface.'[39] Many critics have remarked on the way in which Arikha's use of graduated shades of black, grey and white produces the effect of colour values, 'suggesting colour without using it' to produce a 'tonal painting', as he put it.[40] Effects that were thus implied in the graphic work become central to the painting that he was to resume in 1973. The principles that he discovered through his graphic work, those of harmonisation and contrast across the surface of the paper, of alternation between the foregrounding of the material and technique of the work and that of the depiction that emerges from them, may have offered Arikha the means to return to painting emancipated from the Cézannian colour-grammar of his abstractions. The paintings of the ten years or so after his return to the medium in 1973 display a new sense of how to dispose of 'various colours on a surface' without losing the kinds of vital tensions between material and image that his drawings had set in play and equally without abandoning the acute formal and spatial sense that he had clearly developed as an abstract painter.

Approaching almost any of the paintings of the 1970s, it is evident that despite his new insistence on depiction and observation, Arikha remained a painter with an acute awareness of the purely formal qualities of balance, rhythm and construction. The dialectic of strict formal composition and observation that characterises his drawings is no less operative in the paintings. Taking just a handful of examples from that extraordinarily vital decade, such as *La Demie-Baguette* [*Half a Loaf*] (1973), *Glass of Whiskey* (1974), *Box and Pitcher* (1975) and *Black Mat and Dry Bread* (1979) (Figs 3.9 to 3.12), it is almost impossible not to see in them the elements of abstract paintings. The precise geometrical arrangements and divisions of the canvases, the astonishingly bold points of view that allow for proportionally huge planes of colour varied only by implied shadow or by the mixing of adjacent white and beige pigment in the off-white wall of *La Demie-Baguette* or the tablecloth of *Black Mat and Dry Bread*, the daring juxtaposition of white tablecloth and black napkin or table mat, all counterpoint with striking effect the intensely precise depiction of the texture of a slightly burnt crust or the light reflecting off a glass of whiskey. In the latter work, the red tablecloth and dark grey wall establish two distinct planes of colour that dominate almost the entire painting, almost flaunting the bold 'saturation' of these fields with unified colour against which the glass of whiskey stands forth in all its reflective luminosity and transparency, occupying like Beckett's glass of wine the virtual centre of the painting. Arikha was fully conscious from the very outset of the challenge such works presented not only to abstraction but to the Cézannian conventions that underlay both abstract and figurative work. As he later remarked, 'Where I started was in contradiction to the Cézannien code: I am not afraid of local colour, unbroken forms, saturations, all those things which were made taboo in Cézanne's legacy.'[41]

And yet Arikha was not averse to incorporating with a certain bravura the lessons both of abstraction and of the traditions of still-life painting that are almost impudently staged in the cylinders, cubes and spheres that structure the objects in *Box and Pitcher*. The peculiar line of sight in *Glass of Whiskey* interrupts the perspectival depth that might have projected the surface of the table and instead poses the glass as if it were on the very edge of both table and canvas; the corner of the wall paradoxically pushes the stool and the baguette lying on it forward, almost out of the picture plane: such tours de force of spatial manipulation are not unwitting of their relation to the whole lineage of

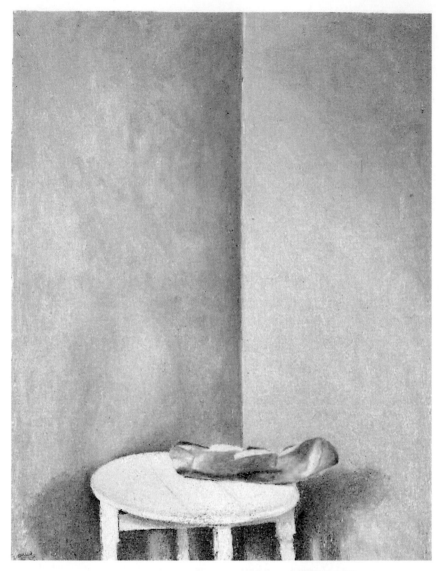

Fig. 3.9 Avigdor Arikha, *La Demie-Baguette* [*Half a Loaf*] (oil on canvas, 116 × 89 cm, 1973), © Artists Rights Society (ARS), New York/ DACS, London, 2016.

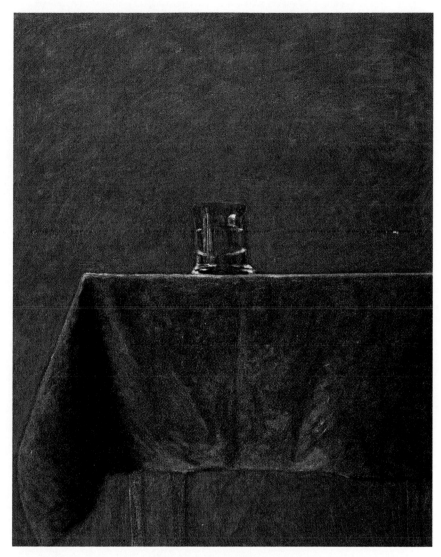

Fig. 3.10 Avigdor Arikha, *Glass of Whiskey* (oil on canvas, 81×65 cm, 1974), © Artists Rights Society (ARS), New York/DACS, London, 2016.

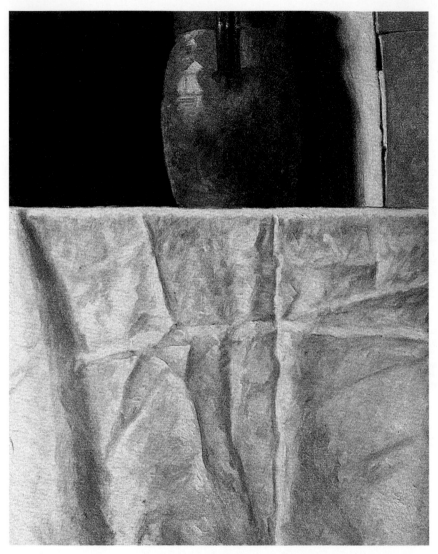

Fig. 3.11 Avigdor Arikha, *Box and Pitcher* (oil on canvas, 73 × 60. cm, 1975), © Artists Rights Society (ARS), New York/DACS, London, 2016.

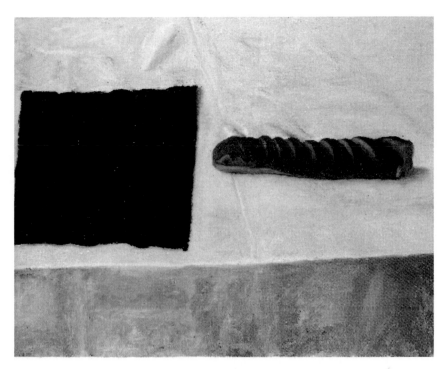

Fig. 3.12 Avigdor Arikha, *Black Mat and Dry Bread* (oil on canvas, 65 × 81 cm, 1979), © Artists Rights Society (ARS), New York/DACS, London, 2016.

twentieth-century and earlier still lifes and, indeed, bespeak a very learned eye. On the one hand, they allude to the genealogy of abstraction itself, for, as Barbara Rose points out:

> the development of abstract art was as much involved in the development of a new kind of pictorial space as it was in the abandonment of representation. Indeed it has been argued by Clement Greenberg that the development of this new type of space, beginning with Manet's initial self-conscious flattening of the pictorial cavity, precluded the representation of fully three-dimensional forms [in] painting, rather than vice versa.[42]

Arikha's heightened consciousness of this tradition results in 'depictions' that nonetheless demand to be looked at simultaneously as abstractions, while his equal awareness of the still-life tradition leads him to draw out of its emphasis on the undisguised flatness of the canvas those effects of spatial ambiguity that are achieved by painting objects as if they stand at the very edge of the surface – the retreating visual plane – on which they precariously rest, flattening forward the visual plane into the field of the viewer even while ostentatiously presenting those objects in all their volume and dimensionality.[43] The effect recalls the experiments with space, perspective and volume in the still lifes of both Cézanne and Matisse in the early part of the century, sharing their phenomenological ambiguities, yet Arikha achieves this while at the same time insisting not – as they and, indeed, van Velde do – on the formalisation or schematisation of the represented fruits, but on their precise depiction. The almost vertical disposition of the plate and tabletop in *Three Apples and One Pear* (1978; Fig. 3.13), counterpointed by the fleshy, almost spherical volume of the fruits, makes this abundantly clear. The perspective in this instance is flattened forward into the picture plane, not by a view from beneath that cuts off the surface, but by a view from above that seems to tip the whole surface forward. For all their rotund gravity, the fruits seem at moments to be falling forward off the plate on which they are arranged, until the eye reorients its sense of perspective and point of view.

At times, Arikha synthesised both effects, as in the astonishing painting *Fruit on Silver Plate* (1981; Fig. 3.14). Here, one plump pear seems to balance on the very edge of a table that is covered by a red tablecloth in contrast to which a white linen napkin's fall seems to emphasise the perpendicularity of the canvas and the depicted scene alike. The convex mirror of the silver bowl, which extends over the table's edge and thus apparently into the plane of the viewer, reflects and distorts the napkin in a way that highlights its own volume. The rich and saturated colouration of the painting – the red of the tablecloth and grey of the wall here setting off the white napkin and the near-black silver bowl – is not accidentally reminiscent of the fabrics and metallic surfaces of a baroque painting. Arikha, indeed, has commented that 'what constitutes the greatness of European painting, is the *round*, "*la ronde-bosse*"', not, of course, the *trompe-l'oeil* type of illusionism, but the mastery by the brush of the concave and the convex forms', a quality he attributes in particular to Velázquez, but which is even more famously associated with Caravaggio.[44] *Fruit on Silver Plate*, for all the 'presentness' of its depiction of very actual fruits, is nonetheless a highly erudite and allusive painting, a characteristic that becomes increasingly apparent in Arikha's work. Here we

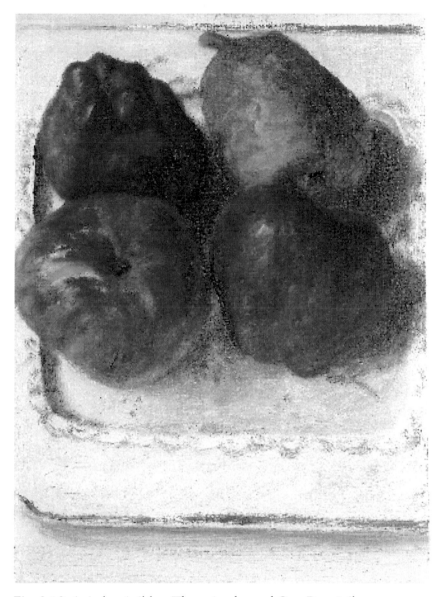

Fig. 3.13 Avigdor Arikha, *Three Apples and One Pear* (oil on canvas, 33×24 cm, 1978), © Artists Rights Society (ARS), New York/DACS, London, 2016.

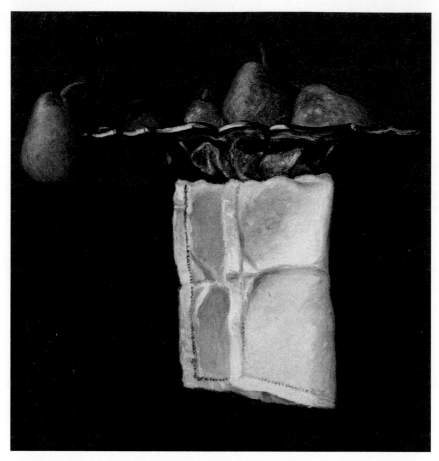

Fig. 3.14 Avigdor Arikha, *Fruit on Silver Plate* (oil on canvas, 60 × 60 cm, 1981), © Artists Rights Society (ARS), New York/DACS, London, 2016.

see precisely what he means by reverting to earlier principles of painting through the experience of the twentieth century. *Fruit on Silver Plate* alludes almost certainly to Caravaggio's *Basket of Fruit* (c. 1599; Fig. 3.15), not only in what is represented in each, but in the mode of presentation, in the formal organisation of the work. Caravaggio's still life also poses its basket of fruit on the edge of the table or shelf on which it rests, which forms a thin, scarcely visible line right at the very edge of the picture plane over which the base of the basket seems to project. Catherine Puglisi, his critic and biographer, suggests that its 'unusually low viewpoint' presumes that it will be hung high, perhaps even over a doorway, from which position the ragged vine leaf to the right of the painting and the bunch of grapes to the left of the basket would seem to stretch forward in a *trompe l'oeil* effect not dissimilar to the way in which Arikha's bowl seems to project beyond both table and canvas.[45]

More than once, Arikha cites the celebrated dictum that Caravaggio 'came into the world to destroy painting', a remark that paraphrases his early biographer and rival Giovanni Baglione and was attributed by André Félibien to Poussin.[46] For Arikha, Caravaggio's example is in the first place his defiance of mannerism, his capacity to paint '*mal armé*':

> Caravaggio defied the norms of *buonmaniera* and accepted no other master than the model. He disarmed art in disarming himself before the visible, and imitated art without art. In doing so, he 'destroyed' painting: by discarding *maniera* he made its code obsolete and no longer credible.[47]

But the spatial play in Arikha's allusion to *Basket of Fruit* is a reminder that what he learnt from Caravaggio's example was not merely, as most of Arikha's critics emphasise, the art of depiction, of painting from observation, but, more importantly, a sophisticated sense of how to integrate in the same painting a high degree of formal organisation with observation from life acute enough to suggest immediacy and ephemerality. It is clear, moreover, that Caravaggio's example affected deeply Arikha's understanding of space and of the possible theatricality both of the painting itself and of the act of painting. Ultimately, this has, for both Arikha and Caravaggio, as much to do with point of view and perspective as it has with the deployment of colour relations.

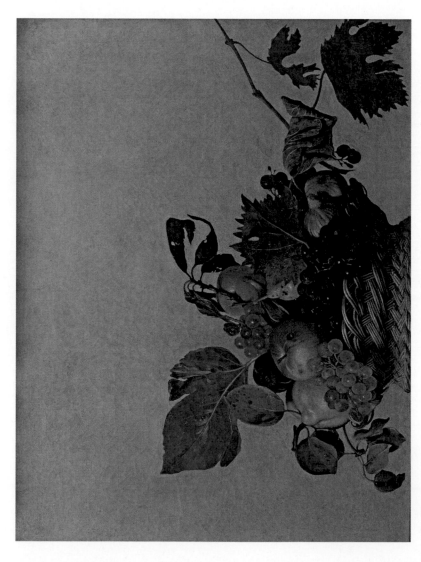

Fig. 3.15 Michelangelo Merisi da Caravaggio, *Basket of Fruit* (oil on canvas, 47 ×62 cm, c. 1599), © Veneranda Biblioteca Ambrosiana (Inv. 151), 2016.

We can see this through a painting of Caravaggio's that Arikha expressly admired and would have seen in the 1965 Louvre exhibition, *The Resurrection of Lazarus* (c. 1608–9; Fig. 3.16). We know that Arikha was in the first place struck by Caravaggio's use of colour: 'the treatment of the body of Lazarus, the chromatic accord between the ochres, the lamp blacks and white and the creation of cold greys – made the deepest impression,' according to Duncan Thomson.[48] He may have been struck, too, by the unifying power of Caravaggio's deployment of various shades of red in a diagonal across the painting, which recalls the similar use of colour in Arikha's abstract work. Indeed, as Arikha remarked, 'Caravaggio's *Resurrection of Lazarus* contains more abstraction than an abstraction.'[49] In *The Resurrection of Lazarus*, the diagonal of red hues draws the viewer's gaze downwards towards the figure of Martha supporting Lazarus's head in her lap from a starting point in Christ's pointing arm, for which the deepest red is reserved, and counterpoints the morbidly gold hue of Lazarus's naked flesh that crosses it, forming a second diagonal. This bright diagonal moves across the surface of a canvas that is otherwise peculiarly dark, rather than inscribing any sense of perspectival depth. This spatial peculiarity of Caravaggio's use of chiaroscuro, a technique that could equally well lend itself to producing the sense of a receding landscape or a hierarchy of significance in the figures, struck even his earliest critics. One of them, Giovanni Pietro Bellori, commented that Caravaggio

> never brought any of his figures out into the daylight, but found a way to paint them against the darkness of a closed room, taking a high lamp that hung vertically over the principal part of the body, and leaving the rest in shadow, so as to give force by the power of light and dark.[50]

The resultant diagonal 'cellar' light[51] that often appears to emanate from a high window outside the frame of the picture not only allows for the striking contrasts of highlight and shadow so characteristic of many of Caravaggio's paintings, like the *Lazarus* or the earlier *Calling of St. Matthew* (1599–1600). It also produces the no less powerful effect of thrusting the figures in the scene forward on to a horizontal plane parallel with the viewer and at the surface of the canvas. As Louis Marin put it:

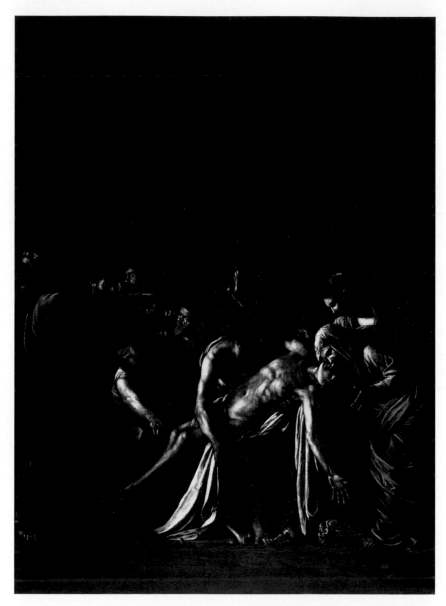

Fig. 3.16 Michelangelo Merisi da Caravaggio, *The Resurrection of Lazarus* (oil on canvas, 380×275 cm, c. 1608–9). Museo Nationale, Messina, Italy. Photo credit: Scala/Art Resource, New York.

A painting's black ground is much more than a 'background' or scenic space. The ground is, ultimately, the very surface of the painting. As a result, the projection of the beam of light onto the painting's plane leaves only the very edge of the surface for the arrangement of the figures and objects. Only the very first line of the painting remains: the figures are constantly pushed forward; the scene on which they stand is a kind of apron or *forestage*. It is as though we were looking at figures in bas-relief standing out from a solid wall, the wall of an arcanian tomb.[52]

In such paintings, chiaroscuro is that effect by which the figures 'stand forth', to use again Heidegger's apt phrase for the appearance of the thing as opposed to the representation of an object, and are then disposed across the surface of the canvas rather than receding into a perspectivally organised distance.

Caravaggio's flattening of space, which tended to reverse the *trompe l'oeil* effects of his earlier paintings, though these operated also on the frontal edge of the canvas, was almost immediately, and mostly negatively, viewed as depriving the painter of the means to narration.[53] His religious paintings present the paradox of a supposedly 'historical' or narrative painting that portrays an instant without the implied past and future actions it entails. Giulio Mancini, Caravaggio's contemporary and early biographer, commented like Bellori on the painter's 'use of a constant source of light that illuminates from above without reflections, just as this might occur in a room with only one window and with walls painted black'. But he went on to insist that this technique is entirely unsuitable for narrative painting, 'for it is impossible to arrange within a single room illuminated by only one window a large group of figures who enact the story'.[54] Caravaggio's supposed inability to tell a story is thus intimately linked to his deployment of spatial relations and especially to his refusal to subserve the illusion of both spatial and temporal depth for which punctiform perspective had come to supply the conventions.

Hence it was less on account of his choice of humble models and insistence on a kind of social realism that Caravaggio was so denigrated by subsequent painters and critics than it was for his refusal of a carefully articulated convention for the representation of the ideals of narrative painting. It is precisely this quality in Caravaggio that led Poussin to declare that he 'had come into the world to destroy painting'. What matters is not only that he painted from life, choosing vulgar subjects, or infusing sacred ones with vulgar personages, or depicting saints with dirty feet, but more crucially the two-fold objection that he lacked ideas and could not tell a story. According to Marin, 'we are told that Caravaggio never articulated an idea of his own, that he lacked the ideas needed to choose between options, and that he had no beautiful ideas.' Moreover:

> Caravaggio cannot tell a story; he only knows how to paint one or two isolated figures. When he tries to tell a story, he places these figures in the foreground so that it looks as though they have been shoved forward by the density of the neutral background, that black box having an absolute density.[55]

'Beautiful ideas' and 'narrative' or history are here intimately related, the 'idea' being that which is revealed in the harmonious disposition of the narrative. It is precisely this art-historical demand that leads Arikha, in turn, to oppose Caravaggio to Poussin. In his essay 'On Abstraction in Painting', Arikha sees Western painting as having been captured, at least since the Renaissance, by the related aims of *representing the ideal* rather than the actual, and of *moralising or instructing*:

> Art had to instruct and delight, and improve mankind through its moralizing power, by illustrating the loftiest and most heroic actions. It was believed that this sort of painting would perpetuate more vividly than the written word, the *immortal principle of a mortal creature* [Plato, *Timaeus*, 42e]. In other words, painting was to be judged essentially on *what* it represented and not so much on *how* it represented it.[56]

And 'what' is represented is an *action*, a narrative, through which the ideal was displayed both as example and as form. For Poussin, it was the capacity to represent 'the loftiest and most heroic actions' that makes the painter of history, *istoria*. Crucially, as Arikha points out, that capacity was inseparable from the artist's more or less geometrical capacity to create the 'visual pyramid' that Alberti thought lay at the heart of perspective and proportion in painting.[57] Alberti's 'visual pyramid', painstakingly elaborated in his work *On Painting*, enabled at once the presentation of spatial depth and the harmonisation of the various implicit temporal moments of the narrative through their distribution in several planes of the canvas. Arikha shows in almost equally painstaking detail how Poussin's *Rape of the Sabines* conforms in every element of its composition to this visual pyramid. On the other hand, this visual pyramid, says Arikha tersely, 'was not really Caravaggio's concern'.[58]

Caravaggio's capacity for observation thus coincides with his refusal of the perspectival effect of 'depth' that makes the ideal historical painting. What he achieves instead is the depiction of the moment of a happening itself. As Marin comments:

> It is now impossible to show a *differentiated but single action* unfolding in both its syntagmatic power and its diachronic potency. Instead, representation represents but a single moment. This instant is seized the way a snapshot instantaneously captures a flash of a second.[59]

The dramatic tension of such painting lies in its depiction of seeing as a kind of attentive seizure of a moment like that of the awakening of Lazarus – the instantaneous registering of an *istoria* before it has become an event. It is well known that Caravaggio frequently incorporated his own self-portrait as spectator into such paintings, turning back from the door in *The Martyrdom of St Matthew* (1599–1600) as if to take in the details of the saint's murder, or gazing over Judas's head at Christ's face in *The Betrayal of Christ* (1602–3). In *The Resurrection of Lazarus*, Caravaggio's self-portrait not only gazes towards Christ's pointing finger; it simultaneously seems to take part in a kind of self-conscious commentary on the spatial relations of the painting as a whole. The orientation of his gaze and the height of his head place him almost exactly midway between Christ's face and Lazarus's upraised right hand which, occupying the exact centre of the painting, faces Christ's finger in a gesture that is ambiguously one of refusal or salute. The placement of the hand with its palm facing Christ also orients it in line with what would be the perspectival vanishing point of the painting were it not that Caravaggio's spatial logic flattens the action so dramatically forward on to the surface of the painting.[60] This hand that does not point substitutes, then, for the axis of depth in the painting, signalling its absence at the very heart of the work, while at the same time emphasising the horizontality of the line of vision that runs through Caravaggio's gaze towards that of Christ which meets it along the foreground of the painting.

What results is a tableau, in a sense very close to that of Bertolt Brecht: a stilling or, to invoke the inevitable pun, a friezing of the action. Genevieve Warwick points out that 'tableaux formed part of Caravaggio's visual inheritance':

> His paintings resist the word/image parallel of academic *ut pictura poesis*, as Poussin recognized. Instead of historical narrative it is tableau. It was this that critics like Mancini faulted in their judgment that Caravaggio's paintings were not fully narratives but stilled scenes.[61]

And, as in Brecht, what emerges from that tableau is a highly ambiguous set of relations of looking that manage to create what Leo Bersani and Ulysse Dutoit have called 'a profound uncertainty about relational priorities', both socially and aesthetically.[62] We can see here precisely why the scandal of Caravaggio's vulgar subjects or models is inseparable from that of his formal tendencies as a painter. The refusal of the ideal and of the *istoria* that conveys it is one with the refusal of the perspectival system that dominated Western art from the Renaissance down to Cézanne and the grid or 'chequerboard' that came to organise twentieth-century pictorial space. The dominant code of spatial organisation is one of a handful of what Arikha terms 'key forms' in painting that determine the devolution of innovation into mannerism, and Caravaggio's spatial and temporal challenges to convention were at one in effecting the rupture that he initiated in early seventeenth-century painting. That he remained for so long on the sidelines or in obscurity in the history of European art may be due to the fact that he challenged not just the stylistic mannerism of his moment, but the key forms of a longer epoch in that history. It was not only painting that Caravaggio came to destroy, but the inaugural representative codes of what Heidegger called the 'world picture' of modernity. In destroying the dominant mode of 'representing-producing' of his epoch, he questioned the procedure by which the thing perceived became a historical object for the subject, captured in the perspectival grid that, more or less at that same moment, secured the place of the sovereign subject.[63]

Caravaggio's impact on Arikha would appear to have exerted itself through a no less complex set of effects and on corresponding dimensions of his work, not merely on what Arikha calls the 'what' of painting, but equally on its formal and ethical aspects.

Determinant as the decision to return to depiction may have been, and crucial as Caravaggio's choice of 'vulgar' subjects may have been to Arikha's interest in everyday objects, in 'ordinary, even unnoticed things',[64] his influence – or the two artists' visual affinities – can be read in both the spatial or organisational and what we might call the temporal dimensions of Arikha's work. These are inseparable from his consistent refusal of both narrative and image, or representation. It is clear, to commence with, that Arikha intensely shares Caravaggio's interest in moments that suggest the 'about to happen' or the 'just happened', in what Marin, speaking of Caravaggio's infamous self-portrait as a Medusa's head, terms the moments 'just before and after' the event.[65] Even his apparently quietest paintings can be saturated with an implied drama: again and again, Arikha's glance falls obliquely on those overlooked points where something might be about to happen, on points of passage, aperture or entry beyond which or through which an event might arrive. The resultant paintings are imbued with a kind of waiting, an utterly secular advent that may be the correlative of Arikha's often-remarked sense that the moment of painting itself arrives unexpectedly, 'like a call': it summons the immediate response of the artist that determines the 'high velocity' of his brush or stylus, even as Caravaggio's dependence on the actual presence of models in the studio required his own rapid handling and speedy brushwork.

It is appropriate, then, that what Arikha claimed to be the first painting that he undertook after his long dedication to graphic work was *The Corridor* (1973; Fig. 3.17), a subject whose 'call' was apparently so urgent that he flew back from a commission in Freiburg simply in order to paint it.[66] This relatively large canvas (it is over a metre in height) depicts the view along a short, almost empty corridor at the end of which a door stands ajar, the light that filters through it forming a kind of inner frame at the end of the corridor. Everything in the painting seems conducive to speed of execution: the reduction of the palette to three, maybe four colours, and the rapid brushwork that textures the bold fields across which those colours are applied – the three walls and ceiling as well as the open door forming almost monochromatic panels that lead the eye rightwards in a rhythm of dark turning to light, punctuated by the bright L-shape where the light filters through, and by the vertical crack of light at the door frame. At the same time, the painting, with its austere refusal of any event or figure

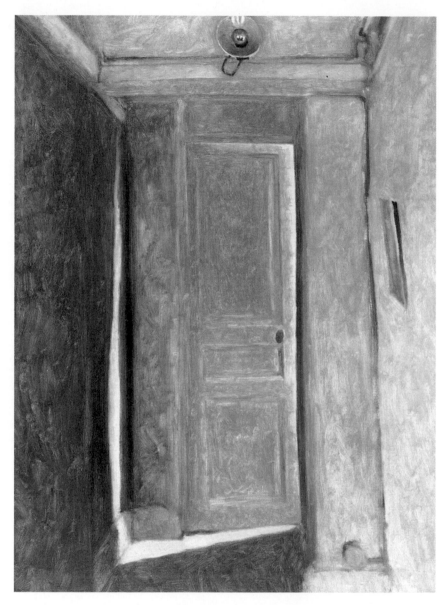

Fig. 3.17 Avigdor Arikha, *The Corridor* (oil on canvas, 116 × 89 cm, 1973), © Artists Rights Society (ARS), New York/DACS, London, 2016.

that would supply an extraneous source of interest, communicates a profound stillness, a rest in the midst of things, 'the space of a door / that opens and shuts', as Beckett had put it in one of his poems.[67] This corridor that leads to a door ajar is the scene of an instant 'just before and after', where something may have happened or be about to happen – it is, literally, a passage between times.

The Corridor establishes a visual motif that was particularly prominent in Arikha's work in the decade following his recommencement of painting. A striking number of his paintings offer glimpses of or through a partly open door, suggesting but not revealing what might be passing beyond that door, whether what happens is happening elsewhere or has happened before or after the moment of the painting. These paintings seem like responses to Beckett's imagined subjects for paintings in his review of MacGreevy's essay on Yeats, 'The being in the street, when it happens in the room, the being in the room when it happens in the street', but they are far from images in the negative sense that Arikha gives to a term that was at one point so significant to Beckett.[68] Rather, as with the still lifes, paintings like *Open Door into the Visitor's Studio* (1976; Fig. 3.18) and *Glimpse into the Garden* (1979; Fig. 3.19) are profoundly painterly works that maintain an extraordinary equilibrium between the scene depicted and their technical means, between meticulous visual observation and bold, saturated fields of colour. Precisely their attention to the generally overlooked point of view, the downward gaze at the floor of the former, or the centring of a corner by the door rather than the doorway or even the wall in the latter, demands that we engage with the visual field by accommodating those elements that we normally dismiss as lacking interest. At the same time, Arikha's gaze at what seems empty, void of activity, permits abstraction and depiction to subsist together in the kind of vital oscillation that characterises his work. The flat black of the floor or carpet in *Open Door*, which occupies almost the whole bottom third of the painting, counterpoints the modulating shades of white that form the wooden panels of the doorway and the pinkish-grey wall and doorway glimpsed in the shadows beyond it. The painting is thus a study in chiaroscuro, but one with a construction that is the reverse of that which Marin notes in Caravaggio. Here, the deep black, far from forming the background, is pushed forward into the viewer's plane of vision and the downward glance it

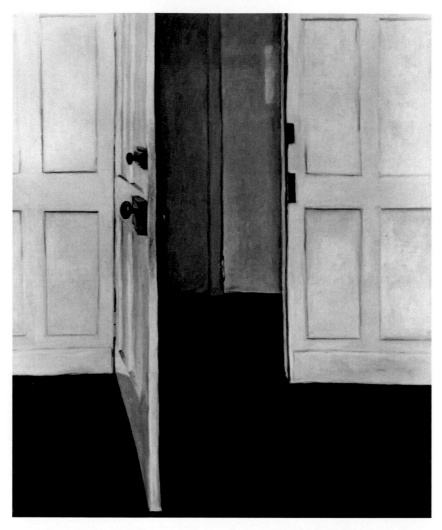

Fig. 3.18 Avigdor Arikha, *Open Door into the Visitor's Studio* (oil on canvas, 183×152 cm, 1976). Milwaukee Art Museum. Gift of Jane Bradley Pettit M1980.197. Photo credit: P. Richard Eells. © the Artist/ Artists Rights Society (ARS), New York/DACS, London, 2016.

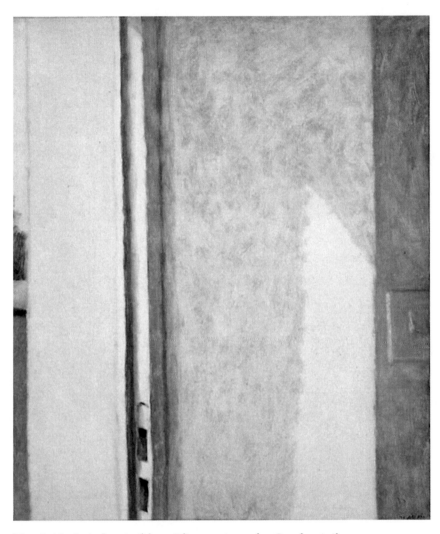

Fig. 3.19 Avigdor Arikha, *Glimpse into the Garden* (oil on canvas, 65 × 54 cm, 1979), © Artists Rights Society (ARS), New York/DACS, London, 2016.

obliges foreshortens the perspective such that a paradoxical play of horizontals and verticals results. The short arm of the inverted black T functions at once as a horizontal bar leading to the flattened interior and as a vertical thrust of black into the otherwise white and grey upper region of the canvas. At the same time, the foreshortened vertical of the open door, which reaches out so as to intersect directly with the viewer's line of sight, implies a perspectival depth that the painting refuses to deliver. The door, angled out from the painting, operates, indeed, much as Lazarus's hand does in Caravaggio: it focuses the play between the two-dimensional surface of the painting and the appearance of depth, and does so while the whole canvas is projected forward to the very surface of the pictorial space. It is, of course, an aspect of Arikha's virtuosity that, even while engaging in such formal playfulness, the very precisely depicted black door handles and plates become colorific and formal echoes across the white spaces of the canvas that prevent it from falling into two simply contrasting visual halves.

Glimpse into the Garden is even more startlingly foreshortened, offering a view that is almost myopically pressed against the wall and doorway. Perspective is at first hard to capture in this painting, given that the line of sight leads not to the visual centre of the work but dramatically across to the left, where the most remote depth of the picture, the green lawn and pinkish wall that are all that can be glimpsed of the garden, forms a single, narrow vertical stripe that leads at once upwards into the pale blue strip of sky and outwards along the grass. At the same time, the angle of the wall that protrudes furthest into the viewer's space occupies nearly the far right of the canvas, demarcating the borderline of shadow and light and opening a large stretch of white to pink vertical bands of colour that are almost entirely devoid of visual 'information' except for the meticulously depicted slots in the door frame. The painting may allude glancingly to Matisse's *The Piano Lesson*, given the column of green that suggests an ambiguously horizontal counterpoint to the rhythmic disposition of the vertical columns that here, as in Matisse's canvas, march across the flattened surface of the picture. And yet such an allusion to Matisse, and to the whole tradition of rethinking pictorial space that he represents, is held in an almost witty equilibrium with the commitment to an exact and even pedantically sober depiction of the actual.

These paintings, indeed, suggest a certain ethical commitment that permeates Arikha's approach to painting and, indeed, to the visual field in general. Consistently, his work is marked by a singular degree of attention (and, indeed, this is as much a characteristic of his precise and illuminating critical reflections as it is of his painting and other graphic work). His attention, moreover, tends to be directed over and over again to spaces that are 'in between', occulted not so much by being hidden as by being overlooked in our habitual attention to the spectacular or to the eventful, even to the extent that, as we have seen, he directs his gaze to places that might even be considered 'blank'. More than once he has given his attention to the corner of a room or to the space between a window and a mirror, rather than to either of those visually saturated objects; by the same token, his eye will fall on a discarded object, or, perhaps more pertinently, some object that is at that moment in disuse, an old umbrella or a pair of gloves.[69] In so far as Arikha's commitment is to bring the viewer to see the world anew – even as learning to draw was for him learning to see again – the continuity of his work with the formalist project of 'estrangement' may seem paramount. It is the purpose of his work not to symbolise or even to express, but to renovate our capacity to see in ways that, as his remarks regarding the ways in which abstraction had become mannerism suggest, the practice of painting in its increasing self-referentiality had abandoned. Such formalist commitment to making the familiar strange is congruent with another such dimension of his work: its continual and even dramatic posing of an almost abstract formal equilibrium in tension with a meticulous accuracy in depiction. In this respect, for all Arikha's engagement with actual objects depicted in uninterrupted and unrevised sessions, there is nothing either naturalist or naturalising about his work. It is absolutely not photographic or even realist, always drawing attention with one eye, so to speak, to the formalising necessity of painting and to the materials which are its means – brushstrokes, textures of ink and paper or oil and canvas, flat and abraded surfaces – while with the other seeking to seize the visible as it appears.

Such an acute and always doubled apprehension of the world demands a quality of attentiveness that Walter Benjamin once described in a compelling locution as 'the natural prayer of the soul'.[70] Both in terms of the constraints it imposes on medium and materials and in terms of a certain austerity of visual style that refuses either colorific elaboration or photorealist gloss, Arikha's attentiveness is at one with his deliberate aesthetic simplicity. His technical means are deliberately pared down, whether in the initial self-limitation to ink and paper or in the restricted palette that rarely deploys more than four or five colours, and his imagination is disciplined by its commitment solely to the actually visible. If what results might be called a 'poor painting', it would be so not by analogy with the contemporaneous *Arte Povera* movement, with its emphasis on found and everyday materials, but rather with Jerzy Grotowski's concept of poor theatre, a theatre reduced in its means precisely in order to uncover the essence of the theatrical rather than competing with the technical and material means of film.[71] As Arikha commented on the 'emancipation' of painting by its return to its own essential means and aims:

> Much of the need to hold the visible, such as of historic or tragic events, once satisfied by painting, is now satisfied by photography. The need for the heroic image, as a 'signifier of the signified', is now satisfied by film. In this respect painting gained a lot from the advent of photography. One can at last be moved by a painting without 'reading' it. At last the painting is separated from the image, the 'what' does not determine the 'how'. Painting has lost one part of its public, but has gained its autonomy.[72]

This gained or regained autonomy of painting lies in the conviction that, freed from its role as a medium of representations, painting opens again to the act of *seeing*. Hence the centrality to Arikha's remarks on painting of the distinction he draws between Poussin's moral aims, achieved through historical painting, and Caravaggio's emphasis on observation. Even more than Caravaggio, whose work was still largely commissioned for ecclesiastical purposes, Arikha's work refuses any symbolic or allegorical function, a function that for a secular artist is defined by what he terms the 'image', something which points beyond itself to a designated meaning. The image, as Arikha put it, is 'about information. It designates more than it contains. It's a reminder of something it does not contain.'[73] Rather than being a sign or image, representing things in the world beyond it, the painting is itself a thing in the world, a 'mark', as Beckett puts it. Where an image conveys information, a mark is the trace of a thing that has happened, at once the happening and its effect, and therefore a thing that happens in its own right. Both the production of the painting and its reception or viewing depend on a complete immersion in the moment of seeing itself: painting, accordingly, is a thing that happens, and no longer the record of a happening, an *istoria*. In that respect, it most surely comes to destroy representation.

III

Arikha's remarks on his painting's refusal of any representative function powerfully resonate with Beckett's often-cited dismissals of symbolic interpretations of his own work – 'no symbols where none intended', as the addenda to *Watt* conclude with character-istic ambiguity.[74] Beckett's warding off of symbolic interpreta-tions of his work, which every reader or director of his plays who inquired unfailingly met, is, like Arikha's refusal of the image, equally a refusal of *reading*, a reluctance to allow the attention to turn from the work itself to extraneous sources of authority or explanation. The degree of convergence between what we might term their 'aesthetic ethics' is perhaps marked most clearly in the increasing painterliness of Beckett's theatre as it evolved and as his experiments with the possibilities of drama became ever more radical. Where, for Arikha, the particular emancipation of paint-ing that allowed him to return from abstraction to depiction, from mannerism to seeing, was the abandonment of *istoria* and its allegorical or symbolic functions, for Beckett, the equivalent emancipation of his theatre was, as we have seen, bound up with his gradual departure from those constituents of drama that con-tinued to shape his work of the 1950s, the remains of narrative, symbol and the dramatic image. In both artists, we are thus con-fronted with the paradox of a painting and a highly visual theatre that are radically opposed to the work of representation as it has been articulated in the history of modern aesthetic practice.

Crucial in the development of the painterliness of Beckett's drama may have been his own emphasis as a director on reworking these earlier plays around a rhythmic series of tableaus, a practice that seems to have been related to his desire to draw out of them effects that were musical rather than narrative or symbolic, precisely in order to undercut the audience's uneasy reaching after meaning.[75] Theatrically, however, musicality is realised through visual effects: the notion of a musical effect or structure necessarily finds its reali-sation through visual patterns of repetition or through the periodic suspension of the action in the tableau, which, like a cinematic still, highlights the synchronic relations of disposition or gesture of characters and properties on the set. It is striking, indeed, to what an extent Beckett's later theatrical works can be arrested at almost any point and appear as if they were paintings. The word 'still', which nicely condenses the contradictory senses of what continues or goes on with that which is arrested or silent (as in the late work *Stirrings Still*), resonates in Beckett's vocabulary. Visually, it is deeply connected to the fundamental paradox of painting itself, which seeks to represent living and moving beings on the two dimensions of an unmoving canvas, a paradox which finds expression in the *still life* or *nature morte*.[76] It is in his approach to theatre as a visual art, as a kind of painting, that Beckett most successfully resolves this paradox, coming to 'write painting', as one of his favourite actors and collaborators, Billie Whitelaw, put it.[77] But if Beckett thus resolves one element of the paradox, by producing the visual representation that moves in time, the theatrical still or tableau has the power to foreground that element of the paradox which is not merely formal, but addresses the radical connection between still life and dead nature, between the human and the thing.

We can grasp how such a concern binds the work of Arikha and Beckett at a profound level by passing to Beckett's theatre by way of one more painting of Arikha's, his remarkable *Anne Leaning on Table* (1977; Fig. 3.20). The powerful initial impact of this painting probably comes from the astonishing effect of the huge expanse of creased linen that virtually marginalises the painter's wife's black head of curls. Yet those dark locks in turn anchor what would otherwise be a study on whites, playing on the contrast between the off-white tablecloth, with its grey folds and shadows, and the cooler tones of the nightgown with its purplish grey shadings, but the overall effect of the painting, whose dispassion seems emphasised by its rapid, sure brushwork and thin and fluid impasto, is to render the human figure a mere element in the composition, absorbed, if not overwhelmed, by the visual prominence of the things that abut and support it. To Arikha's refusal of *istoria* and of symbol or image, to his emphasis on the things that lie at the margins of perception, corresponds something that may be yet more uncanny in its effect – this radical displacement of the human in relation to the frame. There is, indeed, something inhuman about this painting, in the relation it proposes between the human figure and the things of the world, but at the same

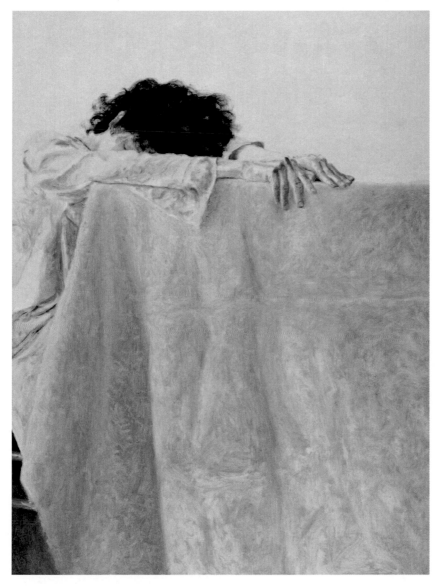

Fig. 3.20 Avigdor Arikha, *Anne Leaning on Table* (oil on canvas, 130×97 cm, 1977), © Artists Rights Society (ARS), New York/DACS, London, 2016. Digital Image © 2016 Museum Associates/LACMA, licensed by Art Resource, New York.

time nothing inhumane: rather, it seizes with almost appalling dispassion the vulnerable thingliness of the human. This is communicated not least in those hands, at first overlooked, whose precisely drawn inertness seems at once to grasp the tablecloth and, formally speaking, to make the colour-bridge between the white nightshirt and the off-white linen, sharing the pigment tones of the latter (see Fig. 3.21: *Anne Leaning on Table* [detail]). They rest, expressing in a manner the hidden face cannot, a peculiar combination of stubborn thingliness and human passivity, on the very edge of the invisible tabletop, on the horizon of this strongly foreshortened visual space.

These hands and head resting on a table resonate forcibly with the same gesture as it appears over and over again in Beckett's theatre and prose. In *Stirrings Still*:

> There had been a time he would sometimes lift his head enough to see his hands. What of them was to be seen. One laid on the table and the other on the one. At rest after all they did. Lift his past head a moment to see past his hands. Then lay it back on them to rest it too. After all it did.[78]

But no less in the description of Listener and Reader in *Ohio Impromptu*, 'Bowed head propped on right hand. Face hidden. Left hand on table', or the similar posture of the sleeper in *Nacht und Träume*. But perhaps the most striking resemblance would be to the final fadeout of *Krapp's Last Tape* in that 1972 BBC production with Patrick Magee, directed by Donald McWhinnie. This was a peculiarly painterly production of the play whose visual effects were emphasised in its adaptation for television. In keeping with stipulations that Beckett clearly articulated to American director Alan Schneider, after working with McWhinnie in 1959, the colours of both costume and set were reduced to a starkly contrasting black and white motif, against which the few brightly coloured things, such as the bananas Krapp consumes or the red and gold tobacco tins in which he stores his spools, stand out in dramatic relief, highlighting the darkness that surrounds them.[79] Beckett's directions emphasise this light-dark contrast in ways that recall Caravaggio's 'cellar light'. His stage direction positions the *'Table and immediately adjacent area in strong white light. Rest of stage in darkness'*, an instruction that – as we might expect – not only produces a strong chiaroscuro effect, but also reinforces the

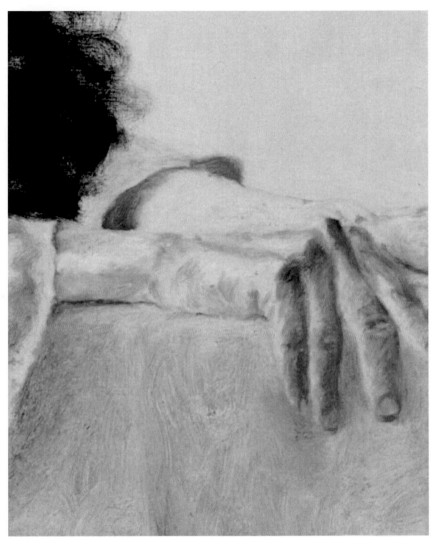

Fig. 3.21 Arikha, *Anne Leaning on Table* (detail).

high degree of foregrounding of the action of the play.[80] On stage, the table is positioned 'front centre', with the only light source hanging directly above it, so that the action is performed almost entirely on a relatively thin strip of the actual stage space, pushed forward, as it were, by the darkness massed behind it. In the TV production, the single lamp above the table is counterpointed by a distant light source from the kitchen doorway which appears at the end of a virtual corridor of dim light into which Krapp recedes with rhythmic regularity to drink or gather his equipment. That rhythm of disappearance rhymes gesturally with the *fort-da* motifs of Krapp's reminiscences (the black ball, the swaying boat and so forth) and amplifies the gathering stillness that takes over as the action slows and Krapp subsides at his table. The powerful chiaroscuro of the set, establishing the implied depth against which the instant of the present stands forth in every sense, spatial and visual, thrusts forward the final still that the long fade of the end effects. It becomes graphically evident that the power of the play resides in the balance between its utter formal and visual beauty and Magee's startlingly ugly, sweating, snarling Krapp as that dynamic tension reaches a point of suspension in the conclusion. A peculiarly unsentimental pathos unexpectedly precipitates in this TV production, as the slow close-up focuses in gradually to an extended virtual still of Krapp's head displaced by the still-turning spool of the tape recorder, the scene's only moving thing, and his hand curved gently, helplessly, around the body of the machine. This final still resumes a motif that has been insistent throughout this production: the repeated alignment of Krapp's listening head with the tape recorder in such a way that it is the latter that dominates, displacing his anxious, desiring, mourning human form to the very margin of the screen. Just as the formal exactness of the play counterpoints his raging self, so the technical means he uses to contain his memories takes on an autonomous life in relation to which Krapp seems to fade and slip away, a thing among the things of his world.

It is hard to establish how far Beckett's knowledge of Caravaggio influenced the set and lighting of *Krapp's Last Tape*, however 'Caravaggiesque' in a quite precise sense its effects are. Even James Knowlson, the biographer who is always most authoritative regarding Beckett's knowledge of painting, records no definitive viewing by Beckett of any painting by Caravaggio before his trip to Malta in November 1971, where he saw *The Beheading of St John the Baptist* (1607–8). As Anne Atik also records, this painting had a profound influence on his setting of *Not I*, the play in which he explores to the furthest extent the possibilities of extreme chiaroscuro effects on the stage.[81] It is difficult to imagine that he did not attend the Louvre show which so excited Arikha, or that he would never have seen the *Doubting Thomas* in Potsdam during his German itinerary, or the *Death of the Virgin* in the Louvre, however difficult of access other major paintings of Caravaggio's may have been. Satisfying as it might be to document specific instances of any painter's influence on the visual aesthetics of Beckett's drama, even the few documented instances of the direct impact of a specific work – as in the case of *Godot* and Caspar David Friedrich's *Two Men Contemplating the Moon* – offer little that helps us comprehend how the dramas might work on stage as visual work. Indeed, the painting of artists in whose work Beckett had a long-standing interest, as with Caravaggio or Arikha, teaches us less about particular pictures than about how the visual resources of the stage – depth and foreground, lighting and darkness, movement and stillness, colour and gesture – compose the larger effect of the play, as theatre and not as a translation of an image. In *Krapp's Last Tape* we can see very clearly the potential of a darkened stage to thrust the action forward, almost into the space of the audience, or to focus attention on the relation among the different human and material elements of the play. The effect resembles those that Marin describes in his analysis of Caravaggio's 'black box' or arcanum or that we observe in Arikha's foreshortened perspectives and in his play with the disposition of objects on the surface of the canvas: they succeed in freezing the action into moments of significant tableau.

Krapp's Last Tape, written in the late 1950s, remains a play dominated by a dramatic narrative, even if it is reduced to the relation of a single figure to a past self. Beckett's plays in the following decades become increasingly invested in the question of visibility itself, of what it is to be present or to appear, almost as if what fascinated him was not what Krapp could relate or recall, but his movement as a figure across the space of the stage, his comings and goings.[82] This deepening of the visual emphasis in the composition of the late plays corresponds to the emphasis Beckett placed on the visual aspects of his works in his increasingly active practice as a director.[83] Between the first stage performance of *Krapp* and its subsequent TV productions falls the 'dramaticule' *Come and Go*,

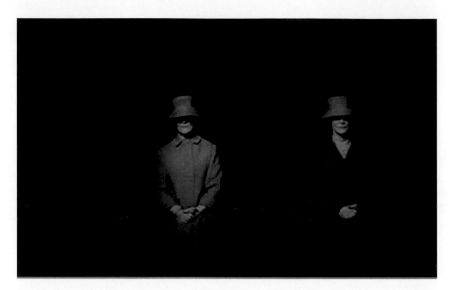

Fig. 3.22 Paola Dionisotti, Anna Massey and Sian Phillips in *Come and Go*, directed by John Crowley, 2000.

a work in which Beckett achieves some of the most painterly stage effects in his oeuvre, reducing narrative and back-story to an absolute minimum. On a low and nondescript bench, foregrounded at the very front of the stage and faintly illuminated from above against a pitch-black stage, sit three women, each dressed in a differently coloured coat and hat that almost entirely cover their bodies. Turn by turn, each rises and heads slowly towards the back of the stage on one or other side of the bench, disappearing into the dark (see Fig. 3.22). As each one disappears, one of the other women slides along the bench to whisper a scarcely audible remark in the third woman's ear about some apparently catastrophic event or change that has overcome the one who has disappeared. We can only judge from the brief, shocked response of the auditor the depth of the catastrophe. Even the victim, it seems, is in each case unaware of what has happened. Slowly returning from the darkness, the absent woman now returns, taking her place beside the one who has moved to the centre, whose turn it now is to depart. This recurs three times with minor variations in the words spoken. At the end of this ten-minute play, the women sit together, holding hands 'in the old way', criss-crossing one another and feeling for rings on their fingers that are clearly not to be seen.

In terms of gesture and movement, the play or 'dramaticule' is breathtakingly simple, based on a very simple algorithmic choreography and a repeated 'coming and going'. Verbally, it is of exceptional simplicity: by producing the ghost of a narrative (and, of course, these women may indeed be ghosts), it offers the audience a kind of essence of drama, a tantalising situation that provokes both pity and fear without the desire for resolution or explanation ever being fulfilled.[84] Even the brief allusions – to Eliot's women who come and go in *The Lovesong of J. Alfred Prufrock* and, perhaps, to the witches of *Macbeth* – are so attenuated as to dissolve almost as soon as they are noted. And yet the play retains a peculiarly powerful impact, its brevity and slowness leaving a sense of aesthetic suspension that has virtually no equal even in Beckett's oeuvre. To a great extent, its impact must derive from his extraordinary sense of colour relations in space: as each woman, dressed in her distinct colour, disappears into the dark, she disappears, so to speak, in a different tone. Each colour fades differently into darkness, at a different pace and leaving a different after-image to hang briefly upstage before the other women move. Beckett will, of course, exploit this phenomenon again, in the wordless dance-play for television *Quad*, in which four dancers in differently coloured robes rhythmically criss-cross a dark square, appearing from and disappearing into the deep black of the surround. But whether his acute sense of how colour works onstage came from his direct observation as a director of actors coming and going in darkened theatres or from his life-long attention to painting would be impossible to determine. Certainly, Atik refers to several of his conversations with Arikha about colour, and we know by now just how attentively he observed the work and effect of paintings.[85] As we have seen, Arikha's own work depends to a great extent on his refined sense of how colour and tone work in combination, often in ways strikingly akin to the colorific effect of *Come and Go*. What is most striking, however, given the powerful theatrical images that Beckett's earlier plays presented, is the shift in his visual vocabulary. *Come and Go* reduces not only word and gesture but also set to a minimum – even the bench, as the stage directions emphasise, is to be as unremarked as possible, unlike Estragon's stone or mound, which retained a symbolic function. Already, in his directorial work, Beckett had come to emphasise the tableaus implicit in the action of *Godot* or *Endgame*, introducing *Wartestelle* or resting points in order to signal their importance. In *Come and Go*, the principal visual mode of the play is the tableau against which the stylised movements of the women are thrown into relief.[86] Here, everything turns around darkness and colour set in motion in such a way that their modulating juxtapositions dramatise precisely what it is to 'stand forth': precisely the relations of figure and colour to dark ground that Caravaggio exploited in order to thrust forward the action of *The Resurrection of Lazarus*, or that juxtaposition of tone and hue Arikha achieves in his boldly saturated colour fields, Beckett achieves in having his women actually move up- and downstage as coloured figures enacting the spectral appearance of the phenomenon over and over again.[87] It is as if the stilled and frieze-like action in one of Caravaggio's later paintings were suddenly counterpointed by a movement deep into the darkness on whose surface it is painted, translating the vibrancy it lends to the brilliant reds and golds of the *Lazarus* out of stasis into time.

Krapp (1959), *Come and Go* (1965) and *Not I* (1972) form a continuum of plays that radically and unprecedentedly exploit the possibilities of darkness in the theatre rather than assuming that the visible space of the stage is to be maximised and filled with action and gesture. Through each, the lighted area is reduced steadily to a minimum, whether – as in the case of *Not I*'s Mouth – it seems to loom out of the depths of the darkness, or whether – as in *Krapp* and *Come and Go* – Beckett establishes a kind of dialectic of surface and depth by having his characters appear and disappear 'vertically' upstage while the action unfolds along the front of the stage in a dimly illuminated strip. *Footfalls* (1975) is a play which seems to belong to this continuum but more starkly divides the lit frieze from the darkness that surrounds it. It is, to be sure, another play that dramatises appearance and disappearance and turns on insistently repeated words and movements. May, a prematurely aging woman of around forty, paces back and forth, exactly nine steps in each direction, along a narrow band of light downstage. Her pacing along this strip, which she leaves only to fade into the darkness at the end of each section or movement of the play, places her in a kind of reverse 'cellar light': the stage direction insists that the lighting be '*dim, strongest at floor level, less on body, least on head*'. Behind it, all is dark, except – in the film version – for a crack of light that marks the slightly open door of a room.[88] There, it seems, May's mother, never visible to the audience and designated in the stage directions only as 'Woman's

Voice', lies in her sickbed and either responds to May's half-hearted proposals to nurse her or narrates her own version of the events that seem to have led to this enigmatic situation. It seems that May has been pacing in this way since childhood, though the traumatic event that initiated her withdrawal into this narrow space remains unnamed. Whatever 'it' was that May gestures towards recounting in the fragment of novelistic narrative about a girl called 'Amy' that she takes up in the second movement, it remains 'unworked through': she 'never stops revolving it all', as the Voice claims in the third movement.

The burden of the play is, however, hardly May's attenuated quasi-Gothic narrative, as cliché-ridden and outmoded as the adulterous tale babbled in *Play*. Indeed, May's tale, a decayed remnant of nineteenth-century fictional conventions, is as much a ghost of a genre as May and the mother are themselves ghosts of characters, almost as much 'not there' as the girl Amy claims to be.[89] If it is about anything, *Footfalls* – as its title suggests – is about the repetitive pacing of her 'revolving it all', May's steps falling distinctly on the wooden boards as a percussive counterpoint to her voice, with its own patterns of repetition. In this respect, it is among the most purely musical of Beckett's plays, utterly dependent on a precise and exacting rhythmic performance. For all that, it is no less strikingly visual, suggesting a world reduced to this faint horizontal

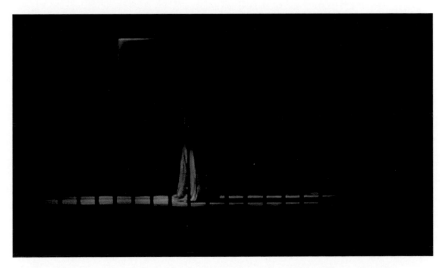

Fig. 3.23 Susan Fitzgerald as May in *Footfalls*, directed by Walter Asmus, 2000.

strip of light at the very edge of darkness into which, between movements, May disappears. Its bold counterpointing of the light and the darkness out of which, in the strongest sense, May's figure comes and goes resonates powerfully with the play of intense black and white spaces through which, in Arikha's drawings of the 1970s, figures emerge and ephemerally, fragilely, breathe. For both Arikha and Beckett, the reduction or refusal of *istoria*, of a narrative investment in signification, coincides with a profound attention to the moment of appearance itself, in which the thing – human or nonhuman – stands forth. In play as in painting or drawing, no referent beyond the moment of attentive apperception can be invoked, any appeal beyond that moment to an extraneous context being a refusal of the utter immersion both artists demand as the ethical condition for the reception of their work.

We are aware that a highly concentrated and ideally unbroken act of concentrated engagement with the visible was the constraint that Arikha imposed on himself as the means to a renewal of seeing, a constraint that, as Peggy Phelan astutely observes, makes the act of painting as depiction as performative as 'action painting' itself.[90] For Beckett, an analogous formal constraint structures the relation both of the artist to his dramatic materials and of the audience to the play as it unfolds in the theatre. Almost from the start, as we have seen, Beckett cleaves with rigorous fidelity to the Aristotelian unities, from *Godot* onwards obeying them with scarcely a deviation. Almost without exception his plays never involve more than a single line of action in a single space. More importantly, the plays invariably unfold in exactly the time taken to watch them: they dissolve any distinction between the time of watching and the time of action, thus ensuring the immersion of the spectator in the instant of the drama itself, increasingly unsupported and undistracted by any ulterior knowledge or by any appeal to allegorical or symbolic meaning. As Ulrika Maude has put it, Beckett incorporates the 'viewer's process of viewing into the drama'.[91] The degree of immersion in the work as an event in itself that both artists demand of themselves and of their viewers makes it tempting to refer to both Arikha's painting and Beckett's drama as 'happenings', were it not for the connotations that have accreted to that word in consequence of its use in the performance art of the 1960s.[92] In a very different sense, theatre for Beckett is the space in which what takes place is the happening of the moment as a thing in and of itself. The more he reduces their narrative dimensions, the more, indeed, that he reduces the stage space in which narrative might unfold as gesture and interaction, the more the plays produce moments of suspension, suspension of breath, perhaps, which calls forth attention precisely by refusing any 'outside', spatial, temporal or allegorical, to the moment of the performance. In light of such work, 'Art is nothing', as Arikha has put it. 'It is a breath, it passes through the breath and stays in the breath.'[93]

For both artists, this moment of breath, or of suspension of breath, corresponds to the call for sheer attentiveness to what Beckett terms in 'For Avigdor Arikha' the 'unself'. We may recall that Beckett deliberately revised the English text of his tribute to the artist in order to replace the term 'not-self' that first came to hand, a term that would have retained the sense of an object or material still available for appropriation by the subject. 'Unself', on the contrary, implies that which is alien or strange precisely by virtue of our incapacity to reappropriate it as a material in which our image is given back to us. if only for a space, the appropriativeness that constitutes selfhood and possession in the self-same moment as it constitutes objects and properties is foreclosed. And should we not continue to ask, then, what is this space that each in his own way shapes, this space of a 'truce' where the feverish work of the gaze is suspended, having made its provisional mark? And what is it that appears there in the very *suspension*, the erasure, of the need for the idea, for history, for the object?

Suspension is the condition of attentiveness in Walter Benjamin's sense. It is an attentiveness that makes of seeing itself a sense more akin to listening than to the capture of the object by the sovereign eye: if Arikha's paintings come in response to a call, it is equally true that in face of them we take the attitude of the listener, paradoxical as that may sound. The same holds true of the visual appearance of Beckett's late plays which demand not only that we listen to what remains of speech or dialogue, but also that we apprehend their visual quality as dispersed, suspended in the frieze that is painted across the arcanum or black box of the stage. As Jean-Luc Nancy puts it, the sonorous is opposed to the '*theoretical* sense' of sight:

> In terms of the gaze, the subject is referred back to itself as object. In terms of listening, it is, in a way, to itself that the subject refers or refers back. . . . Or, in semi-Lacanian terms, the visual is on the side of

an imaginary capture (which does not imply that it is reduced to that), while the sonorous is on the side of a symbolic referral/*renvoi* (which does not imply that it exhausts its amplitude).[94]

The sonorous, Nancy goes on, has to do with 'participation, sharing, or contagion', rather than with the mimetic tendency of vision. To *listen in* to the visual is to become attuned to that quality of dispersal that demands our 'referral' through the diverse elements, the things that constitute its appearance, rather than to seek a point from which to 'capture' the image. That is, in turn, to be displaced by the gaze, not secured in the sovereign centre as the 'prince of rays'.

Art, according to Emmanuel Levinas, 'lends things a face'.[95] If so, it does so precisely in order to endow those things, like the 'figures' or vestigial faces that circulate through Bram van Velde's canvases, with the power of the Other, the power which, in looking back, undoes the sovereignty of the subject. For Levinas, that sovereign I 'is put in question before the face of the other, in the ethical vigilance in which the sovereignty of the *I* recognizes itself as "hateful," and its place in the sun "the prototype and beginning of the usurpation of the whole earth"'. What challenges the subject 'in the face of the other' is not so much the 'plastic forms of [its] representation' but the surplus 'that cannot be represented'.[96] In lending a face to things, then, art does not humanise them, but takes the excess of the thing over representation into itself. The sense of the uncanny that we may feel in the face of Arikha's paintings, of Beckett's late plays, is what it is to *be in face of*: not to seek the figure of the human, not, indeed, figuration at all, or the possessive relation it grounds, but to be scored by the marks of the thing itself as it 'stands forth', *la chose même*, as Beckett elsewhere puts it. The stakes of these artists' work become those of the question of what it is to live beyond the guarantees of history, of the concept, of the subsumption of every particular into universal equivalence, as symbol or sign. That means passing beyond the claims of the human into that uncanny space where the human takes its place again as a thing among other things and art summons that suspension of the breath in which attentiveness comes to: 'Dull with breath. Endless breath. Endless ending breath. Dread darling sight.'[97]

Notes

1. Samuel Beckett, 'For Avigdor Arikha', in *Disjecta*, p. 152.
2. See, for example, his letter to Duthuit, 28 June 1949, in *The Letters of Samuel Beckett, Volume II: 1941–1956*, p. 169: 'I have done everything it is in my power to do for Bram, but it is all over. The harm I have done him is over too.' Rémi Labrusse has documented this gradual distancing from both van Velde and Duthuit in 'Beckett et la peinture'.
3. For biographical information on Arikha, we are indebted to Duncan Thomson's indispensable *Arikha*, from which I have drawn extensively here.
4. Barbara Rose, 'Avigdor Arikha Interviewed by Barbara Rose', in Richard Channin et al., *Arikha*, pp. 90–2.
5. See Jane Livingston, 'Thoughts on Avigdor Arikha', in Channin et al., *Arikha*, p. 102, and Joseph Shannon, 'An Interview with Avigdor Arikha', ibid., p. 166.
6. Avigdor Arikha, 'On Drawing from Observation', in *On Depiction: Selected Writings on Art, 1965–94*, pp. 109–10.
7. Beckett to Hans Naumann, in *Letters, Vol. II*, p. 462.
8. Arikha, 'On Drawing from Observation', in *On Depiction*, p. 109; Maurice Tuchman, 'A Talk with Avigdor Arikha', in Channin et al., *Arikha*, p. 49.
9. Rose, 'Avigdor Arikha Interviewed', in Channin et al., *Arikha*, p. 90.
10. Shannon, 'An Interview with Avigdor Arikha', in Channin et al., *Arikha*, p. 166.
11. Thomson, *Arikha*, p. 76.
12. As Barbara Rose has put it, 'Because form in Arikha's drawing is not mass but surface, these ephemeral mists, clots, bursts of ink, appear as fragile and delicately connected as a spiderweb. Matter is dematerialized into film, becoming a hazy atmosphere or an insubstantial mirage about to dissolve once more into air.' See Rose, 'The Drawing of Avigdor Arikha', in Channin et al., *Arikha*, p. 18. The intensity and the unrelenting objectivity of Arikha's self-portraits recall most forcefully those of Rembrandt, to which, indeed, *Self-Portrait with Open Mouth* almost certainly alludes. See, for example, Rembrandt van Rijn, *Self-portrait, open mouthed* and *Self-Portrait, frowning*, both from 1630 and exhibited in Het Rembrandthuis, Amsterdam.
13. Avigdor Arikha, 'Alberto Giacometti: A Creed of Failure', in *On Depiction*, p. 211.

14. Rose, 'The Drawing of Avigdor Arikha', in Channin et al., *Arikha*, p. 18.

15. Anne Atik, *How It Was: A Memoir of Samuel Beckett*, p. 29.

16. Atik, *How It Was*, pp. 30–1.

17. Beckett, 'Three Dialogues with Georges Duthuit', in *Transition Forty-Nine*, p. 98 and *Disjecta*, p. 139. Beckett's critique of Western pictorial space is discussed in the previous chapter.

18. Leon Battista Alberti, *On Painting*, pp. 43–4. Atik records somewhat ironically a conversation on Alberti, Vasari and other Italian art theorists and mentions that Beckett gifted his own copy of Vasari to Arikha. She does not specify the texts in question. See Atik, *How It Was*, p. 52.

19. Tuchman, 'A Talk with Avigdor Arikha', in Channin et al., *Arikha*, p. 43, and Robert Hughes, 'Avigdor Arikha', ibid., p. 34.

20. Tuchman, 'A Talk with Avigdor Arikha', in Channin et al., *Arikha*, p. 46. The remark is quite precise, despite the casual context. For Arikha, Velázquez's work lies somewhat to the side of the dominant post-Renaissance traditions of Western painting, especially in its relation to Italian practices of perspective and historical painting. Though it is unlikely that he was much influenced by the Italian painter, this location aligns Velázquez with Caravaggio, whose importance to Arikha and Beckett we will be considering further. On these issues, see Arikha, 'Velazquez, *Pintor Real*', in *On Depiction*, pp. 45–60. His interest in the Spanish painter had actually preceded his 1965 encounter with Caravaggio: see Thomson, *Arikha*, p. 45, and Rose, 'The Drawing of Avigdor Arikha', in Channin et al., *Arikha*, p. 17.

21. 'My brush drawings are postabstract, and could not have come into being without abstraction.' Avigdor Arikha, cited by Robert Hughes, 'Feedback from Life', in Duncan Thomson and Stephen Coppel, *Avigdor Arikha from Life: Drawings and Prints, 1965–2005*, p. 10. Cf. Stephen Coppel, 'The Prints', ibid., p.23: 'Arikha made it plain that the programme he had set himself was not a return to "representational" or "figurative" art but a move forward to post-abstract naturalism—a progress that could only have developed out of the modernist achievements of abstraction, particularly by Mondrian.'

22. Arikha, 'On Abstraction in Painting', in Channin et al., *Arikha*, p. 204. On 'literariness', see Clement Greenberg, 'The Case for Abstract Art', in *The Collected Essays and Criticism, Vol. 4*, pp. 77–9.

23. Arikha, 'On Drawing from Observation', in *On Depiction*, p. 133.

24. Thomson, *Arikha*, p. 39.

25. See Arikha's remarks on Matisse in Tuchman, 'A Talk with Avigdor Arikha', in Channin et al., *Arikha*, p. 46. His comment there on Matisse's linking back to 'the colour-grammar of the *Beatus Apocalypse of Saint-Sever*' is amplified in his essay 'Matisse's *Jazz* and the *Beatus Apocalypse of Saint-Sever*', in *On Depiction*, pp. 183–93.

26. Hughes, 'Avigdor Arikha', in Channin et al., *Arikha*, p. 31.

27. Thomson, *Arikha*, p. 39, describes Arikha recalling the date 'with a commemorative precision that is almost liturgical', a phrase that may miss a more specifically Jewish attention to the significance of dates. The date 10 March 1965 recurs for Arikha much as 20 January does for Paul Celan throughout his essay 'Meridian'. On the significance of the repetition of such dates, both in Celan and in the Jewish tradition, see Jacques Derrida, 'Shibboleth: For Paul Celan'.

28. Hughes, 'Avigdor Arikha', in Channin et al., *Arikha*, p. 32.

29. As Stephen Coppel remarks, 'Arikha has never denied the lessons he learnt from abstraction, particularly from Mondrian: a respect for the edges of the plate, sheet, or canvas; an awareness of the flatness of the picture plane, and the formal elements of the composition.' See Coppel, 'The Prints', in Thomson and Coppel, *Avigdor Arikha from Life*, p. 32.

30. Rose, 'Avigdor Arikha Interviewed', in Channin et al., *Arikha*, p. 81.

31. Beckett, *Watt*, p. 379.

32. Thomson's characterisation of such paintings, *Arikha*, p. 34, is precise: 'Particularly among such earlier paintings as *Noirs* [1959], there is a complex and intricate articulation, where forms that are more obviously organic advance and retreat and seem to change places. A painting like *The Fall* (1958) has a tumultuous quality, where the pale forms at the top crash into a darker pile at the bottom.'

33. John Ashbery, 'Paris Notes', cited in Thomson, *Arikha*, p. 35.

34. Arikha, 'Cézanne: From Tremor to Chequerboard', in *On Depiction*, p. 178. The term 'colour-grammar' Arikha uses in Tuchman, 'A Talk with Avigdor Arikha', in Channin et al., *Arikha*, p. 46.

35. Arikha, 'Cézanne: From Tremor to Chequerboard', in *On Depiction*, pp. 180–1.

36. Hughes, 'Avigdor Arikha', in Channin et al., *Arikha*, p. 34.

37. Arikha, 'On Nicolas Poussin's *The Rape of the Sabines* and Later Work (The Louvre Version)', in *On Depiction*, p. 88. This work was initially published in 1983 as *Nicolas Poussin: The Rape of*

the Sabines (The Louvre Version). In this earlier essay, he remarks specifically on Poussin's colour harmonies as being attained by 'an *equalization of intensities*, as in stained glass' (Arikha's emphasis), an observation that may be relevant to the balancing and echoes of intensities in the greys of his own graphic work. See *Nicolas Poussin*, p. 23. His allusion to stained glass, on which he was working across this period of transition, may suggest the bridge between the techniques of abstraction and those of his black and white drawings.

38. Arikha, 'On Nicolas Poussin's *The Rape of the Sabines*', in *On Depiction*, pp. 99–100.

39. Arikha, 'On Nicolas Poussin's *The Rape of the Sabines*', p. 101.

40. Arikha, cited in Thomson, *Arikha*, p. 74.

41. Tuchman, 'A Talk with Avigdor Arikha', in Channin et al., *Arikha*, p. 46.

42. Rose, 'The Drawing of Avigdor Arikha', in Channin et al., *Arikha*, p. 17.

43. Joseph Shannon remarks on this trait in his interview with Arikha, in Channin et al., *Arikha*, p. 166: 'In your work you so often place things close to an edge to create tension or you'll use a straight edge, deeply foreshortened where there is none of the top showing—ambiguous. Isn't that to build this kind of reduced, Mondrianesque composition but with your own images?'

44. Arikha, 'On Abstraction in Painting', in Channin et al., *Arikha*, p. 203. Genevieve Warwick discusses Caravaggio's use of the convex mirror as being in deliberate antithesis to Albertian perspective, in 'Introduction: Caravaggio in History', in Warwick (ed.), *Caravaggio: Realism, Rebellion, Reception*, pp. 18–20.

45. Catherine Puglisi, *Caravaggio*, p. 215. This is not the first time that Arikha seems to allude to this painting, which is not surprising, given Caravaggio's seminal importance for him. A simple watercolour, *Apple half-peeled on a black plate* (1976), which similarly plays with one's sense of perspective and viewpoint, depicts a half-peeled apple with a blemish in precisely the same place as the blemish on the apple in the foreground of Caravaggio's still life. Such blemishes traditionally were a moral reminder of mutation and decay, a *memento mori* in the midst of life and fruitfulness, and Arikha's version of this is fittingly a meditation on the rapidity required of the painter in capturing an ephemeral moment: not only is the apple blemished; caught half-peeled, it is also just on the point of turning brown from exposure to the air. The painter has to try in vain to capture its whiteness before this chemical reaction takes place.

46. Arikha, 'On Nicolas Poussin's *The Rape of the Sabines*', in *On Depiction*, p. 94. See also Giovanni Baglione, 'Life of Caravaggio', Appendix II of Puglisi, *Caravaggio*, p. 415: 'some people consider him to have been the ruination of painting.'

47. Arikha, 'Cézanne: From Tremor to Chequerboard', in *On Depiction*, p. 177. His expression here interestingly echoes Beckett's remark about wishing to be 'mal armé'.

48. Thomson, *Arikha*, p. 39.

49. Arikha's comment, in Rose, 'Avigdor Arikha Interviewed', in Channin et al., *Arikha*, p. 81.

50. Giovanni Pietro Bellori, 'Life of Caravaggio', Appendix III of Puglisi, *Caravaggio*, p. 416.

51. The phrase is from Timothy Wilson Smith, *Caravaggio*, p. 36.

52. Louis Marin, *To Destroy Painting*, p. 163.

53. See Puglisi, *Caravaggio*, pp. 92 and 333.

54. Cited in Marin, *To Destroy Painting*, p. 150.

55. Marin, *To Destroy Painting*, pp. 100 and 161.

56. Arikha, 'On Abstraction in Painting', in Channin et al., *Arikha*, p. 201. See also his similar comments on the Platonic origins of this idea of painting in 'On Drawing from Observation', in *On Depiction*, p. 113.

57. Alberti, *On Painting*, pp. 65 and 54. For a good account of Alberti's system of painting and its socio-historical account, see Graham L. Hammill, *Sexuality and Form: Caravaggio, Marlowe and Bacon*, pp. 35–40.

58. Arikha, 'On Nicolas Poussin's *The Rape of the Sabines*', in *On Depiction*, p. 83. Warwick comments on 'the artist's challenge to the Albertian system of pictorial representation' and continues: 'He commonly eschewed that tradition in favor of bas-relief compositions, with the figures close to, even pressing through, the picture plane and a dark background immediately behind them closing off any illusion of deep spatial recession.' See 'Introduction: Caravaggio in History', in Warwick (ed.), *Caravaggio*, p. 18.

59. Marin, *To Destroy Painting*, p. 163.

60. Lazarus's hand thus also displaces Caravaggio's head from the place that it (or, properly, Christ's head) should occupy according to Albertian prescriptions, where the centric point should occupy a position at the height of the central figure, in both meanings of the term 'central': 'The suitable position for this centric point is no higher from the base line than the height of the man to be represented, for in this way both the viewers and the objects in the paint-

ing will seem to be in the same plane.' Alberti, *On Painting*, p. 54. On the placement of Lazarus's hand and of Caravaggio's alignment with it, see Puglisi, *Caravaggio*, pp. 323 and 327.

61. Warwick, 'Introduction: Caravaggio in History', in Warwick (ed.), *Caravaggio*, p. 19.

62. Leo Bersani and Ulysse Dutoit, *Caravaggio's Secrets*, p. 23.

63. See Martin Heidegger, 'The Age of the World Picture', and my discussion of this text in the introduction. Bersani and Dutoit, in their *Arts of Impoverishment: Beckett, Rothko, Resnais*, pp. 88–9, emphasise the way in which, in the Western canon, 'the accuracy of art's imitation of reality is intimately connected to narrative modes of imitation'.

64. Thomson, *Arikha*, p. 76.

65. Marin, *To Destroy Painting*, p. 139.

66. Thomson, *Arikha*, p. 75.

67. Beckett, 'my way is in the sand . . .', in *Grove Centenary Edition, Vol. IV*, p. 39.

68. Beckett, 'MacGreevy on Yeats', in *Disjecta*, p. 97.

69. See, for example, the oil painting *August* (1982), the pastel *Studio Corner with a Crack in the Wall* (c. 1985) or the etching *Pair of Gloves* (1972), among a myriad of works in different media.

70. Walter Benjamin, 'Franz Kafka: On the Tenth Anniversary of his Death', p. 134. Benjamin is citing the French theologian and philosopher Nicolas Malebranche.

71. See Jerzy Grotowski, *Towards a Poor Theatre*. Beckett had in some ways anticipated Grotowski in calling for a 'poor painting'. See his remark in a letter to Duthuit, 9 June 1949, *Letters, Vol. II*, p. 166: 'Does there exist, or can there exist, or not, a painting that is poor, undisguisedly useless, incapable of any image whatever: a painting whose necessity does not seek to justify itself?'

72. Arikha, in Shannon, 'An Interview with Avigdor Arikha', in Channin et al., *Arikha*, pp. 170 and 173.

73. Arikha, in Rose, 'Avigdor Arikha Interviewed', in Channin et al., *Arikha*, p. 81.

74. Beckett, *Watt*, p. 379.

75. Cited in Dougald McMillan and Martha Fehsenfeld, *Beckett in the Theatre: The Author as Practical Playwright and Director, Vol. 1*, p. 89.

76. Beckett's sensitivity to this dilemma is explicit in his critical essay on the van Velde brothers, 'La Peinture des van Velde, ou Le Monde et le Pantalon', in *Disjecta*, p. 126: 'In what have the representative arts

been bogged down, since forever? In wanting to arrest time in representing it.' My translation. See the discussion of this observation and its critical consequences in Chapter 2.

77. Billie Whitelaw, cited in Peggy Phelan, 'Beckett and Avigdor Arikha', p. 99.

78. Beckett, *Stirrings Still*, in *Grove Centenary Edition, Vol. IV*, p. 488.

79. Beckett, letter to Alan Schneider, 4 January 1960, in Maurice Harmon (ed.), *No Author Better Served: The Correspondence of Samuel Beckett and Alan Schneider*, p. 60.

80. Beckett, *Krapp's Last Tape*, p. 221.

81. James Knowlson, *Damned to Fame: The Life of Samuel Beckett*, pp. 520–2; Atik, *How It Was*, pp. 4–6.

82. On the increasing visuality of Beckett's late theatre, see *The Theatrical Notebooks of Samuel Beckett, Volume 4: The Shorter Plays*, p. xv. See also Gerhard Hauck, *Reductionism in Drama and the Theatre: The Case of Samuel Beckett*, pp. 175–6.

83. Dougald McMillan and Martha Fehsenfeld document in great detail Beckett's 'preoccupation with giving the play a visual form' in *Beckett in the Theatre*, p. 91 and passim.

84. Ruby Cohn refers to the women in the first French production of *Come and Go* as 'softly gliding phantoms, feet invisible under the long coats': 'Beckett Directs *Endgame* and *Krapp's Last Tape*', in S. E. Gontarski (ed.), *On Beckett: Essays and Criticism*, p. 294. Anna McMullan sees *Come and Go* as anticipating what she calls 'Beckett's ghost plays of the 1970s and 1980s, which are concerned with the borders between the visible and the invisible, presence and absence, sound and silence'. See McMullan, *Theatre on Trial: Samuel Beckett's Later Drama*, p. 84.

85. See, for example, Atik, *How It Was*, p. 97, where Beckett and Arikha discuss Goethe's colour theory and Beckett remarks on the 'small patch of yellow wall' in Vermeer's *View of Delft*.

86. On these *Wartestelle* and their relation to the production of tableaus, see McMillan and Fehsenfeld, *Beckett in the Theatre*, pp. 115–19. Mark Nixon comments perceptively on the sources of Beckett's interest in the tableau: 'In the late drama and television plays, the linear and geometric composition of stage and scene reformulate the Renaissance notion of a "tableau vivant".' See his *Samuel Beckett's German Diaries, 1936–1937*, p. 148.

87. I allude here both to Jacque Derrida's compelling discussion of 'the apparition form, the phenomenon of spirit' in *Specters of Marx: The*

State of the Debt, the Work of Mourning and the New International, p. 135, and to Neary's well-known remark on 'figure and ground' in *Murphy*, p. 4.

88. See *Footfalls*, directed by Walter Asmus (2000), in *Beckett on Film*, produced by Michael Colgan and Alan Moloney (Blue Angel Films, 2001). Given Walter Asmus's long association with Beckett's own directing, it is perhaps not surprising that this is one of the most effective transpositions of Beckett's theatre to film, even in its slight deviation from Beckett's meticulous lighting directions.

89. On the Gothic dimension of *Footfalls*, see my essay 'Frames of *Referrance*: Samuel Beckett as an Irish Question', pp. 43–7.

90. Phelan, 'Beckett and Avigdor Arikha', p. 99.

91. Ulrika Maude, *Beckett, Technology and the Body*, p. 120. Both Graley Herren, *Samuel Beckett's Plays on Film and Television*, p. 173, and Anna McMullan, *Theatre on Trial*, p. 25, discuss this effect in terms of the disturbing 'entrapment' of the audience of *Play*.

92. On the 'happening', especially in the context of participatory art practice and theory in Paris in the 1960s, see Claire Bishop, *Artificial Hells: Participatory Art and the Politics of Spectatorship*, pp. 93–101.

93. Arikha, 'Looking at Painting', in *On Depiction*, p. 221.

94. Jean-Luc Nancy, *Listening*, p. 10.

95. Emmanuel Levinas, 'Is Ontology Fundamental?', p. 128.

96. Levinas, 'Philosophy and Transcendence', pp. 32–3. The internal citations are from Blaise Pascal, *Pensées*, and read in full: 'My place in the sun, the beginning and the archetype of the usurpation of the entire world' (p. 23). My claim is not that either Beckett or Arikha would have endorsed the larger context of Levinas's thinking, but that there is a very precise convergence between what Levinas here claims about the effect of 'being in face' and what Beckett claims specifically about Arikha's work.

97. Beckett, *Ceiling. For Avigdor. September 1981*, in Channin et al., *Arikha*, p. 12.

Conclusion: The Play's the Thing

The play's the thing
Wherein I'll catch the conscience of the King.

Shakespeare, *Hamlet*, II, ii, 594–5

Among the last three plays that Beckett wrote are two of his most explicitly political works: *Catastrophe* and *What Where*. *Catastrophe* was written in 1982 for the Avignon Festival and, unlike any other of his plays, was dedicated to a specific individual, Václav Havel. Havel, at the time incarcerated for his political activism, was a playwright and a leading figure in the Czech civil society movement. *What Where*, written and first staged in 1983, and then reconceived for German television in 1986, extends Beckett's enduring concern with scenarios of interrogation and torture that received its most elaborated treatment in the prose text *How It Is*, at the time of the French debates on torture that were provoked by the Algerian War. *What Where* explicitly echoes the series of protagonists of that work – Pim, Pom and Pam – in the quartet of characters Bam, Bem, Bim and Bom.[1] Indeed, in so far as *Catastrophe* too stages the spectacle of a person reduced to a captive and manipulable thing, one could say that it participates equally in that strand of Beckett's work. It goes without saying, as many critics have already pointed out, that neither play is solely, maybe not even foremost, concerned with politics: *Catastrophe*, with its self-important director and stage hands, has been read as an allegory of the playwright's work, for example, while *What Where* belongs with Beckett's 'memory plays' and may also explore the writer's practice – as *How It Is* had earlier done – as a mode of extorting speech or determining truth, of obliging expression where there is nothing to be expressed and no desire to express.[2] It would be surprising if this were not the case: virtually all of Beckett's works condense specific sets of interrelated and overlapping concerns that provide analogies for one another. The resistance to or the difficulty of including politics among those concerns lies not only in Beckett's all-embracing resistance to 'the craze for explicitation', as *Catastrophe*'s director puts it, but also in a limited sense of what the concept of the political might entail, given its customary reduction to the advocacy of explicit commitments or the treatment of recognisable ideological positions or debates. The sense in which these are political plays is largely tangential to such accepted understandings of the term: the political effect of Beckett's work in general takes place not at the level of the statement, but in its steady dismantling of the regime of representation that each work seems to push yet further.

My aim in this conclusion is to explore the direction that Beckett's dramatic work opens for thinking the domain of the political as it intersects with those of the ethical and the aesthetic, even to the point of their inextricable co-implication. I seek, that is, to pursue the consequences of Beckett's staging of the human as thing and to elaborate how it passes beyond his early recognition of the crisis of representation, or what he termed the 'new thing that had happened' in the subject-object relation that had structured the conception of the human in each of these domains. Beckett's 'thing' was consistently articulated and enacted alongside the dialogue with painting in which he found the terms to approach the broad field of his concerns. Through painting also he defined the relation of his aesthetic concerns to what we might call the whole existential field of his work, including its insistently ethical and the political implications. That field is constituted by a reconception of the human as one thing among others, a conception that does not shirk the fatally destructive and reifying consequences of modernity but passes by way of them along the *via negativa* of his work. Continually he found the crisis of subjectivity registered in painting, as a crisis of visuality, and found in painting the most acute engagement with that crisis. As we have seen throughout, the metaphors and the practices of painting, those that situate the subject in space and capture the object, those that organise the 'possessive space' of subjectivity, are the most powerful correlatives of the philosophical account of the subject's dominance over its object and therefore, when thrown into crisis, offered the most vivid apprehension of the rupture through which what Beckett terms 'the thing' emerges. It is therefore appropriate to approach it once again through these late plays which, along with his penultimate work, the television play *Nacht und Träume*, continue to extend his apprehension of drama as visual art. If in van Velde's painting he was able to see 'the thing immobile in the void', increasingly his own dramatic work becomes the space in which the thing appears and can be thought.

In its brevity as in its staging, *Catastrophe* is the play in which theatre itself becomes the scene, not so much of a performance (or of a *représentation* in the French sense of a theatrical performance) as of spectacle. What is being prepared for us in this process of rehearsal or *répétition* is not a narrative, a theatrical *istoria*, but a moment in which the object who is the Protagonist will appear captured, 'in the bag' and exposed, standing on a plinth for all the world like a sculpture. Hands, legs and cranium whitened, he is of course also a canvas, and in either case a secular and anonymous Ecce Homo exhibiting the appearance of this human thing as an image of catastrophe. At certain moments, indeed, the play strikingly recalls Caravaggio's *Ecce Homo* (1605; Fig. 4.1), where Christ stands with head bowed and hands crossed at his waist as an 'assistant' removes a dark cloak to expose him to the crowd that is the implied audience of the tableau. An opulent Pilate gestures toward him with startlingly dirty hands, gaze raised to the viewer's eyes, as if to direct our own gaze. Yet it is precisely the dispersal of the gaze in this painting, that of each of the figures turned in different directions so that we ourselves no longer know where to rest our eyes, that betrays the viewer's own implication in the scene. The viewer is situated not in the punctual position of the sovereign – a position in any case denied by Caravaggio's typically dramatic foregrounding and flattening of the painting's tableau – but among the shifting crowd that fatefully bays for possession of Christ's body beyond the frame of the picture. *Catastrophe* in turn is the only one of Beckett's plays that demands the rupture of the fourth wall, the Director finding his seat among the audience, at first in the front, 'in an armchair downstairs, audience left', and later speaking from 'the front row of the stalls'.[3] While the Assistant remains on the stage, the voice of Luke, the lighting technician (both *Lux* and St Luke, patron saint of the arts?), is heard from the rear of the auditorium (C, 488). As the latter appears only in the split between the sound of his voice from the rear and the light that he supplies falling on the Protagonist on stage, the audience no longer knows where to look for an 'overview' of

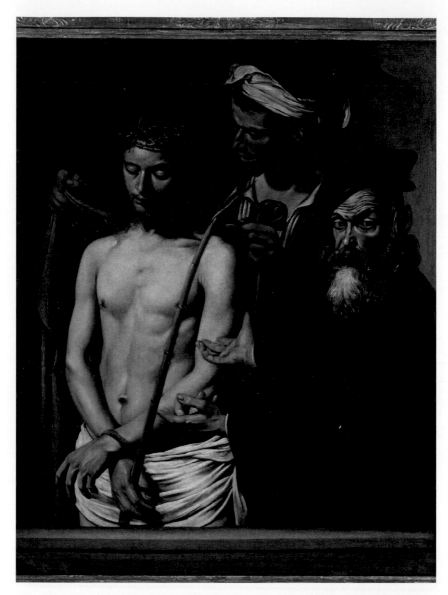

Fig. 4.1 Michelangelo Merisi da Caravaggio, *Ecce Homo* (1605). Musei di Strada Nuova—Palazza Rosso. Photo credit: Scala/Art Resource, New York.

the performance. The movement of the Director, stand-in for the sovereign subject who acts out the search for a totalising point of view, denies the audience any imaginary identification with a single perspective that could secure it in place before the spectacle. Turning back towards the Protagonist, as we are directed to do by the muted but telling violence of the Director's 'let 'em have it' (C, 489), we find ourselves implicated in the brutality of this spectacle and captured by the sound of a 'distant storm of applause' (C, 489) that anticipates our own, among us and remote at the same time. Our dwelling in the unfolding time and dispersed space of this happening implies us 'in the picture', but doubled: at first apparently as subjects of spectatorship, and then, in the last brief seconds, as the object of the Protagonist's gaze that 'fixes' us, with all the force of ambiguity that stage direction musters (C, 489).

The uncharacteristically jagged language of the play, largely lacking the rhythms and stylisation of most of Beckett's late plays, betrays its saturation not only with theatrical cliché but with the trite casualness of a routinised brutality, accustomed to the curt imperatives of power and the instrumentalisation of the body: 'Lose that gown. Step on it. I have a caucus' (C, 486); 'Not a squeak' (C, 487). Theatre as spectacle is both the metaphor and the fact

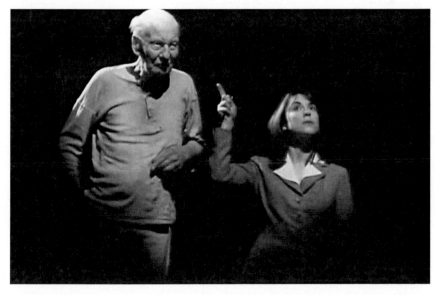

Fig. 4.2 Sir John Gielgud as the Protagonist and Rebecca Pidgeon as the Director's female assistant in *Catastrophe*, directed by David Mamet, 2000.

of a reification that is not only general but mutual and embraced: 'He'll have them on their feet' (C, 489). And this self-satisfied representation of 'our catastrophe' is, accordingly, the real catastrophe. The play's title designates not so much the Protagonist who is manipulated to be the image of catastrophe as it does the whole spectacle of an instrumentality in which it participates by exhibiting catastrophe as just a commodity, 'in the bag'. Its minimal action and effects unspectacularly reveal the logic of the spectacle. And the resistance of the Protagonist, the residual recalcitrance of a human thing denied utterance, is not a manifestation of the survival of some residuum of the subject in the face of its annihilation, but that resistance of the object to representation in which it finds its obdurate thingliness. It is the excess of the thing in the subject over the object as which it appears. The Protagonist gestures not as subject to subject, or even as object speaking back to subjects, but from the far side, from the place of the thing that is unredeemed and has no desire to be redeemed. It looks back in the form of that profoundly Beckettian thing, the gaze. It is a gaze that does not meet our gaze in the form of recognition, but in that of petrification, a Medusa's gaze that comes not with the last breath of the subject but from the stone into which it has been transformed. The Protagonist realises himself as the sculpted thing he was intended to be.

Catastrophe, nonetheless, is a performance that never quite takes place, never fully arrives and by the same token never ends. It is, as the French would have it, the staging of a *répétition*, of a rehearsal, destined to that other repetition-with-a-difference, night after night, that is the condition of the peculiar ephemerality of live theatre. Still implicit in *Catastrophe* is the repeated unfolding of the series of acts of domination that characterises Beckett's staging of the human as a thing subjected to coercion – interrogation, torture, or merely the apparent compulsion to repeat that produces the haunting effects of *Footfalls*, *Ohio Impromptu* and *Nacht und Träume*. Beckett's last play, *What Where*, and its television version in German, *Was Wo*, resume and extend that work into its most etiolated form, that of a musical round or canon in which each part takes the other's place. In the stage version, the rectangle where this round plays itself out – what Beckett called the 'field of memory' – is located '*stage right as seen from the house*', while Voice, identified in the directions as the voice of Bam, emanates from a dimly lit space downstage left.[4] As always in Beckett's later plays, physical action and voice are separated as much as is feasible, here spatially as well as temporally divided.[5] The action unfolds with Voice playing a role as impresario like that of the Opener in the much earlier radio play about coerced speech, *Cascando*. Repeatedly, Voice observes the passing of time through the cyclical series of the seasons and 'switches on and off' the action upstage, first as mime, 'without words', then 'with words', as if in a distant echo of the dumb show that precedes Hamlet's production of *The Mousetrap* in which the King is caught. Voice introduces the action of the play as a segment of a possibly endless series of repeated and virtually identical acts: 'In the end Bom appears. Reappears' (WW, 498).

The play's action outlines a scenario of torture and interrogation. Bom reappears to report to the figure of Bam, hitherto alone in the playing area, on his progress with an unnamed victim to whom he has 'given the works' (WW, 499), reducing him to weep, scream and beg for mercy. But the victim has refused to 'say it' (WW, 500) and Bom, accused by Bam of lying, is taken away by Bim to be given the works until he confesses 'That he said it to him' (WW, 501). When Bim reappears, the cycle begins again, only this time what Bim has failed to extract from Bom is 'where' he said it. In his turn, Bim is taken away by Bem, who, after failing once again, reappears for a fourth cycle, at the end of which it is Bam himself who exits to take him away for interrogation. Voice remains alone, to 'switch off' after delivering the tantalising line 'Make sense who may' (WW, 504). There is no reason, of course, to assume that the action will not recommence, as it does in so many of Beckett's plays from *Godot* onwards, not least because the fifth player mentioned in Voice's first line ('We are the last five') has not yet physically appeared. But even should it repeat, it would remain an action that brings us no closer to the nameless thing that is the ostensible goal of the interrogations – the 'it' or 'what' that has been uttered, the 'where' in which the utterance took place. By the same token, the other action that is designated by the quartet's words remains resolutely absent, offstage or 'obscene': the scene of torture is never enacted. The action circles around it as the speech circles around the unnamed 'it'. In much the same way, the dancers in *Quad* circle around the unseen thing at the centre of the stage, 'supposed a danger zone', in the course of their appearances and disappearances, and May 'revolves' around the unmentionable 'it all' of her narrative in *Footfalls*.

One could, of course, read this all as an allegory of torture in actual practice: 'enhanced interrogation' rarely produces any 'actionable intelligence', the thing that it pursues, and generally remains an obscenity that is rarely exhibited in public. Be that as it may – and make sense who may – torture is as much an allegory for the existential situation the play stages as it is the referent of the play's allegory. It is the certainty of the dominating subject that torture seeks to secure and that the thing that resists utterance refuses to it, categorically, one might say. Torture in the pursuit of its certainty effectively shatters the subject that would be the guarantee of any truth it extorted. Accordingly, as Alain Badiou says of *Texts for Nothing*, 'The only result of the torture is the desolate and desert-like injunction that one must subject oneself to torture again.'[6] The voice that speaks and the sense that it makes cease to emanate from the depths of an expressive subject and become detachable things in themselves, divorced from any anchorage in time and space that might be occupied by a unitary 'I'. There is something profoundly unsettling in the way Beckett's late plays

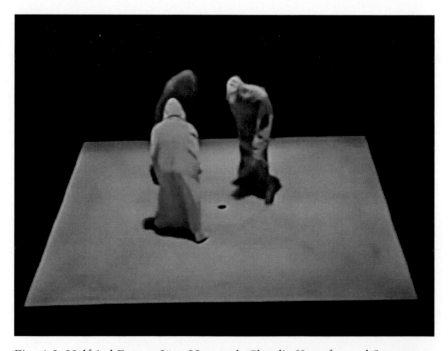

Fig. 4.3 Helfried Foron, Jürg Hummel, Claudia Knupfer and Susanne Rehe in *Quadrat I* [*Quad I*], television production directed by Samuel Beckett for Süddeutscher Rundfunk, 1981.

thus turn repeatedly around a deixis without referent – the it, the where, the thing – which finds a peculiarly embodied correlative in these constantly shifting personages whose differences never amount to distinct identities.[7]

Beckett's final reduction of *What Where* for German television, *Was Wo*, emphasises this: the space of the play dispenses even with the structurally convenient depth of the theatrical version's upstage and downstage. The personages, reduced to disembodied faces with 'bodies & movement eliminated', loom out of the flattened darkness of the screen, a 'black ground unbroken', as Beckett's production notes describe it.[8] Their grey faces, aligned in a frieze across that black screen, fade up and down on the surface of the dark, rather than receding into or emerging from its depths. This purely abstract, depthless space, devoid of location, is not therefore to be mistaken for a representation of some inner, mental or psychic space.[9] Gone is any semblance of the mind-body split with which Beckett has so often been associated, the mental interior that *Murphy* rendered as 'a large hollow sphere, hermetically closed to the universe without'.[10] Voice, which could be imagined either as that which recalls all that passes in the play or as a mental projection of any or all of the characters, emanates from an enlarged, blurred and dimly illuminated 'death mask' in the upper left, suspended like a partially occluded moon above the smaller and fitfully appearing other faces. From this 'rond lumineux', as Beckett's French director Pierre Chabert described the 'ring of diffuse light' that replaced the original loudspeaker in his 1986 stage production, emanates the colourless voice that regulates and judges the action (WW, 451).

How should we read this peculiar distribution of space, of sound, of light in *What Where*? It is a vivid reminder that Beckett's late plays do not merely offer the image of an instrumentalised humanity within the classic pictorial space of the theatre. They shatter and disperse both the subject and its space and produce a thoroughly reconceived, alternative spatiality in which a radically different construction of the human comes into play. This alternative theatrical space begins to emerge in *Krapp's Last Tape*, *Film* and *Play*, with their initial experiments in separating out the elements of performance and set – the voice that speaks from the tape recorder, the spotlight or camera that functions as an effective character – and in their disaggregating of motion and speech, action and word. *Was Wo*, indeed, appears as a fundamental

Fig. 4.4 *Was Wo* [*What Where*], directed by Samuel Beckett and Walter Asmus for Süddeutscher Rundfunk, 1985.

reduction of *Play*, both in its trio of faces suspended in the dark and in its staging of an interrogation that seems aimed at eliciting some unspoken and unspeakable 'thing'. We may recall the ambiguity of the woman W1's invocations to the light which suggest that both the spotlight and the matter it seeks are the thing in question: 'but it will come, the time will come, the thing is there, you'll see it, get off me, keep off me' (147) and 'Yes, and the whole thing there, all there, staring you in the face' (157).[11] This thing is at once the externalised light that interrogates, object of her perception as much as she is of it, and at the same time the thing it seeks 'within' her or, rather, in the words she is obliged to speak. But in *Play*, as we saw, the light still emanates from a single source, forming a beam that fixes its objects turn by turn from the same perspectival space as the audience occupies. We are indeed implicated in the 'play' of interrogation and in the space of its unfolding, but the spatial relations of spectator and spectacle, subject and object, remain in place. *What Where* in its various redactions pushes this ambiguity of spatial location considerably further, dissolving interior and exterior, locating this phenomenal voice and the light from which it emanates in a space that is, like a psychotic hallucination, neither inner nor outer.

Beckett's thing is, then, not to be defined as 'a certain carving out of the real' or even 'a compromise between mind and matter, the point of their crossing one into the other'.[12] His apprehension of it in the 1940s almost certainly emanated from his pre-war readings of Kant and approximated the noumenal 'thing in itself', the object that both eludes and resists representation, as he put it of van Velde's paintings. But the critical destruction of pictorial space that he undertook across this post-war period, the dismantling of its 'possessive' assault on its objects, equally dissolves the subject that, situated at the apex of the visual pyramid, regulated this visual grid. To Beckett's unrelenting apprehension of the objective reification of the human corresponds, then, what we might provisionally term an inner dissolution of the subject; provisionally, because the ultimate effect of that dissolution is not simply to evacuate some interior space or to pursue – as the essay on Proust had projected – 'the core of the eddy', but to reconceive the human as a constellation or assemblage of things that are at once inner and outer. This Voice that speaks out of its diffuse ring of light is at once a percept in the external world and a projection perceived as an inner voice. In this respect, Beckett's thinking of the thing converges most pertinently with that of Jacques Lacan's reading of Freud's *Beyond the Pleasure Principle* in the seminar on the ethics of psychoanalysis of 1959–60. There, the thing, *das Ding*, stands as the unrepresentable nub around which the subject's relation to its objects circulates. *Das Ding* is at once at the centre of psychic formation and that which is excluded and lost to representation, an irreducible element of the real through whose negation the subject's sense of interiority and exteriority is forged. It functions, indeed, as does that invisible and uncanny 'danger zone' of *Quad*, a point that, precisely in being dodged, constitutes the form of the dance, compelling its repetitive rhythms and circulations. As Lacan remarks, thus conceived, the thing offers real difficulty to any 'topological representation', to being staged, we might say:

> For this *das Ding* is rightly at the center in the sense that it is excluded [from the subjective world of the unconscious]. That is to say that in reality it ought to be posited as exterior, this *das Ding*, this prehistoric Other that is impossible to forget and whose primal position Freud affirms for us, in the form of some thing that is *entfremdet* [alienated, estranged], foreign [*étranger*] to me even as it is at the heart of me, something which, at the level of the unconscious, only a representation represents.[13]

This strange thing, being at once interior and exterior, constitutes the self as similarly exterior and interior, as a thing distributed among its things, and, perhaps, as the thing that hides the thing. 'The *Ding* is the element originally isolated by the subject, in its experience of the *Nebenmensch* [neighbour, next-person], as being of its nature strange [*étranger*], *Fremde*.'[14] Alien and unrepresentable at the heart of the self, the thing's first appearance for the subject is, according to Lacan, a thing that may even emanate from the self, the cry. This cry is a thing quite independent of any meaning it may bear or object it may designate. It is, like the voice or the gaze, a phenomenon that occupies the peculiar interior-exterior space in which the human as itself a thing is suspended. It could be no more, as Beckett intimated, than a breath.

In this, Lacan reiterates, this thing is distinct from the subject's objects, which serve 'more or less as his image, his reflection'.[15] That instrumental relation of subject to object Beckett regarded as untenable from a very early point in his career, and his refusal led him from the objective, and often negative, perception of the human's reduction to thing to an alternative apprehension of human being that is at once aesthetic, political and ethical. Already in *How It Is*, as I have argued elsewhere, he had found in the scenario of tortured speech the means to grasp the abstract 'inner voice' of the Kantian moral law as itself a thing for the subject and had projected from the conditions of its object, the pathological subject, the possibility of a quite other 'life in common', another 'good'.[16] The plays that follow that work, from the early 1960s through to *What Where*, furnish the spatial and visual coordinates of a human being and a human community imagined and imaged otherwise. They destroy theatre in a sense analogous to that in which Caravaggio was said to destroy painting – by departing from both the narrative investments and the spatial relation of spectacle to spectator that in most regards continue to structure it. Beckett's work dismantles the figure of Man that was, for Schiller, the culminating revelation of every drama that made the stage a 'moral institution', and shatters the theatrical space in which that figure could appear as the apex of a quite painterly visual pyramid that united the several gazes of the audience in a single and representative object, their common image and reflection.[17] This destruction of theatre is a profoundly social act. It shatters what Guy Debord, capturing the way in which Schiller's stage had become the figure for a general mechanism of reification, described as 'spectacle', 'a social relation among people, mediated by images'. In that spectacle, 'what binds the spectators together is no more than an irreversible relation to the very center which maintains their isolation.'[18] Beckett's anti-spectacular theatre thus shatters equally that relation to the centre in which the illusory sovereignty of the subject is secured. Theatre accordingly becomes the medium in which he most powerfully advances and broadens a critique of representation that he had launched in his writings on visual art.

His thoroughgoing dismantling of the regime of representation is not confined to his antagonism, from the very start, to mimetic or realist art. It fractures not only the aesthetic but with it the political and ethical dimensions through which the modern subject is articulated. Following Kant, it is in the aesthetic domain that this subject is realised as the disinterested and universal subject of common sense. This 'common sense', abstracted from the particularities of the actual senses or tastes of the individual, is the condition of possibility for any political or ethical subject, the *sine qua non* of their claims to universality. It transforms the singular and 'pathological' subject into the subject of representation, in both senses: the subject who can be represented and the subject who regulates representation.[19] This tightly interwoven complex of representation is what Beckett's work rips apart. Taking the side of the pathological subjects in the extreme, of the derelicts and wasted beings, the disabled and disintegrating, that populate his plays, he refuses to evade the all but ineluctable logic by which the enlightenment subject of emancipation devolved into the alias of domination. Rather than seek compensation for domination in the aesthetic dimension, to cite a peculiarly affirmative work of Marcuse's, he pushes the aesthetic of representation to the point that it begins to unravel the whole complex that it had sustained, 'reducing the dark where there might have been, mathematically at least, a door'. This is the necessity of the negativity of his work, which refuses any convenient exit.

And yet it is this negativity that brings him to the threshold of another imaginable community for whose outlines the experience of his own theatre may offer some analogy. Deprived of the spectacle, of even the integrated theatrical image of humanity that his first great plays projected, the audience is obliged to confront, in the time and space of the performance, a vision of 'humanity in ruins' whose dispersed and fragmented elements refuse to cohere into any representative 'image or reflection'. They fracture and shift with the murmur of some disintegrating ice floe. The subject in the theatre is not unified by its gaze or by its ear, but is itself suspended in face of the strangeness of the thing it finds there. That strange thing is the distant echo of the *res* of the dissident republic that Beckett encountered in the form and the matter of Yeats's painting and of the thing suspended in the void that was what survived of van Velde's assault on representation. It is also the condition for the community that might yet come for a humanity that has lived through the experience of its own reduction to its thingliness, beyond subject or object, inner or outer, and re-emerges from the *disjecta* of our collective catastrophe.

Notes

1. For an analysis of *How It Is* and of Beckett's virtually life-long concern with torture and incarceration, see my 'On Extorted Speech: Back to *How It Is*', in *Irish Culture and Colonial Modernity, 1800–*

2000, pp. 198–220. My argument here will resume some of the arguments of that chapter.

2. See, for example, *The Theatrical Notebooks of Samuel Beckett, Volume 4: The Shorter Plays*, p. 452; S. E. Gontarski, *The Intent of Undoing in Samuel Beckett's Dramatic Texts*, p. 181; Anna McMullan, *Theatre on Trial: Samuel Beckett's Later Drama*, pp. 33–45. Graley Herren suggests that *What Where* belongs to a series of plays in which Beckett explored 'torture as a metaphor for creativity' in *Samuel Beckett's Plays on Film and Television*, p. 184.

3. Beckett, *Catastrophe*, pp. 485 and 487. Cited in the text hereafter as C.

4. Beckett, *What Where*, in *The Grove Centenary Edition, Vol. III*, p. 497. Cited in the text hereafter as WW. For the 'field of memory', see Beckett's *Theatrical Notebooks*, p. 450.

5. Gontarski describes this as 'one of Beckett's most persistent theatrical axioms', in Beckett's *Theatrical Notebooks*, p. 311.

6. Alain Badiou, 'Tireless Desire', in *On Beckett*, p. 54.

7. This shifting sense of identity in difference would be far more apparent to the audience of the theatre version of *What Where* than that of its television rendering, where the differences in the appearances of the quartet are far more apparent, despite all efforts to disguise them. In the theatre the players, described as 'alike as possible', would be remote enough to disguise those differences.

8. See Beckett's revised text of *What Where*, prepared for Süddeutscher Rundfunk as *Was Wo* in 1986, in *Theatrical Notebooks*, pp. 427 and 431. The headnote to the notebook for this production, 'Process of elimination', is, as Gontarski notes, 'one of Beckett's most succinct summaries of his late aesthetics' (p. 450).

9. Badiou would doubtless see this as what he calls the 'grey black place of being'; *On Beckett*, p. 6 and passim.

10. Beckett, *Murphy*, p. 63.

11. Beckett, *Play*, pp. 356 and 365.

12. See Elizabeth Grosz, 'The Thing', pp. 170–1. Beckett's thing is equally not the mere datum of sense perception that, as it were, awaits subsumption into the concept, Hegel's *Sache*: cf. G. W. F. Hegel, *Phenomenology of Spirit*, p. 58.

13. Jacques Lacan, *Le Séminaire VII: L'éthique de la psychanalyse*, p. 87. My translation and interpolations.

14. Lacan, *L'éthique de la psychanalyse*, pp. 64–5. My translation and interpolations.

15. Lacan, *L'éthique de la psychanalyse*, p. 133. My translation.

16. See Lloyd, *Irish Culture and Colonial Modernity, 1800–2000*, pp. 209–17.
17. For an analysis of the significance of Schiller's concept of the work of theatre in 'The Stage as Moral Institution', see David Lloyd and Paul Thomas, *Culture and the State*, pp. 53–7. Daniel Albright traces the origins of the theatrical space that Schiller assumed to Renaissance stagecraft, relating it clearly to painting's perspectival grid: 'The proscenium stage was devised to intensify the visual aspect of the theatre: Inigo Jones and other Renaissance state architects carefully arranged the scenery and the backdrop so that there was one point in the audience (occupied, say, by the king) from which the vanishing point of the perspective, the whole impressive stage machinery, made sense.' See Albright, *Beckett and Aesthetics*, p. 79.
18. Guy Debord, *Society of the Spectacle*, n.p., theses 4 and 29.
19. For a summary of Kant's complex of representation, see Lloyd, 'Representation's Coup', pp. 11–15. This notion of representation is distinct from Jacques Rancière's 'representative regime' of the arts as laid out in *The Politics of Aesthetics*, pp. 21–2, which identifies representation with mimesis and separates it conceptually and historically from 'the aesthetic regime of the arts'.

Bibliography

Acheson, James, and Kateryna Arthur (eds), *Beckett's Later Fiction and Drama: Texts for Company* (London: Macmillan Press, 1987).

Ades, Dawn, *André Masson* (New York: Rizzoli, 1994).

Adorno, Theodor W., *The Jargon of Authenticity* (Evanston: Northwestern University Press, 1973).

—— *Sound Figures*, trans. Rodney Livingstone (Stanford: Stanford University Press, 1999).

—— 'Trying to Understand *Endgame*', in *Notes to Literature*, vol. 1, trans. Shierry Weber Nicholsen (New York: Columbia University Press, 1991), pp. 241–75.

Alberti, Leon Battista, *On Painting*, trans. Cecil Grayson, intro. and notes by Martin Kemp (Harmondsworth: Penguin Books, 2004).

Albright, Daniel, *Beckett and Aesthetics* (Cambridge: Cambridge University Press, 2003).

Alechinsky, Pierre, et al., *Celui qui ne peut se servir des mots (pour Bram van Velde)* (Montpellier: Éditions Fata Morgana, 1975).

Allen, Nicholas, *Modernism, Ireland and Civil War* (Cambridge: Cambridge University Press, 2009).

Amiran, Eyal, *Wandering and Home: Beckett's Metaphysical Narrative* (University Park: Pennsylvania State University Press, 1993).

Arikha, Avigdor, *Nicolas Poussin: The Rape of the Sabines (The Louvre Version)* (Houston: Museum of Fine Arts, 1983).

—— *On Depiction: Selected Writings on Art, 1965–94* (London: Bellew, 1995).

—— *Peinture et regard* (Paris: Hermann, 1991).

Arnold, Bruce, *Jack Yeats* (New Haven: Yale University Press, 1998).

Ashbach, Charles, and Victor L. Schermer, *Object Relations, the Self, and the Group: A Conceptual Paradigm* (New York and London: Routledge & Kegan Paul Ltd, 1987).

Athanassoglou-Kallmyer, Nina Maria, *Cézanne and Provence* (Chicago: University of Chicago Press, 2003).

Atik, Anne, *How It Was: A Memoir of Samuel Beckett* (London: Faber and Faber, 2001).

Auerbach, Erich, *Scenes from the Drama of European Literature*, foreword by Paolo Valesio (Minneapolis: University of Minnesota Press, 1984).

Badiou, Alain, *On Beckett*, ed. and trans. Alberto Toscano and Nina Power, with Bruno Bosteels (Manchester: Clinamen Press, 2003).

Baker, Phil, *Beckett and the Mythology of Psychoanalysis* (London: Macmillan Press Ltd, 1997).

Barrell, John, *The Dark Side of the Landscape: The Rural Poor in English Painting 1730–1840* (Cambridge: Cambridge University Press, 1980).

Beckerman, Bernard, 'Beckett and the Act of Listening', in Enoch Brater (ed.), *Beckett at 80/Beckett in Context* (New York and Oxford: Oxford University Press, 1986), pp. 149–67.

Beckett, Samuel, *As the Story Was Told: Uncollected and Late Prose* (London: Calder, 1990).

—— 'The Capital of the Ruins', in *As the Story Was Told: Uncollected and Late Prose* (London: Calder, 1990), pp. 17–28.

—— *Catastrophe*, in *Samuel Beckett: The Grove Centenary Edition, Volume III: Dramatic Works*, ed. Paul Auster (New York: Grove Press, 2006), pp. 483–9.

—— *Disjecta: Miscellaneous Writings and a Dramatic Fragment*, ed. Ruby Cohn (New York: Grove Press, 1984).

—— *Endgame*, in *Samuel Beckett: The Grove Centenary Edition, Volume III: Dramatic Works*, ed. Paul Auster (New York: Grove Press, 2006), pp. 89–154.

—— *Film*, in *Samuel Beckett: The Grove Centenary Edition, Volume III: Dramatic Works*, ed. Paul Auster (New York: Grove Press, 2006), pp. 369–88.

—— *The Grove Centenary Edition, Volume III: Dramatic Works*, ed. Paul Auster (New York: Grove Press, 2006).

—— *The Grove Centenary Edition, Volume IV: Poems, Short Fiction, Criticism*, ed. Paul Auster (New York: Grove Press, 2006).

—— *Krapp's Last Tape*, in *Samuel Beckett: The Grove Centenary Edition, Volume III: Dramatic Works*, ed. Paul Auster (New York: Grove Press, 2006), pp. 219–30.

—— *The Letters of Samuel Beckett, Volume I: 1929–1940*, ed. Martha Dow Fehsenfeld and Lois More Overbeck (Cambridge: Cambridge University Press, 2009).

—— *The Letters of Samuel Beckett, Volume II: 1941–1956*, ed. George Craig, Martha Dow Fehsenfeld, Dan Gunn and Lois More Overbeck (Cambridge: Cambridge University Press, 2011).

—— *Molloy*, in *Samuel Beckett: The Grove Centenary Edition, Volume II: Novels*, ed. Paul Auster (New York: Grove Press, 2006), pp. 1–170.

—— *Murphy*, in *Samuel Beckett: The Grove Centenary Edition, Volume I: Novels*, ed. Paul Auster (New York: Grove Press, 2006), pp. 1–168.

—— *Play*, in *Samuel Beckett: The Grove Centenary Edition, Volume III: Dramatic Works*, ed. Paul Auster (New York: Grove Press, 2006), pp. 353–68.

—— *Proust*, in *Samuel Beckett: The Grove Centenary Edition, Volume IV: Poems, Short Fiction, Criticism*, ed. Paul Auster (New York: Grove Press, 2006), pp. 511–54.

—— *The Theatrical Notebooks of Samuel Beckett, Volume 4: The Shorter Plays, with revised texts for* Footfalls, Come and Go *and* What Where, ed. S. E. Gontarski (London: Faber and Faber and New York: Grove Press, 1999).

—— 'Three Dialogues', in *Samuel Beckett: The Grove Centenary Edition, Volume IV: Poems, Short Fiction, Criticism*, ed. Paul Auster (New York: Grove Press, 2006), pp. 555–63.

—— 'Three Poems', *Transition Forty-Eight*, 2 (1948): 96–7.

—— *Waiting for Godot*, in *Samuel Beckett: The Grove Centenary Edition, Volume III: Dramatic Works*, ed. Paul Auster (New York: Grove Press, 2006).

—— *Watt*, in *Samuel Beckett: The Grove Centenary Edition, Volume I: Novels*, ed. Paul Auster (New York: Grove Press, 2006), pp. 169–379.

—— *Worstward Ho*, in *Samuel Beckett: The Grove Centenary Edition, Volume IV: Poems, Short Fiction, Criticism*, ed. Paul Auster (New York: Grove Press, 2006), pp. 471–85.

—— and Georges Duthuit, 'Three Dialogues', *Transition Forty-Nine*, 5 (1949): 97–103.

Benjamin, Walter, 'Franz Kafka: On the Tenth Anniversary of his Death', in *Illuminations: Essays and Reflections*, ed. Hannah Arendt, trans. Harry Zohn (New York: Schocken Books, 1969), pp. 111–40.

Bersani, Leo, and Ulysse Dutoit, *Arts of Impoverishment: Beckett, Rothko, Resnais* (Cambridge, MA: Harvard University Press, 1993).

—— *Caravaggio's Secrets* (Cambridge, MA: MIT Press, 1998).

Bignell, Jonathan, *Beckett on Screen: The Television Plays* (Manchester: Manchester University Press, 2009).

Bishop, Claire, *Artificial Hells: Participatory Art and the Politics of Spectatorship* (London: Verso, 2012).

Casanova, Pascale, *Samuel Beckett: Anatomy of a Literary Revolution* (London: Verso, 2006).

Celan, Paul, 'Meridian', in *Collected Prose*, trans. Rosemarie Waldrop (Manchester: Carcanet Press, 1986), pp. 37–55.

Channin, Richard, et al., *Arikha* (Paris: Hermann, 1985).

Connor, Steven, 'Beckett and Bion', available at: <http://stevenconnor.com/beckbion.html> (last accessed 2 March 2016).

Corkery, Daniel, *Synge and Anglo-Irish Literature* (Cork: Mercier Press, 1966).

Croke, Fionnuala (ed.), *Samuel Beckett: A Passion for Paintings* (Dublin: National Gallery of Ireland, 2006).

Cronin, Anthony, *Samuel Beckett: The Last Modernist* (New York: Harper Collins, 1997).

Dayan, Colin, *The Law Is a White Dog: How Legal Rituals Make and Unmake Persons* (Princeton: Princeton University Press, 2011).

Debord, Guy, *Society of the Spectacle* (Detroit: Black and Red, 1983).

Deleuze, Gilles, and Félix Guattari, *Kafka: pour une littérature mineure* (Paris: Éditions de Minuit, 1975).

Derrida, Jacques, 'Shibboleth: For Paul Celan', in *Sovereignties in Question: The Poetics of Paul Celan*, ed. Thomas Dutoit and Outi Pasanen (New York: Fordham University Press, 2005), pp. 1–64.

—— *Specters of Marx: The State of the Debt, the Work of Mourning and the New International*, trans. Peggy Kamuf (New York: Routledge, 1994).

Dobbins, Gregory, 'Whenever Green Is Red: James Connolly and Postcolonial Theory', *Nepantla: Views from the South*, 1.3 (2000): 605–48.

Dolar, Mladen, 'The Object Voice', in Renata Salecl and Slavoj Žižek (eds), *Gaze and Voice as Love Objects* (Durham, NC: Duke University Press, 1996), pp. 7–31.

du Bouchet, André, 'Three Exhibitions: Tal Coat – Masson – Miró', trans. Dorothy Bussy, *Transition Forty-Nine*, 5 (1949): 89–95.

Duthuit, Georges, 'Matisse and Byzantine Space', *Transition Forty-Nine*, 5 (1949): 20–37.

Esslin, Martin, 'A Poetry of Moving Images', in Alan Warren Friedman, Charles Rossman and Dina Sherzer (eds), *Beckett Translating/ Translating Beckett* (University Park and London: Pennsylvania State University Press, 1987), pp. 65–76.

—— 'Towards the Zero of Language', in James Acheson and Kateryna Arthur (eds), *Beckett's Later Fiction and Drama* (London: Macmillan, 1987), pp. 35–49.

Foucault, Michel, *The Order of Things: An Archaeology of the Human Sciences* (New York: Vintage Books, 1973).

Friedman, Alan Warren, Charles Rossman and Dina Sherzer (eds), *Beckett Translating/Translating Beckett* (University Park and London: Pennsylvania State University Press, 1987).

Gibbons, Luke, *Transformations in Irish Culture* (Cork: Cork University Press, 1996).

Gontarski, S. E., 'Crapp's First Tapes: Beckett's Manuscript Revisions of *Krapp's Last Tape*', *Samuel Beckett Special Number*, special issue of the *Journal of Modern Literature*, 6.1 (1977): 61–8.

—— *The Intent of Undoing in Samuel Beckett's Dramatic Texts* (Bloomington: Indiana University Press, 1985).

—— (ed.), *On Beckett: Essays and Criticism* (New York: Grove Press, 1986).

Greenberg, Clement, *Art and Culture: Critical Essays* (Boston: Beacon Press, 1989).

—— *The Collected Essays and Criticism, Volume 4: Modernism with a Vengeance, 1957–1969*, ed. John O'Brian (Chicago: University of Chicago Press, 1993).

Grosz, Elizabeth, 'The Thing', in *Architecture from the Outside: Essays on Virtual and Real Space* (Cambridge, MA: MIT Press, 2001), pp. 166–82.

Grotowski, Jerzy, *Towards a Poor Theatre* (New York: Routledge, 2002).

Guilbaut, Serge, 'Disdain for the Stain: Abstract Expressionism and Tachisme', in Joan Marter (ed.), *Abstract Expressionism: The International Context* (New York: Routledge, 2007), pp. 29–50.

—— *How New York Stole the Idea of Modern Art: Abstract Expressionism, Freedom and the Cold War* (Chicago: University of Chicago Press, 1985).

Hammill, Graham L., *Sexuality and Form: Caravaggio, Marlowe and Bacon* (Chicago and London: University of Chicago Press, 2000).

Harmon, Maurice (ed.), *No Author Better Served: The Correspondence of Samuel Beckett and Alan Schneider* (Cambridge, MA: Harvard University Press, 1998).

Harvey, Lawrence E., *Samuel Beckett: Poet and Critic* (Princeton: Princeton University Press, 1970).

Hauck, Gerhard, *Reductionism in Drama and the Theatre: The Case of Samuel Beckett* (Potomac, MD: Scripta Humanistica, 1992).

Hegel, G. W. F., *Phenomenology of Spirit*, trans. A. V. Miller (Oxford: Oxford University Press, 1977).

Heidegger, Martin, 'The Age of the World Picture', in *Off the Beaten Track*, ed. and trans. Julian Young and Kenneth Hayes (Cambridge: Cambridge University Press, 2002), pp. 57–85.

—— 'The Origin of the Work of Art', in *Off the Beaten Track*, ed. and trans. Julian Young and Kenneth Hayes (Cambridge: Cambridge University Press, 2002), pp. 1–56.

—— 'The Thing', in *Poetry, Language, Thought*, trans. Albert Hofstadter (New York: Harper Colophon, 1975), pp. 165–82.

—— *What Is a Thing?*, trans. W. B. Barton Jr and Vera Deutsch (Lanham, MD: University Press of America, 1967).

Herren, Graley, *Samuel Beckett's Plays on Film and Television* (New York: Palgrave Macmillan, 2007).

Homan, Sidney, *Filming Beckett's Television Plays: A Director's Experience* (Lewisburg: Bucknell University Press, 1992).

Joyce, James, *Dubliners* (Harmondsworth: Penguin, 1975).

Kalb, Jonathan, *Beckett in Performance* (Cambridge: Cambridge University Press, 1989).

Knowlson, James, *Damned to Fame: The Life of Samuel Beckett* (New York: Simon and Schuster, 1996).

—— *Light and Dark in the Theatre of Samuel Beckett* (London: Turret Books, 1972).

Labrusse, Rémi, 'Beckett et la peinture', *Critique*, 46 (August/September 1990): 670–80.

Lacan, Jacques, *The Four Fundamental Concepts of Psychoanalysis*, Book XI of *The Seminar of Jacques Lacan*, ed. Jacques-Alain Miller, trans. Alan Sheridan (New York: W. W. Norton, 1981).

—— *Le Séminaire VII: L'éthique de la psychanalyse* (Paris: Éditions du Seuil, 1986).

—— 'The Subversion of the Subject and the Dialectic of Desire in the Freudian Unconscious', in *Écrits: A Selection*, trans. Alan Sheridan (New York: W. W. Norton, 1977), pp. 281–312.

Laporte, Roger, *Bram van Velde ou cette petite chose qui fascine* (Montpellier: Éditions Fata Morgana, 1980).

Levinas, Emmanuel, 'Is Ontology Fundamental?', *Philosophy Today*, 33.2 (1989): 121–9.

—— 'Philosophy and Transcendence', in *Alterity and Transcendence*, trans. Michael B. Smith (New York: Columbia University Press, 1999), pp. 3–37.

Lloyd, David, *Anomalous States: Irish Writing and the Post-Colonial Moment* (Dublin: Lilliput Press, 1993).

—— 'Frames of *Referrance*: Samuel Beckett as an Irish Question', in Sean

Kennedy (ed.), *Beckett and Ireland* (Cambridge: Cambridge University Press, 2010), pp. 31–55.

—— *Irish Culture and Colonial Modernity, 1800–2000: The Transformation of Oral Space* (Cambridge: Cambridge University Press, 2011).

—— *Nationalism and Minor Literature: James Clarence Mangan and the Emergence of Irish Cultural Nationalism* (Berkeley: University of California Press, 1987).

—— 'Representation's Coup', *Interventions*, 16.1 (2012): 1–29.

—— 'Rethinking National Marxism: James Connolly and "Celtic Communism"', in *Irish Times: Temporalities of Modernity* (Dublin: Field Day, 2008), pp. 101–26.

—— and Paul Thomas, *Culture and the State* (London: Routledge, 1997).

Lyons, Charles R., *Samuel Beckett* (New York: Grove, 1983).

MacGreevy, Thomas, *Jack B. Yeats* (Dublin: Victor Waddington, 1945).

McHugh, Roger (ed.), *Jack B. Yeats: A Centenary Gathering* (Dublin: Dolmen, 1971).

McMillan, Dougald, 'Samuel Beckett and the Visual Arts: The Embarrassment of Allegory', in S. E. Gontarski (ed.), *On Beckett: Essays and Criticism* (New York: Grove Press, 1986), pp. 29–45.

—— *transition: The History of a Literary Era, 1927–1938* (London: Calder and Boyars, 1975).

—— and Martha Fehsenfeld, *Beckett in the Theatre: The Author as Practical Playwright and Director, Volume 1: From* Waiting for Godot *to* Krapp's Last Tape (London and New York: Calder, 1988).

McMullan, Anna, *Theatre on Trial: Samuel Beckett's Later Drama* (London: Routledge, 1993).

Marin, Louis, *To Destroy Painting*, trans. Mette Hjort (Chicago: University of Chicago Press, 1995).

Marter, Joan, 'Introduction: Internationalism and Abstract Expressionism', in Marter (ed.), *Abstract Expressionism: The International Context* (New Brunswick, NJ: Rutgers University Press, 2007), pp. 1–12.

—— (ed.), *Abstract Expressionism: The International Context* (New Brunswick, NJ: Rutgers University Press, 2007).

Mason, Rainer Michael (ed.), *Bram van Velde, 1895–1981: Rétrospective du Centenaire* (Geneva: Musée Rath, 1996).

Maude, Ulrika, *Beckett, Technology and the Body* (New York: Cambridge University Press, 2009).

Monahan, Laurie, 'Violence in Paradise: André Masson's *Massacres*', *Art History*, 24.5 (2005): 707–24.

Morris, Frances, 'Bram van Velde (1895–1981)', in Morris (ed.), *Paris*

Post War: Art and Existentialism, 1945–1955 (London: Tate Gallery, 1993), pp. 171–2.

—— (ed.), *Paris Post War: Art and Existentialism, 1945–1955* (London: Tate Gallery, 1993).

Mueller, F. Max, *Persona* (Chicago: Open Court Press, 1908).

Nancy, Jean-Luc, *Listening*, trans. Charlotte Mandell (New York: Fordham University Press, 2007).

Nixon, Mark, *Samuel Beckett's German Diaries, 1936–1937* (London: Continuum, 2011).

Oppenheim, Lois, *The Painted Word: Samuel Beckett's Dialogue with Art* (Ann Arbor: University of Michigan Press, 2000).

—— (ed.), *Palgrave Advances in Samuel Beckett Studies* (Basingstoke: Palgrave Macmillan, 2004).

—— and Marius Buning (eds), *Beckett On and On . . .* (London: Associated University Presses, 1996).

Pettit, Philip, *Republicanism: A Theory of Freedom and Government* (Oxford: Oxford University Press, 1997).

Phelan, Peggy, 'Beckett and Avigdor Arikha', in Fionnuala Croke (ed.), *Samuel Beckett: A Passion for Paintings* (Dublin: National Gallery of Ireland, 2006), pp. 99–101.

—— 'Lessons in Blindness from Samuel Beckett', *PMLA*, 119.5 (2004): 1279–88.

Pountney, Rosemary, *Theatre of Shadows: Samuel Beckett's Drama, 1956–76, from* All that Fall *to* Footfalls *with Commentaries on the Latest Plays* (Gerrards Cross: Colin Smythe, 1988).

Puglisi, Catherine, *Caravaggio* (London: Phaidon, 1998).

Pyle, Hilary, *Yeats: Portrait of an Artistic Family* (London: Merrell Holberton, 1997).

Quigley, Mark, *Empire's Wake: Postcolonial Irish Writing and the Politics of Modern Literary Form* (New York: Fordham University Press, 2013).

Rancière, Jacques, *The Politics of Aesthetics*, trans. Gabriel Rockhill (New York: Continuum, 2006).

Salecl, Renata, and Slavoj Žižek (eds), *Gaze and Voice as Love Objects* (Durham, NC: Duke University Press, 1996).

Schermer, Victor L., 'Building on "O": Bion and Epistemology', in Robert M. Lipgar and Malcolm Pines (eds), *Building on Bion: Roots – Origins and Context of Bion's Contributions to Theory and Practice* (London and New York: Jessica Kingsley Publishers, 2003), pp. 226–53.

See, Sarita Echavez, *The Decolonized Eye: Filipino American Art and Performance* (Minneapolis: University of Minnesota Press, 2009).

Sharkey, Rodney X., 'Heidegger, Beckett and Beaufret', *Samuel Beckett Today/Aujourd'hui*, 22 (2010): 410–22.

Stoullig, Claire (ed.), *Bram van Velde*, catalogue of the 1989 exhibition, Musée national d'art moderne, Centre Georges Pompidou (Paris: Éditions du Centre Pompidou, 1989).

Tal-Coat, Pierre, *Tal-Coat*, catalogue of the exhibition at the Grand Palais, Paris, 1976 (Paris: Centre national d'art et de culture Georges Pompidou, 1976).

Thomson, Duncan, *Arikha* (London: Phaidon, 1994).

—— and Stephen Coppel, *Avigdor Arikha from Life: Drawings and Prints, 1965–2005* (London: British Museum Press, 2006).

van Velde, Bram, 'Some Sayings of Bram van Velde', *Transition Forty-Nine*, 5 (1949): 104.

Warwick, Genevieve (cd.), *Caravaggio: Realism, Rebellion, Reception* (Newark: University of Delaware Press, 2006).

Wilson Smith, Timothy, *Caravaggio* (London: Phaidon, 1998).

Wynans, Sandra, *Iconic Spaces: The Dark Theology of Samuel Beckett's Drama* (Notre Dame, IN: University of Notre Dame Press, 2007).

Zarrilli, Philip B., 'Acting "at the nerve ends": Beckett, Blau, and the Necessary', *Project Muse: Theatre Topics*, 7.2 (1997): 1–11.

Index

Page numbers in *italic* indicate illustrations.